CONSENT

NONFICTION

Sex and the Soul: Juggling Sexuality, Spirituality, Romance, and Religion on America's College Campuses

The Happiness Effect: How Social Media Is Driving a Generation to Appear Perfect at Any Cost

Consent on Campus: A Manifesto

FICTION

The Possibilities of Sainthood
This Gorgeous Game
The Survival Kit
Gold Medal Summer
The Tenderness of Thieves
Unplugged
Gold Medal Winter
The Healer

CONSENT

A MEMOIR OF UNWANTED ATTENTION

DONNA FREITAS

Little, Brown and Company

New York Boston London

Little, Brown and Company
Hachette Book Group
1290 Avenue of the Americas, New York, NY 10104
littlebrown.com

First Edition: August 2019

Little, Brown and Company is a division of Hachette Book Group, Inc. The Little, Brown name and logo are trademarks of Hachette Book Group, Inc.

The publisher is not responsible for websites (or their content) that are not owned by the publisher.

The Hachette Speakers Bureau provides a wide range of authors for speaking events. To find out more, go to hachettespeakersbureau.com or call (866) 376-6591.

ISBN 978-0-316-45052-2
LCCN 2018956641

10 9 8 7 6 5 4 3 2 1

LSC-C

Printed in the United States of America

This is a complicated book to dedicate because it's about something so dark and ugly in my life. Who, exactly, wants a book like this to be dedicated to them?

But then, there are so many people in my life who let the light back in, people to whom I feel so grateful, some women in particular (and one man). Molly, Miriam, Michele, Carlene, Rene, Marie, Kylie, Frances, Daphne, Alvina, Jill, Rebecca, Eliot. Also, Professor C. and Professor L. from Georgetown, for believing me and believing in me, and for being the women I so longed to become.

CONSENT

AUTHOR'S NOTE

Trauma is a jumble. Of feelings, of memories, of nausea and sickness in a person's gut, of confusion in the mind.

This memoir is about a trauma in my life, a state of siege that began one spring and that was not alleviated until nearly two years later. By the end of it, I was in a heap.

I've done my best to put what happened in order, but I'm not sure if I got everything and its timing exactly right. There was so much of it to make sense of, a labyrinth, really, that sometimes I get lost in its twists and turns. When I try to remember what happened, as it happened, often what I get is one big flood of memories, all piled on top of one another, melted together, the layers difficult to distinguish.

But know this: each event I describe is one that is seared in my brain and, sadly, likely always will be.

THE MONSTER IN THE HOUSE

The package sat, unopened, on the coffee table.

It had been there for days. Through sun and rain and summer thunderstorms. Next to it was a fat candle from Pottery Barn that I'd bought on sale and a stack of books I was reading for graduate school. In front of the table was an old, wood-framed couch. I'd thrown a thick blanket over it to hide its cheap cushions, stained from former occupants of my university-issue apartment, with its cinder-block walls and tall bright windows that I loved with all my heart. It was the first place I'd ever had all to myself. Behind the table was the hulking television set I'd won during my first year of college and had lugged around for years. It was from my residence-hall lounge, and the RAs had raffled it off at the end of the semester. I was the lucky winner they'd pulled from the hat.

The package was thin, a rectangular manila envelope, my address handwritten on the front in careful script. Its contents could have been anything. Happy photos of friends or pictures from a wedding. But there was an article sealed within that dull yellow envelope. The draft of one.

I knew this because the author, who was also my mentor, told me so, along with his directive that I read the essay inside of it, that he *needed* me to read it. I would be a bad person, a bad student, a bad friend if I ignored this duty as I'd ignored so many other needs and requests from him lately.

He sent it to me on the day he left for a monthlong trip. It was the end of July, it was hot and humid, the blacktop outside my apartment literally steaming with the heat. He called to inform me the article was on its way, that I had the entire month to get to it. Maybe he believed that lack of time or warning was behind my failure to read anything else he'd sent recently. Maybe he thought that allowing me a whole month was a kindness.

During the four weeks he was away, he called to ask if I was reading, if I had already read. He called over and over and scolded when it became clear that I had not yet fulfilled this simple obligation. Time was running out, August was waning, and I hadn't even opened the envelope.

"Don-*na*," he'd say over the phone in that singsong way he always spoke my name. "I'm coming home. I want to be able to talk about this when I get back."

Why, why, *why?* I wondered, silently, as I promised him—because I did promise him—that I would get to it soon, maybe today. Why *me?* I was a nobody graduate student. He was an important professor, famous in certain circles. Didn't he have colleagues whose opinions he could solicit? Why did he care about mine?

By then I knew the answers to my own questions. The desperation in his voice was evidence enough. But still, the knowledge was murky and vague, fearful and suspicious. I'd pushed it deep into the recesses of my brain, done my best to kill it. I was in denial and I relished this denial, so fierce and powerful that it was almost magnificent.

As I sat there, watching television on my couch, that ugly manila envelope taking up space on my table next to the remnants of my latest take-out dinner, a part of me was still hopeful that I was wrong; that the nagging feeling consuming my insides would turn out to be a product of my melodramatic imagination.

Day after day I rose from bed, walked out into my living room, wishing that the envelope had vanished overnight. But no, it sat there, among my things, just steps from my hideous Pepto-Bismol–colored kitchen, where I cooked lavish dinners for friends, for my RA staff, for myself. Seeing the envelope each time I came in the door was like discovering someone had left a ticking time bomb in my apartment while I was out buying Advil at CVS. I would agonize over its presence in my house and my life, doing my best to disarm it.

It was *just* an article. An innocent thing. A stack of papers, typed up and printed out and stapled together. Strings of words in black and white. What was I afraid of? What, really, was the big deal? I read articles all the time. I was a graduate student, a voracious reader. Reading was my calling, my purpose, my joy.

Just do it already, my mind would push, one minute. *But I don't want to,* it would tug, the next. *Come on, Donna,* I would admonish myself. *It's not like an article can actually hurt you. It's not like it's packed with knives and bullets and poison.*

Back and forth, back and forth went this spiral of thoughts. As the days marched forward, the questions of how I'd gotten to this place, and whose fault it was, plagued me. Whose responsibility was it, really? Mine? His? The answer was so hard to parse out, but parse it out I did, and then I did again.

I allowed the article in my house. (Consent?) *I* placed it on the coffee table. (Also consent. Right?) I answered the phone when he called, pleading with me. (Consent, technically. But there was no caller ID back then, so maybe not?) I made him promises that I would read. (Is there consent when there is also cringing? When he is begging?) But I also *resisted* touching that yellow envelope. (I did not *want* to consent to it.) I didn't open it for nearly a month. (This was a silent no. But do silent nos count?) I scowled when I looked at it. (A bodily gesture of resistance. But then, it wasn't like he was in the room and could see me scowling. Thank God.) I did my best to ignore its presence, its persistence, I didn't move it, didn't touch it, not at first. (Does the absence of a response imply a yes?)

The mere sight of the article on my coffee table filled me with a dread so profound I'm not sure I can ever convey its depths. Words are not enough. Then again, shouldn't I have used my words? Shouldn't it have been *that* easy, just saying the word *no* loud and clear and true like a bell?

I waited until the day before he returned from his trip to open the envelope, to take out the article, to actually touch it with my fingers. I held it as if I might be allergic to the paper, averting my eyes. It was like readying myself to take the most disgusting medicine in the history of the world, medicine you know is going to make you sick but somehow you have to get it down your throat. You have to take a deep breath, close your eyes, and swallow it, then do your best to distract yourself from such a pervasive level of disgust that you know gagging and retching are inevitable.

I turned on the television so there was noise around me, so it felt like there were other people nearby. I didn't want to be alone with it, not any bit of it, not the envelope, the paper, the article, not the words on the pages.

Then, finally, I started.

After so much resistance, I let my eyes settle on the first word and then the second and the third, until I was allowing them inside my brain, inside my body, where they would cohere into sentences that would take on meaning. I convinced myself that after so much melodrama I was about to find out the article was as benign as the stack of books I read for my classes, that soon I would be laughing at how silly I'd been to make such a big deal over nothing, that I would be rolling my eyes at the way I'd fought this article off as though it were a mugger in a dark alley. I'd realize that the author really did mean well, that he had no ulterior motives or harmful agenda.

I waited for the relief to hit, for the cool wave of it to flow through me in the oppressive August heat.

But as those words entered me one by one, piling up into a massive heap of sentences that became paragraphs that became sections, it turned out that the article was poison after all, that it really was going to make me sick. So ill that I got up from my couch and lay down flat on my back on the floor of my apartment, holding my stomach.

The article was a confession of love.

But it wasn't a direct confession. There was no *Dear Donna* at the beginning, or sentences that included the words *I've lately realized that I'm in love with you.* He'd told me he loved me without telling me directly, while cloaking it in a lengthy, lofty reflection—no, an honoring—of a real-life love between an older man, a famous writer and thinker, and a young woman thirty years his junior, with whom this man began a passionate and clandestine affair, one that was revealed to the public only many years after his death. The essay was about forgiving this man the transgression of loving the younger woman, of pursuing her, of being unable to stop himself from doing so, from corralling his desires. The article justified his love for her, praised it as virtuous, even divine, and exulted in the fact that she reciprocated that love, forbidden as it was to both of them because the man was also a priest. I imagine my mentor believed this was the ultimate romantic gesture, to craft an essay about the love he felt for me, but to do so metaphorically. To invite me into a sexual relationship through the poetry of a well-written paper. For him, a deeply thought-out intellectual essay was the equivalent of a sonnet.

It was sneaky and convoluted and, ultimately, cowardly, though it was like everything else that he did, which was also sneaky and convoluted and just indirect enough to leave me doubtful, to make me question my instincts, my judgment, my intuition, that something was deeply wrong with his behavior toward me. His movements were always just shy of obviously inappropriate, they were always potentially completely innocent; acts that *could* be interpreted as overtures of something romantic, yet that also could be misinterpreted as such.

There was always room for doubt with him, and this was part of his talent as a stalker of me.

Eventually I got up from the floor and sat on the couch again. I tossed the papers onto the coffee table and they fanned across it, obscuring the cheap wood. My dread ballooned outward to encompass the entire apartment, oozing through the screens of my open windows and poisoning the humid summer air.

What was I going to do? What was my plan?

He was going to call me the second he returned home and push for a face-to-face meeting so we could "discuss" his article. Not answering the phone wouldn't do any good, since he would simply show up at my door and wait for me to come out. I could deny that I'd read it. I could deny and deny, but then he would just badger and badger until I couldn't deny any longer. I could say yes to him, I could have the conversation and act like I didn't see any connection between his essay and the situation I now found myself in. That *he'd put me in.*

As these thoughts flew through my head, my entire being revolted. My entire self, my body, my brain, my heart, my soul, were one big *no.* No, no, no, *no.* I cannot do this. I can*not.* I wanted to die. I wanted to die rather than deal with what was looming.

The phone rang.

I considered not picking up because, you know. It was probably him.

But I did pick up, because what else was I going to do? Never answer the phone again? I had a job to do, with RAs who depended on me. Friends. Family. A boyfriend.

It was my father on the line.

"Your mother has cancer," he told me the moment I said hello, his voice thick with grief. "It's not good. You have to come home. She's having surgery tomorrow. She might not make it. Your mother might die."

I listened to him, barely comprehending his words, their terrible meaning. As I held the phone to my ear, already beginning to pack my things, something incredible registered inside of me. I would not be here tomorrow because my mother was having surgery. Major surgery. For cancer. She might *die.* This was the ultimate excuse to be away when he came back. There could exist *no better excuse* to avoid the dreaded conversation. To *never ever* have that discussion he was so desperate to have.

As my father continued to talk, I thought to myself: *I am a horrible daughter.* And later, as I hung up the phone and zipped up my travel bag, I thought to myself:

I am saved.

WHAT THEY TOOK
AND HOW I LET THEM

I am not supposed to be telling you any of this.

In exchange for my graduate school eventually making the harassment from my mentor stop, and a very small sum of money, I agreed to pretend that none of what I am about to tell you ever happened. I agreed to absolve my university of all wrongdoing. I agreed to be silent forever.

At the time I didn't care what I had to do or sign. The only thing I wanted was for this man to go away, this man who was supposed to be my mentor, my shepherd throughout the years of graduate school and onward into my professional future. I would have signed anything back then, a paper that called me a harlot, that said my mother was a whore. I would have paid the school if need be, if it finally made him go away. I would have taken out my checkbook and emptied my savings account into the school's. I would have handed them anything they asked of me, if only I could finally be free.

But what they wanted was my voice.

So I gave it to them. I cut out my tongue in the university's office of human resources and offered it to the woman whose job it was to take it. I mutilated myself right there, in the middle of the day, in front of her administrative assistant. I didn't even notice the blood. I handed over the most important thing a woman has according to the feminists I was reading for my classes in the building right next door. I did this like it was nothing.

I didn't know what a crime I was committing against myself until much later, didn't realize that my university was requiring me to maim myself, and do so permanently. I didn't know when I was visiting HR that I was dealing with people who worked to protect the institution and its professors at the expense of the vulnerable bodies of its students. Who knew that universities could conspire like gangs of criminals, albeit under the guise of being respectable places of lofty ideals? Who knew that this college where I'd enrolled to get my PhD, this beacon of hope and light, would stoop so low as to ask a young woman to rip her vocal cords from her throat to fulfill this most basic of requests, which was to go to her classes without fear of being stalked?

But then, I am not unique in this experience.

All around the country, at universities far and wide, at workplaces of all sizes and types, at companies that boast of doing good and making the world a better place, there are file cabinets full of the bloody tongues of women. Some are young and tender, others more weathered and battered, but all of them taken from us by people in business-casual attire, in suits and sensible skirts, walking up to us as though what they are about to do is perfectly legitimate, perfectly reasonable, even as they take the long, curving knives from behind their backs, raising them up to strike our faces and our necks. Acting as though this is just business as usual while they disfigure us, and we stand there, letting them, because this seems like our only option.

Once they have our tongues they don't even seal them in a bag, to try to stem the mess. They've grown so used to this procedure that by now they're immune. Instead, they carry our tongues back into the room they've reserved for female body parts, a room with special locks, with sound-proofing to drown out all the things the tongues say to each other at night, in the dark, when everyone else goes home, a cacophony of disembodied voices. But they never stop bleeding. They bleed and bleed for years, so much that more people must be hired to make sure nothing seeps into view. No one wants a public scandal, after all.

Women's tongues are dangerous when they let us keep them. Institutions, workplaces, companies have long known this, which is why they take them from us, why they require that we forfeit them, why they'll pay us so much for them, these blood diamonds mined from our bodies. It's good to see that women are breaking into these locked-away places and taking our tongues back.

I am still getting used to mine again.

It is thick and strange in my mouth.

"You know I was stalked, once, in graduate school."

I remember dropping this line into a conversation with a colleague, Mary, who is now one of my best friends. I said it like this information was no big deal, barely a shrug, even as my blood pressure spiked as it always does when I bring up this topic.

Mary and I had only recently met. We were sitting at a table on the sidewalk in Manhattan on a sunny August day, chatting happily over dishes of pesto spaghetti at my favorite Italian place. We'd hit it off at a conference and decided to hang out when we returned home, the first of what would become many lunches, countless get-togethers, and which now amount to over a decade of friendship. She was seven months pregnant at the time, her cheeks rosy and flushed in the heat. I remember how her stomach was round and bursting from her tiny frame. We were both in summer dresses, sleeveless, clingy, as bare as a person can get and still go out in public. On Mary the effect was dramatic, and on our walk to the restaurant she garnered more than a few stares from passersby and plenty of sympathetic smiles from other women.

Mary stopped eating after I told her this and looked up. "Oh?"

"Yeah. Isn't that weird?" This came out of my mouth as a statement, even though I'd phrased it as a question. Before she could respond I rushed back in to ask her, "So what was grad school like for you?"

She hesitated before answering—of course she did, because how is a person supposed to respond to such an unexpected confession, immediately followed by an abrupt shift in subject? But she let the conversation move forward from there to plenty of more benign topics, putting some distance between what I'd confided and the now of our lunch, padding my comment with other talk like white noise until we almost couldn't hear what I'd said ringing in the air any longer. We slurped our bright green spaghetti and laughed and joked and gossiped, and my blood pressure slowed to a more normal rate.

I cringe even now, many years later, at how I must have sounded that day. The way I told her what had happened to me was so clumsy, everything about it awkward and stumbling and uncomfortable. I'd forced it up from my darkest self and lobbed it onto the table for her inspection without warning or preamble. I was experimenting with "integrating" this fact of my past into my present because of my therapist's advice. She kept urging me to talk about what happened during grad school with other people, with friends, with anyone, so I might better incorporate it into my life and relationships as a way of healing the trauma it caused to my body and brain.

But I've yet to find a way to speak about it that is not clumsy.

How does one become graceful, exactly, when speaking about the ugliest parts of her history? The parts that stir the most shame and blame, the confessions capable of stopping a conversation in its tracks and rendering the other person speechless? Of turning an afternoon of delicious food and newfound intimacy into something off-putting and strange?

"I remember when you told me that," Mary said to me the other day. "And how you told me."

"I'm sorry," I said, trying to laugh it off as a way of staving off the burn that crept into my cheeks. "I can't believe I did that to you, so soon after we met."

Mary has big brown eyes, honest and sincere, soft and quiet. "Donna," she said. "Don't apologize. It made me feel honored."

"Honored?" This was not the word I expected her to use.

"That you felt you could trust me with something so personal, so quickly. It made me realize that you and I were going to be good friends. Real friends."

"Oh," I said, taking this in, trying to let its delicate and beautiful kindness permeate my skin. "I'm still sorry, though," I added. "I'll always be so sorry."

In multiple ways, I am two people.

I am a writer and an academic, I am creative and scholarly. I am a longtime, well-published novelist, and a grown woman with a PhD whose research about sex on campus is widely taught, who has been speaking about this research and sexual assault at universities and colleges across the nation for over a decade. At the same time, I am a person, vulnerable and ashamed about something I lived during my early to mid-twenties, embarrassed by the fault I see in myself for what transpired, at the role I played in all of it, in allowing it to go on for as long as it did. I am someone whose career has flourished in certain regards, and I'm also a person whose career has languished and suffered because of what happened with my mentor. I know that I *should* be capable of telling myself what I tell college students who've been assaulted and harassed like I was:

It's not your fault. Don't blame yourself.

And yet, I am unable to convince myself of this. I am unable to convince that young woman I was and will always be, to a degree, that the statement "It's not your fault" is entirely true in my case. I remain two people, two women who share the same body, same heart, same mind, same soul. This split woman has lived parallel lives, one in public as a confident, authoritative person, capable as a researcher, speaker, and writer on many subjects, including Title IX and assault. The other woman remains hidden, a person insecure and ashamed, whose professional life is irreparably marked by this man, forever changed by his inability to control himself, to abstain from inappropriate behavior, by the manner in which his gaze became fixated on me and I could not turn it away.

I am a survivor, but I also am, and always will be, a victim. I can't speak for others who share this dual identity, but I can say for myself that, while I wish to be the proud person who exclusively occupies the title of survivor, I still claim the territory of the shivering, cowering victim. To say that I am not also her even after two decades have passed would be to lie. Because of my work, because of feminism, because of certain friends who have supported me over the years, I am well aware of the correct things I am supposed to say out loud to others and tell myself in my darkest moments: That everything was *his* fault. That *he* did what he did *to* me. That I should not blame *myself.* I have rehearsed these lines, practiced them like I would for a role in a play, yet there are only fleeting moments when I actually believe they are true. The rest are full of doubt and uncertainty.

So many times I've imagined the self I am now sitting down with that younger self I used to be and telling her all the things we tell young women who've experienced something like I did. I've done this exercise as a means of helping myself, forgiving myself, trying to cope over the years. I've done it because colleagues and friends who know this part of my history have suggested I do it, especially after I've lapsed into monologues of self-recrimination and blame at dinners and over drinks.

"If you sat down with one of your students right now," they'll say, "and heard her describe a similar story to your own, what would you tell her? Would you ever dream of claiming that she is, even partially, at fault?"

The answer, of course, is an unequivocal no. I would never tell one of my students this. I would never tell one of my friends or colleagues this. I would never say such things to anyone who has suffered my particular affliction. I believe in the absolute absence of fault with respect to the experiences of others. I know this completely and without doubt. I am convinced of its reality. So why isn't it unequivocally true in my case? Why can't I make a clean leap from shameful victim to proud survivor? How can I resolve these two competing selves?

Will I ever?

We live in a culture where the harassment and assault of women and girls take place so regularly, so commonly, so consistently, that we need to take stock of the splitting of the person that occurs during acts of trauma. Of the ways that women must learn to become good actresses and excellent liars so they can endure and live as though nothing terrible has happened to them. Of the personal and professional cost of having to live with two brains, be of two minds, of the secrets a person's own body can keep from her for years, of the ongoing feeling that somehow *she is the one who failed* and the damage this does to her sense of self, of her ability to perceive what is true and what is false about who she is and who she is not.

We have made consent out to be something straight-forward, as straightforward as the single word *no,* but we are lying to ourselves and one another about this. If stopping someone's behavior were as magical as uttering a two-letter word, then my professor's behavior would never have gone on as long as it did. The word *no* meant nothing in my case. I paid dearly for this. I am still paying for it.

I am not saying that all I have come to do, to achieve, to accomplish since those years in my twenties has been a lie, or even a performance. I am not saying that the confident, successful woman that I am in so many regards isn't real. She is, *I am,* real. The lie would be to contend that the *other* woman I've been, that I am still, no longer exists. The lie would be to deny her. To claim that the young woman scarred by this man is fully healed. I will always be her. I will always be both women. Even if my friends, my fellow feminists, wish this were otherwise.

In this same vein, I have two brains. Each one hides stuff from the other. Like there are parts of my brain that have been redacted. Like the FBI or the CIA or some secret government agency broke into my mind one night and classified my memories of grad school—my memories of *him*—with a thick, soaking black marker; classified them *from me.*

I have always known I have two sets of memories— one, which is exclusively devoted to this man and all that happened with him, and the other, which is exclusively devoted to everything else that happened in my life during grad school and since. One set is dark and ugly and sickening, and the other is bright and happy and thrilling. The darker set is dangerous; it lies in wait, hidden, lurking, until the moment when the happier side of me least expects, has almost forgotten, it is there, and suddenly it lashes out with the force and violence of a knife slashing through everything else that I am, everything that I've become, wounding me all over again.

My brain, my body, have worked hard over the years to keep these two sets of memories separate, not allowing one to pollute the other—and that is the word for it: *pollution.* I understand this professor as a potentially polluting force, like an insecticide or a putrid, stinking chemical that must be carefully contained. My brain's job, it seems, has been to seal him tight into one corner, protecting the rest of it from any further contamination.

When I try to remember that time in my life, using my brain is like using an Etch A Sketch. When you move the slide across the dull gray screen, it erases whatever had been there so you can start over with a new image. I have one of those slides in my mind, but when I slide it across my memories, on one side there is him and on the other there is everyone and everything else. On one side my life happens and has gone on as though I am completely normal, untouched by this man, successful and happy, but on the other, the girl I see is a pathetic, fearful mess, and she will always remain so.

★ ★ ★

You can view a person through so many different lenses, from so many angles. It depresses me that this ugly part of my history is my lens, my angle, the window through which I am choosing to view all the different aspects of my life, my friends, my family, my faith, my aspirations and hopes and dreams. Then again, writing this *is* a method of capture, of pinning something down. And I'd like to capture this man so I can understand and contemplate him now, from such a distance, who he was and is and how he happened to me. I'd like to turn him into a helpless butterfly pinned to the wall, waiting there for me to study him. I was his reluctant butterfly for far too long, and he held me in his gaze, watched me squirm, and didn't care that I wanted to be free of him.

I've had many years to reflect on what happened during graduate school—how it happened, why it continued for so long. So, I am using my own experience as a case study of sorts, because sadly, there is plenty to study, and however ironically or fittingly, conversations about harassment, assault, and consent have become one of the central aspects of my professional identity. And then, if I learned anything from what I lived, it's that consent is infinitely complex and ongoing, especially when two people are already in a relationship with each other.

There were, quite literally, a range of stages of consent in my case, which gradually shifted to stages of non-consent. Consent is such a tricky, slippery thing, one that can be there one minute and gone the next, that can be murky and vague, that can be given yet given in fear or out of perceived obligation. Because of the difference in power between me and my professor, between me and my mentor, I behaved in a way that shames me and makes me long to go back and do everything differently. And yet it's so much easier to wish I'd acted differently in hindsight now that I am older, now that I know so much more about harassment and how institutions handle it (or don't), now that I am more outside of what was happening.

But when it happens to you and you are young and powerless, and the person who is making it happen holds your dream in his hands, fragile and beautiful and glowing with hope, there is a lot you will do to try to ensure that he doesn't use those hands to crush it.

One last thing, on the subject of dreams.

People often judge the settlements that some women get when they come forward with accusations of harassment and assault, especially when the figures grow into the millions. That's been happening a lot these days, because more and more women are speaking out and our nation is realizing exactly how typical it is for a woman to be subjected to harassment and assault in the workplace, at school, at just about every possible juncture of her life.

In my mind, no settlement is too big or outrageous. No settlement can ever be enough.

What price, really, can you put on the loss, the permanent loss, of a woman's brightest dreams? What cost, truly, is the loss of your future? Your career? Your reputation in the eyes of others?

Even though I've tried to convince myself otherwise, convince myself that this time in my life during graduate school did not determine the course of my future, that it is not at fault for how things turned out for me (or didn't), I am, once again, a woman split in two. Deep down, underneath all the factors that went into my professional decision-making over the years, the bad luck and bad colleagues, the good and serendipitous moments, the choices I made myself, *he* is lurking. Like sludge at the bottom of a lake, hidden and slimy underneath pristine water, he is still there. And when

I acknowledge this truth, I am also able to hear that voice, barely a whisper, telling me that yes, while there are many, many reasons that I did not fulfill the dream of my future, and even though I fulfilled other dreams I didn't yet know that I had, he cost me my one true dream, the purest one, the one whose end still hurts the most and always will.

He broke me in the place I'd once been happiest, where I'd looked inward and had discovered my best self. He took this once-confident, exuberant part of me and turned it into something insecure and anxious, cowering and ashamed, repulsed and sickly. In the process of doing this, he turned everything that had to do with this part of me into a wasteland, full of rubble and hidden mines that I no longer knew how to navigate. That I could not navigate, at least not successfully. That I still can't navigate, if I'm honest.

I had only wanted to be a college professor. That is all. And I am not one. Not in the way that I'd wanted, that I'd hoped. Not in the way my friends are now. And as much as I hate to admit this and wish it were otherwise, that is on him.

PART ONE

1

Rhode Island, where I'm from, is a small place.

That sounds like a joke. It is small in size, yes, but it's also small like a town, a place where everyone knows one another. It's easy to play six degrees of separation, and usually the degrees are just one or two. Rhode Island is working class, it's intimate, it's Catholic, or it was when I was growing up. It is a state full of immigrants, Italians, Portuguese, and Irish. We go to the public beaches in the summers, they fill up with kids and teenagers and parents, men too old to be surfing but there they are anyway, longboards under their arms, weaving their way through the colorful umbrellas dotting the sand like pinwheels.

The lots around my family's house in Narragansett were once wooded places, and my grandmother and I would go blackberry picking for hours, returning only when we'd gathered enough for a pie. There were grapes, blueberries, wild strawberries, too. Depending on the day and the season, my grandmother would be coaxing me into a pair of jeans so my legs wouldn't get cut on the prickers and we would head out into the warm air, past the random, falling-down stone walls that lined the landscape and into the tall grasses where the strawberry plants were hiding.

Someone gave me a sunflower once, I don't remember who, but I was six or seven at the time and I loved that flower like I'd never loved anything. I loved its brightness, its bigness, the way it seemed to be continually bursting into existence, pushing its yellow face into the atmosphere. But because it was a flower I also knew it would die. I mourned its inevitable death before it was close, would stare at it, worriedly, in its vase at the center of the kitchen table. When it finally reached its end, withered and brown around the edges, drooping over after it had been so straight and tall and seemingly invincible, my father lifted it up, took my hand in his, and led me into the vacant lot behind our house. It was dotted with trees and bushes, but mostly grass—grass as tall as me at the time. We laid the wilted sunflower down, gently, reverently, and I thought my father meant for us to hold its funeral since he knew how much I loved it. But instead he looked at me and said, "You wait," and then turned around and led us back into the yard, past the swing set and onto the patio.

The following August and every late summer and fall after that until the lot was paved over to make room for a new house, great, tall sunflowers rose up among the grasses, more and more each year. We could see them from the kitchen through the glass doors at breakfast. I was as certain then as I am now that my father made this annual miracle happen on my behalf, evidence of his love for me multiplying through each new sunflower season like the story of the loaves and the fishes, but far better.

Back in the seventies and eighties, Rhode Island could shelter you like a great big festive tent, full of sea and sand and the simple pleasures of life, noisy with the kind of accents that people make fun of after hearing them on television and in the movies.

"Ray's out pahking the caah," my mother would say all the time when people asked where my father was, after he dropped us off at the door of wherever we were headed, like a gentleman—my father has always been a gentleman. My college roommates used to listen to the messages my mother left on our answering machine in awe, save them to play back again, sometimes for guests, because her accent was so strong it seemed unbelievable to them.

When I was little and learning to spell, taking in the rules about silent vowels and such, I remember my eureka moment when I realized there must be a silent *r*. How else could I account for the fact that words that didn't sound like they had *r*'s in them—*haaht, paaht, caah, prayyah*—were spelled so differently on the page: *heart, part, car, prayer?* Why had nobody taught me this specific lesson about *r*'s in school? When I told my mother about this brainstorm that seemed to solve a great spelling puzzle, she laughed and laughed and explained to me about accents and how they could swallow letters like black holes in people's speech. She was a teacher herself, and I remember how upset I became about how everyone spoke around us, my parents included, like they were trying to trick me, make it harder for children to learn to read and to spell. I told her she should fix this, that it wasn't right or fair to her students that she spoke this way, almost like lying to them, which only made her laugh even more.

Rhode Island could shelter you with its simplicity, its annual rhythms of going to the beach in summer, going to school during fall, winter, and spring, and church on Sundays regardless of the season. It's also the place where I learned in first grade, by accident, right around the time my father was making miracles with sunflowers, that there were gods other than the Catholic God in this world. We were doing a phonics lesson in my Catholic elementary-school classroom, sounding out words, sentence by sentence, working through the textbook readings, which happened to be about Greek gods that morning. Zeus and Athena, Aphrodite and Poseidon, and all of their adventures. The point was to teach us phonics, the lesson to read aloud and do so correctly, but the idea that there were gods other than the one my family and I prayed to on Sundays and before meals and bed was the real lesson I took home that day.

My mother was in her room, folding clothes on the bed.

I climbed up and sat on top of her comforter, legs crossed. Studied her smiling brown eyes, the soft curl of her short dark hair, her colorful clothing, sweaters with flowers stitched into them on one day, animals on another, the bright clothing of a nursery-school teacher.

"You didn't tell me there were other gods," I said to her. It was definitely an accusation.

"What do you mean?" she asked.

I explained about that morning's phonics lesson and what I had discovered. I was shocked to find out that my mother had known about other gods all along, that this was not as surprising to her as it was to me. She asked me a lot of questions that day, what I thought about Zeus and his divine peers, if I liked reading about them and wanted to read more. She would be happy to supply me with books full of stories about Greek gods and other gods, too, if I was interested. But I was stuck on one single question, which I kept asking her over and over.

"What if we believe in the wrong one?"

Since it now seemed the world was full of gods, I could not stop thinking about the possibility that we had picked poorly with the Catholic one. Which god was the right god? We *had* picked, too, my parents and grandmother at least. My family did this without consulting me or revealing what I now saw as essential information before making this choice. How does one make such decisions, anyway, when there are so many gods out there? Why did we pick this Catholic God over the others? What made him better, exactly?

"Well," my mother said, as she continued to fold clothes, little piles stacking up like tiny sand castles across the bed. "That's what faith is." She went on to explain that faith was about believing in something without knowing whether it was true, that leaps of faith were about the very questions I was asking, about deciding it was okay not to know for sure whether the Catholic God was the one "right" god or the one "true" god, accepting that we might never know the answer. That, as a family, my parents and grandmother had faith in the Catholic God and the Catholic Church.

"I don't think I like this," I told her.

Once again, I felt tricked. Like my parents and the Sunday school teachers had intentionally been keeping essential information from me, leaving out data necessary to make an informed decision about God and faith and what *I* believed.

"You can keep asking me questions," my mother said.

She seemed so unruffled, so full of calm as her daughter was making inquiries that could shatter the world as she'd known it since birth. But in truth I think my questions had shaken her. My mother wanted faith for me, faith in the Catholic God and its traditions. Everyone around us had this faith, and she thought it would arm me well as I got older and had to face life's hardships, like padding all over my body, breaking the force of the hurt and the pain.

It's also true that my childish faith in the Catholic God never recovered, that I could never stop thinking about what was true and what might be false when we went to church on Sundays, that I didn't like the idea that we might be wrong, that my parents and grandmother might have made a bad decision faithwise. I never stopped asking questions about other gods, either, both in my head and out in the world, questions that sometimes startled and scandalized my teachers at the Catholic schools I attended my entire life, schools that I loved, full of friends and nuns and priests whom I loved along with them. And though I may have lost my faith in God when I was very young, I never lost my faith in my parents. It was easy. They were always right there.

I was a voracious student during high school, college, graduate school. I still am, to a degree, but not like I was back then. I gobbled up books like the candy my mother forbade me to eat as a child, which only made me a more passionate consumer of all things sugar. I was so precocious at trig and calculus that my math classes conflicted with Honors English, and the AP Lit teacher, Miss H., gave me a private class for years. It was like winning the lottery.

Miss H. was adored at my school for her kindness, her intelligence, for always wearing long, flowing hippie skirts and sweaters, for being stuck in a 1960s time warp, for her pacifism, for her impossibly frizzy, dirty-blond hair that was parted in the middle and framed her weathered face. She smiled a lot, spoke in a soft voice, and had an equally soft laugh. I worshipped her.

She and I read everything together, all the classics. I swooned over Ayn Rand (I was young, I got over it), Dickens, Shakespeare, Steinbeck. My beloved personal teacher would hand me 450-page tomes and ask, quietly, whether I could read them in two, three, maybe four (if I was lucky) days.

Yes, I replied. A thousand times yes!

There was no syllabus, no curriculum, no plan, no structure, only a teetering stack of books in a dim, ugly classroom (for some reason, we never turned on the lights) and conversation, discussion, study, talk. Miss H. would pull up another desk and chair and sit next to me like she was a peer or I was her colleague, and I would forget I was at school and that she was my teacher until the bell rang again. Often she was too busy to meet, and I would sit there alone, reading, working. But she pushed me, hard, on everything, harder than anyone had ever pushed me, especially on my writing. I ate it up, every last crumb, like I was starving, like it was the best meal of my life, like it might be my last, like I'd never tasted good food even though my mother was a gifted Italian cook. I was hungry, and the hunger only grew once I discovered it was there. I learned to love the ache of it.

I had always been a reader, my mother made sure of this with biweekly, even triweekly trips to the library to pick out books and more books. She always made them into these big events, the two of us getting into the car, making sure we had our library cards. I remember, clearly, the day my mother decided I was old enough to strike out on my own into the stacks.

"Why don't you go explore," my mother said to me as if this were no big deal, not a milestone at all, while we were sitting cross-legged on the floor in the children's section, paging through a picture book. "You pick out what interests you, and when you're ready, we'll check it out at the desk together. Take your time."

I got up and stood there, staring at her, not really

believing she was sending me off into the wilds alone with no curfew, thrilled at the promise of secret wanderings. Afterward, I would stagger home with piles of books, as thick as I could manage (Louisa May Alcott was wonderful in this regard, I discovered), as many as the librarians would allow me to borrow, a habit my mother heartily approved of and indulged.

But that private English class with Miss H. marked a shift in my relationship with books and ideas. It was the beginning of everything, my future, my academic desire, my intellectual awakening, my initiation into critical thinking, my joy at learning, searching, questioning, at uncontrolled and unyielding wonder about why, why not, how, who, and what does it all mean, *what?* Miss H. was the reason I got into Georgetown University, a school where it became clear after I arrived that everyone else was more qualified than me to be there. Everywhere I turned were people who'd gone to fancy private boarding schools where they'd had sex and done lots of drugs and taken courses with titles like Life, Death, and Immortality in Greek Literature, or Love and Shakespeare. Where their parents had paid the equivalent or even more than the price of Georgetown for a semester.

I'd gone to the little parochial girls' school affiliated with our equally little Catholic church. This was back when parochial schools cost a few hundred dollars a year, and even this was a stretch, and an ongoing complaint from my parents. We had generic courses like history and English and science, and my fellow plaid-skirted schoolgirls and I often cared more about dances where we could encounter the mysterious species of the high school boy than about academics, and where getting away with wearing boxer shorts under our uniforms or going without socks was a daily occupation. My private English class was a fluke in the grand scheme, a stroke of luck bestowed by a book-loving teacher who'd found the rare student who could keep up with her evening reading, maybe even lap her once or twice in the race.

Compared with everyone around me, I didn't belong at Georgetown, but somehow I was there, and I would make the most of it. I approached my excitingly titled classes with the same gusto I had for all those novels in high school with Miss H., and I approached my new professors in exactly the same way. I showed up to their office hours with my questions, my confusions, my ideas. I went to discuss what we were reading in class and I went to propose ideas for papers they hadn't assigned. It never occurred to me, not once, that I shouldn't go, or that it was strange how often I went, which was very.

I became a regular. Those small, rectangular office spaces with modest desks, impressive bookshelves, and two chairs—one for the professor, another for visitors—were my local watering holes, and I the alcoholic needing my daily drink after work. The more I went, the thirstier I became, and in my professors' offices I found willing and enthusiastic drinking partners. We guzzled down Heidegger and Sartre and Kierkegaard and Charles Taylor, proud lushes of philosophical inquiry. I was drunk and euphoric with the challenges of theory, with the ways my professors pushed my mind, with the discovery that philosophy was akin to the math that had come so easily to me in high school, so easily that it made my classmates angry.

I was *that* student, the one who was always showing up, always devising new and weird ideas, always experimenting, always going above and beyond the regular assignments. Maybe I was also a pain in the ass, but my Georgetown professors were skilled in the art of not showing they felt this way. They humored the enthusiastic, idealistic undergrad that I was. My intellectual awakening was nurtured, fed, given a warm and welcoming home, and raised to become the aspiring, confident PhD applicant I eventually became, a young woman who, shortly after leaving Georgetown, arrived for her first day of graduate school in this new and exciting chapter of her academic life.

My greatest hope was to become like them. My beloved professors, my philosophical guides, my most ardent academic cheerleaders, the reasons I got to be where I now was. They were benevolent gods raining down knowledge and I their most grateful subject. They gave me more than I ever could have asked for, and in that cheesy, idealistic way of the young, I wanted to do the same thing for my own students someday. I was truly lucky to have found these intellectual parents who helped me to become the academic woman I was meant to become.

But on that first day of graduate school, what I didn't know was that all that professorial luck of mine was about to run out.

I took his course because I had to. It was a requirement for my program, one of the foundational classes I needed, and he was an important scholar in the concentration I'd chosen to pursue. He was my newest mentor and I was excited to meet him; excited for all that lay ahead.

I sat down in a chair to his right, nearly next to him but not quite, at the small seminar table around which my peers began to unpack their things. They were decidedly unlike my fellow students at Georgetown and their privileged backgrounds, their glamorous lives and aspirations. I'd chosen religious studies as my general field because it's so interdisciplinary, the kind of PhD where I could let my questions run as wild as they always wanted to, stomping across the various humanities like a happy child through the mud. On that morning I found myself among priests and nuns, some of them in habits and collars, most everyone far older than me. Those who weren't celibate were married with children. I remember looking around the table and thinking, *There is no one here that I could date.* The only other single people I encountered in my program were pursuing other academic concentrations. I was the youngest student in the class.

The room was long and narrow, just wide enough to fit the conference table where we were sitting, waiting for the professor to arrive. Along my back were windows and, in front, a nondescript white wall. But behind the place where the professor was to sit were shelves packed with books. I say this now, though it's possible I'm remembering it incorrectly. Or that I became so accustomed to seeing this man in his office, which *was* overflowing with books, that certain memories of him have seeped into others. But in my mind, behind his chair in that classroom were dark wooden bookshelves, as though to emphasize his role in guarding them, protecting them, speaking for them.

The professor was short, he was unassuming, he had a soft, gentle voice, he smiled at each one of us, he was as friendly as I expected all professors to be, as friendly as my beloved teachers from Georgetown. He had graying hair, cut neatly so that it was flat across the top, and he was dressed in dark, flowing robes. I remember him sitting there at the head of the table like Yoda, layered in fabric, only his small head visible above it, lines running across his face and crinkling around his eyes. Like several of the students, my professor was also a Catholic priest.

There were maybe eight of us in that room, at the most ten. We went around the table, introducing ourselves, explaining our interest in the topic of the course.

"I don't know what I'm doing here," I said when it

was my turn to speak, voicing my uncertainty about the subject matter we were to study that semester, the skeptic among the group. The class involved reading the works of important spiritual figures in history, all of whom had chosen a celibate life themselves. Now that I was studying religion, I felt out of place. How had I, a boyfriend-loving, philosophy-major atheist who had no interest in celibacy, landed myself in a course like this? In a program that *required* a course like this?

"I came to study philosophy and spirituality," I went on. "To try to understand the nature of the divine, of religious experience, of Meaning with a capital *M*." I loved capitalizing words like Being and Connection and Purpose, and giving them extra philosophical oomph. "But I'm not sure what spirituality has to do with these celibate people."

Despite this and even with my reservations about the material, I was, as always, the most eager of students, bright-eyed, bushy-tailed, a veritable rabbit of talkative enthusiasm. I might not have liked the reading list on the syllabus, but I would work hard to unpack it, to try to understand it, open myself to its relevance to my graduate work.

The professor was unfazed by my resistance. He was understanding, sympathetic, generous, patient. The first week of classes, on the very first occasion he offered his office hours, I showed up. It was a big office, far bigger than the offices of my teachers at Georgetown. Big but hideous. The carpet was a terrible burnt sort of color, the walls old and yellowing, the wood dark and masculine and forbidding

During that first visit I challenged, questioned, doubted the material of our class. He was, from the get-go, an engaging conversationalist, lively, pushy in the best of ways. His enthusiasm matched my own, he lit up the ugly space as I did. We were the perfect sparring partners. He encouraged my inquiries, my resistance, my skepticism, and at the same time he helped me to see what I might be missing, what might be worthwhile to think about, what I should possibly reconsider. I appreciated his effort to help me as my other professors had in the past. We agreed I'd come back weekly for a one-on-one discussion.

It was the joy of undergrad all over again, but this time in graduate school. I was thrilled by his attention, his affirmation of my intellectual worth, my academic talent. Right from the start, here was a professor who was investing in me, in my future, a busy, accomplished man who was using his valuable time to talk to a new student, and that student was me. He was like a diminutive and kindly grandfather, taking an interest in a young woman who might remind him of his granddaughter. I believed this and had no reason to think otherwise. All of my other professors had been like him, treating me like a newly dis-covered daughter, albeit an academic one, so his behavior wasn't surprising—it was the norm. I already had fantasies of taking other classes with him in the spring semester, of him becoming my dissertation adviser and my greatest mentor ever.

He planted these possibilities during our weekly chats, too. At the time and in the beginning, these feelings of anticipation and excitement were mutual.

I smiled often that first semester, though not just at him. I could never hide my happiness in the classroom, in read-ing philosophical theory, in asking questions. Why would I have ever thought to hide the rapture on my face when I showed up to his seminar or when I walked in the door of his office? I was grateful to be there. I was lucky, still. The smile on my face, that intellectual insatiability gnawing its way through my insides, I consented to them with gusto. They were the physical, visible manifestations of all that I was feeling.

That smile was, still is, to blame for so much of what came next, I think. The exuberance that was always spilling from my person. It was an outright invitation for him, for anyone, really, to look my way. And once he started looking, he never stopped.

2

I remember being in the car with him, on what could be called "our first date."

It was my car, a crap little black Mazda Protegé that began breaking down nearly the moment I left the lot, my father convinced I'd bought a lemon. It worked fine on this day in January, though, the heat blasting around us in the small space. The air outside was frosty, but there wasn't any snow on the ground. The seats were gray and speckled, the car's only luxuries a tape deck and a radio, which were turned off on this occasion. We were on our way to have a bite to eat, then I was to drive him home to the abbey where he lived with his fellow monks. I was wearing a dress, tights, boots, my hair long and loose. We'd just seen a play at a well-known theater not far from the university, a matinee, and had planned to go somewhere to talk about it afterward.

"I was thinking we could go to this Japanese teahouse," I told him as we filed out of the theater and into the light of day again.

"Wonderful!" His enthusiasm was clear and pure and he was game.

See what I mean by "date"?

To use this word to describe that January day would never have occurred to me back then. Only recently has this term for a get-together, a public meeting at a restaurant or bar between two people with a romantic spark, a kind of erotic frisson, seemed applicable to describe that first outing. A date was something I went on with boys my age, boys in their early to mid-twenties, boys I wanted to go out with, spend time with, to kiss and maybe, eventually, to have sex with. Boys I pursued and boys who pursued me, boys I found handsome, boys who intrigued me.

He was none of those things. He was an old man, not ugly, exactly, but I didn't give his looks any thought because why would I? He was my professor, decades my senior and, even more than this, a Catholic priest. A man who'd devoted his life to celibacy. To me, he was not even a sexual being. In graduate school I was still a young Catholic girl, and priests occupied a different species. They weren't quite human, or prone to human tendencies. They didn't have a sexual identity. They'd been stripped of it completely the moment they took their vows. Like magic, it was gone, evaporated into the ether on the day they stepped into their vocation. To attribute sexual or romantic thoughts to a priest was to transgress in the worst possible way, like showing up to church in a wet bathing suit, clumps of sand caked to your bare legs, leaving a trail of it down the center aisle between the pews. You just didn't do such things.

Teachers and professors occupied nearly the same level of sacred stature in my mind, so to me, this man was doubly safe, an asexual figure on two counts. Not at any point during the entirety of my adolescence and young adulthood had I considered a teacher in a romantic or sexual way. I don't think I even knew it was possible that professors might fall for their students, or students might fall for their professors. Not really.

The only experience I'd had of something close to this was a girl at my high school, someone who seemed far older than us even though she was only a senior when we were sophomores. She'd secretly started dating our gym teacher, a man we called Mr. Z. He was in college at the time, clocking his student-teaching hours, maybe two or three years older than she was. He was good-looking in a jock sort of way, and plenty of girls at my high school lusted after him. Mr. Z. often came up in discussions about hot boys we knew, or would like to know better. The proximity in age made him seem almost attainable, or at least permissible to dream of dating. But when rumors tore through the cafeteria about the secret relationship between him and one of our own, the fact that he was so close in age didn't matter to us any longer. The reality of Mr. Z. taking one of our plaid-skirted sisters up on what had always been a safe, schoolgirl fantasy was scandalous. It was exciting that the impossible had just become reality, it was thrilling to gossip about it, but we also knew it was *wrong* on an objective level. We knew he'd be fired if certain officials heard our whispering. The two of them went out, they broke up, they went out again. We thrilled at the roller coaster of their forbidden relationship. But aside from the fact that he was a teacher and she was a student, if they'd met elsewhere, say, at the beach in the summer, there would be nothing indecent about them going out, because they were practically the same age.

That was the extent of my experience with teacher-student relationships.

I didn't know how these relationships began, I didn't

consider how they might. Back then, on that first outing with my professor, it was like going somewhere with a harmless grandfather.

⁓

That first semester of graduate school, I'd given him things, little presents that weren't physical objects but something far more valuable: personal details, my likes, dislikes, bits of information about my mother, my father, how I spent my time outside class. He tucked them into a special treasure box to use later. I didn't know that what I'd handed over would turn out to be precious, tiny jewels I should have kept to myself, gifts that would make me vulnerable, that would open doors for him, doors I would later find were impossible to shut. He used them like wedges.

It was during our weekly office-hour chats. These personal things came up organically, on my way in from somewhere else, another class, a study session, if I was coming directly from home, or when I was leaving to meet a friend. Just before we began a discussion about the latest reading from the syllabus, or just afterward, the conversation between us would become casual, sparked by everyday questions. It seemed so benign.

Where are you off to? Where are you coming from? Why are you later than usual today?

His questions would prompt me to ask him the same in return. This is what's polite and I was raised to be polite. Also, I was accustomed to learning about the lives of my professors. I typically got to know them well, over time, and he was just the newest one to enter my life. I assumed I'd get to know him. I *wanted* to know him. I *wanted* to tell him things about me because I admired him, and I was excited he'd taken an interest in my academic future.

I not only consented, I *desired*. It feels important to note this fact.

At the end of the fall semester, when he was handing back our final papers, I saw that on mine, at the very end of it, he'd written a short letter about how much he'd enjoyed our weekly conversations, and would I like to go to a play with him in January? A generous couple donated season theater tickets to his abbey, and each time he went he invited a friend or a guest. Would I be his guest at the next one?

Yes, of course, I told him, though I don't remember how I passed on my consent. Was it in words, that same day? In a return note? Over the phone sometime in December while I was on break? All I know is that I agreed to go, and soon after the holidays, just before the beginning of spring semester, I was meeting him at the theater in early January, a decision I would come to regret with all my heart and soul, wishing with everything I am that I'd said no at the time instead.

There was a naked man on the stage.

There we were, this priest and I, sitting next to each other in the darkness of the theater, just a few rows from the front with a prime view of everything, especially of this naked man. Aside from being in the car together, this is my strongest memory of that day. During the play, a play that I can barely recall, not the title, the subject, the plot, nothing, the only thing I remember is that in the second act, the lead actor took off all his clothes. I think he was washing himself from a bucket as he acted out a monologue. When it happened, I wanted to disappear.

I kept my eyes front. I was frozen, hands clasped together in my lap.

I remember thinking: *This is so uncomfortable. The worst.*

It was akin to ending up at the theater with my own father and having to watch a man strip naked, which would have made both of us highly unhappy. I did not have parents who were okay with nudity. All nudity was sexual to them, so it was to be hidden away. This meant that all nudity was awkward for me around adults the same age as my parents or older, whether on the television screen, the movie screen, the beach, and certainly live, at a play. That was perhaps the worst situation in which to witness nakedness: with someone who, as I've already explained, seemed like my grandfather.

With a boyfriend, a friend my age, I would have been fine. I could have enjoyed the daring of it, a man disrobing onstage before all of us while we watched. I might have even contemplated the necessity of his doing this, or whether it was gratuitous to the plot. We could have referred to it afterward, me and a friend or a boyfriend, we could have discussed it, analyzed it. It would have been a blip, no big deal, just another element of the play, albeit a surprising one, since I wasn't prepared for it.

While it was happening and afterward, I wondered if my professor had known the man was going to do this, if he'd realized ahead of time that the play contained an element of nudity and had invited me anyway. But I was far more concerned that maybe he hadn't realized this, that he might be embarrassed to be in this situation, which was sitting in the presence of a naked man alongside a young woman, his student, and forced to act like it was fine. And there I was, eyes on the man's wrinkled backside, his sagging skin, telling myself that I was an adult, that this nudity was in the service of art, that I should not feel embarrassed or awkward, that I was not a little girl, that I did not have to channel the shame that my conservative Catholic parents instilled in me about nakedness. I told myself that the professor sitting next to me was an adult, too, even if he was a priest, despite the fact that he was a priest. That I should do my best to act as though it was totally normal to be sitting next to one of my professors at a play, watching a man disrobe and wash himself, while talking to the audience as if the whole situation weren't a big deal.

Eventually, the man onstage got dressed again. Eventually, the moment passed. Eventually, I could breathe again, I could stretch my fingers, I could relax a bit in my seat.

The entire time I hadn't moved my head, hadn't turned it even slightly. I don't know if my professor turned his, if he looked at me, watched me at all, during the play. It makes me laugh now to think how I'd worried about him that day, about his feelings, his comfort, and whether he might be embarrassed to have invited one of his young female students to a theater production that featured nudity. At the time, I hadn't yet figured out that as a man, he was shameless.

The Japanese teahouse we went to afterward was one of my favorite places.

It was a little café-restaurant of sorts. It was beautiful inside, airy and tall, lots of wooden counters and shelves. It had two floors. You would order on the first floor, then wait until you had your tea, your food, your cookies and sweets, to park yourself and your tray at one of the stools that lined the walls downstairs or carry everything upstairs to grab one of the tables. You were supposed to wait until your order was called to find a seat. They had signs everywhere about waiting, about not taking up a table until you were ready to eat, about how their system worked better if people already had their food when they found a place to sit, that people without their food should patiently leave the tables alone until these circumstances changed.

I always preferred the second floor. It was as serene as the first floor was busy. I loved the tables against each of the walls, especially those closest to the windows. I used to disobey the signs and sneak upstairs right after I placed my order, hoping I'd find a table free, hoping none of the staff would send me back downstairs when they noticed I didn't yet have my tray. Sometimes I went there alone to study, to treat myself to the delicious food and desserts, to the peace and beauty of that upstairs room. It was such a luxury to go there to read, to choose to spend my hard-earned money like this, as though I were much older than my years. When I did go, it seemed that true adulthood had arrived, that I was now a sophisticated woman who went to elegant cafés to study and work and think, like in a French movie or in one of my fashion magazines.

On the afternoon I brought him with me, it had seemed a good option, since it was close to the theater. I found parking and we walked inside to contemplate our order. I described all the things I loved on the menu, and we ended up both getting a chicken-with-yellow-curry dish, one of my go-to items. Then we disobeyed the signs and went straight upstairs to get a table. It was quiet that day, very few people up there with us. As we waited for our food, I kept going back to the first floor to check on our order. This was the downside of ignoring their system. It's not as though they had a speaker upstairs so you could hear your number. The point was serenity, and the point was also that you'd remain downstairs until your order was called, which meant if you didn't, you were stuck checking to see if your food was up, or risk it getting cold.

I was as excited to share this place with him as I would be with any of my other friends. As it happened, I'd invited many of them to this favorite haunt, and we'd spent long lunches and dinners at the very same table where he and I now sat.

I don't remember much about our conversation that day, what was said and discussed, if it was mostly about my graduate program or if it had spilled into more personal subjects. I do remember that I made sure to steer clear of talking about the naked man in the play, that I avoided this at all costs. Otherwise, we might have talked about anything. The weather, books, philosophers, family. All I know for sure is that we went, we were there, and we sat upstairs, eating chicken curry.

I didn't know then that later on I would come to hate him and everything to do with him, everything I associated with him, even what had been one of my favorite places to go and sit with my girlfriends, to talk about our lives while eating our lunch, or to sit by myself in the cherished serenity, feeling like a sophisticated young woman. I used to love these salty oat cookies they always had in a covered dish on the counter, and their ginger scones. I still remember exactly how each one of those tasted and I haven't been back in years. I wish I had known that my decision to drive us there after the play would be the death of this treasured spot for me.

I wonder if I could stomach going there now, so many years later. Exorcise its demons so I could enjoy it again. I honestly can't say. Either way, it will always be tainted.

3

I kissed all the boys in high school, all the boys I deemed worth kissing, which was a long list. I was a kissing bandit. I kissed tall boys, short boys, athletic boys, boys who were like waifs, boys with accents, all-American boys, hot boys, cute boys, not-so-cute boys, boys who were decidedly unattractive, boys who made me laugh, boys who were assholes, boys who I thought might become the love of my life and boys who I absolutely knew would not. Smart, talkative, shy, obnoxious, dense, hilarious, sweet, boring, mysterious, I did not discriminate.

Once after a prom I kissed three different boys in a single night. Two Marks and a Brian. It was exhilarating. The three different kisses, which were really three intense make-out sessions, may have happened within an hour. First, I kissed my date (one of the Marks), then I wandered the hallway of the hotel where the kids at the prom had rented rooms and ran into the second Mark, who'd always made me laugh, and dove right into an enthusiastic lip-locking with him. It was not particularly skillful on either of our parts, but we left giggling and smiling two minutes later to return to our dates. Not long after that on another hallway wander, I ran into Brian, tall, sweet, athletic Brian, who was funny and also somewhat bashful, and found myself reaching up around his neck as he bent down, arms encircling my waist, and shared the most romantic and meaningful kiss of my three-boy evening. That kiss was the beginning of a pre-college romance, doomed once I got to Georgetown and found a new boy I wanted to kiss. But at the time, Brian was lovely.

My senior year in high school I was a shameless flirt, a zealous true believer in the religion of making out, but I hadn't always been that way. At that point, I was making up for lost time, since I was a late bloomer in the boy department.

I'd been a serious gymnast and dancer since I was a child, which also meant that for a long time I had no life at all, at least not socially. I spent too many hours at practice on the bar, the beam, the floor exercise, and the always and increasingly terrifying vault, too many weekends preparing for competitions to ever care to go to a dance or hang out with people after school. But then came an injury and the pain and loss of quitting, and suddenly I had a lot of time on my hands and no idea what to do with it. Soon I discovered the world of "normal" girls my age, a world filled with makeup and dieting and too-short skirts and Friday-night dances and gushing over all the cute boys in my state. (As I said before, Rhode Island is small, so it seemed possible for us to catalog each and every potential crush from towns near and somewhat far.)

I was fifteen and never been kissed, and then I was sixteen and in the same boat. Competitive gymnasts can fly through the air in death-defying somersaults, but put us in front of a boy and we'll likely furrow our brow or run the other way. In my forced retirement I watched, I studied, I learned how to be a girl my age through my growing friendships with other girls my age, girls who were long skilled in the art of boyfriend catching, outfit curating, and getting someone to ask them to dance in those dark gyms with music blaring and bright flashing lights. In my dedicated pursuit of High School Normalcy Studies, I learned to be ashamed of my lack of experience and felt lucky I'd told no one that, in my athletic early adolescence, kissing remained a conspicuous and embarrassing deficiency on my social CV. How does one move from never-been-kissed into the ranks of the finally-been-kissed? It seemed a Heideggerian shift of ontological proportions without a rule book or instructions.

Following a long summer of stumbling flirtations and confusing yet forward banter with an Irish boy who worked at the beach, in the dark hallways of the cabanas I took a deep, courageous breath and proposed to this green-eyed young man that we kiss. I knew he'd say yes, but my heart was pounding. I was concerned about doing things badly, about embarrassing myself terribly. But the kiss happened—it finally happened. It was mostly just tongues pushing around each other in one big, wet mess, but I didn't care. Inside, I was celebrating that I was no longer a kissing virgin. Hurrah! Mission accomplished, ontological shift achieved.

I had finally bloomed. Soon I was a big, glaring poppy.

My kissing career occurred before the existence of slut shaming, at least officially. There wasn't a term for it then, even though the practice existed. Girls shamed each other, they spread rumors, chastised one another, but kissing felt exempt from what counted as slutty behavior. It was so minor, just lips pressed against each other and maybe a little tongue. Nobody was going to get pregnant from kissing, nobody had to take off any clothes. Kissing could be as brief as a few seconds or as intense as a four-hour make-out session. Kisses were innocent and uncomplicated; they were fun, they were playful, they were exciting, and even when they weren't fun or playful or exciting or even slightly good, it still wasn't that big a deal.

This was the perfect sexual activity for someone like me, because I *was* innocent. Life was black-and-white. I had close to zero sexual knowledge and was happy to keep it that way. There was no internet to show me otherwise and very few girls around with enough experience to enlighten me (or few who openly admitted they could). My Catholic parents didn't have a conversation with me about the forbidden subject either, so it mostly remained a mystery, and that was completely fine with me. It was empowering and blissful to run around Rhode Island kissing as many boys as I could find to kiss me back. I was sexually liberated and, somehow, I'd arrived there without having sex at all. The power and freedom came from the joy and pleasure of discovering my own desires, desires that spilled over into the pursuit of the boys I kissed and the boys who chose to kiss me. This power and confidence carried me through college on a thrilling wave that never crashed, even as I expanded my repertoire far beyond kissing.

I was happy in my body, I felt in control of it, and I expressed this faith in the way that I dressed. I became fashionable, as fashionable as a girl on work-study could be. I was clever at shopping at discount stores and finding designer labels at T J Maxx and Marshalls, a fiend during the sales after Thanksgiving and Christmas.

My poor mother frequently expressed dismay at having a clotheshorse of a daughter, at my frivolity and obsession with shopping. She also knew it was her own mother's fault, my beloved grandmother, who lived with us and who planted this seed in me and watered it regularly with our biweekly trips to JCPenney and Woolworths when I was a kid. Shopping was my grandmother's favorite activity. I watched as she bought cheap blouses and purses (my grandmother could never have enough purses), asked my opinion on this and that one, picking out new colors of nail polish to match her latest outfit.

My grandmother worked outside the house for her entire adult life, which was unusual for women of her era, especially Italian immigrant women. She was the first woman supervisor at Raytheon in Newport, a well-dressed, proper lady in a sea of men, put in charge of building submarines. She wasn't about to surrender her inclination to wear skirts just because she was in what was considered a man's job, and she relished all the pretty things we saw at the mall. There was no conflict for her between the stereotypical femininity of the day and being a hardworking woman. I learned this from her, and it stayed with me.

My grandmother was the greatest heroine of my youth. I wanted to be just like her then, and I still do today. She was everything my mother was not—she was relaxed, she was rebellious, she draped herself in costume jewelry to go to the market, she dyed her hair blond. She was funny and quick to laugh, and she moved through a difficult, immigrant life with perseverance and grace. She was stylish, and I wanted to be as stylish as she was. She was the person who renewed my subscription to *Seventeen* each year. I read it the way I'd later read those novels my AP Lit teacher assigned, avidly, studiously, dog-earing the pages with my favorite ensembles, after which I'd rip them out and place them in a file I kept with the pictures of the other clothes I longed to possess. Sometimes I would show my grandmother this collection of dream outfits, and we would ooh and aah over them together.

In high school, during my post-gymnastics years, I learned the art of leaving the house in one outfit, the one my mother approved of, then changing into the outfit she would never let me wear. When I used to try to escape through the door in my little black boots and skirts that barely reached the middle of my thigh, my mother inevitably caught me.

"You look like a streetwalker," she'd scream, literally scream, her arm pointing in the direction of my room, sending me back to change, an early and fervent adopter of slut shaming. *Streetwalker* was my mother's favorite term during my last years of high school, and she would glare accusingly at my grandmother for these transgressions.

In college I became more stylish, less Rhode Island *guido*, more sophisticated young woman of the world, showing off my muscular runner's legs and my petite frame. My magazine reading grew more sophisticated, too, as I let my subscription to *Seventeen* lapse, replacing it with *Vogue* and *Elle* and *Harper's Bazaar*. I loved boots, high-heeled boots, and wore them as often as I could. I loved the way the boys turned their heads, admiringly, as I walked by. I could never have enough of their attention, I was never satiated by it, and I dressed as much for them as I did for me.

I want to be clear about this part. I dressed for myself but I also dressed for them. Even when I had a boyfriend, which I often did, I wanted to look my best, always. I wanted to be noticed and noticed often. I courted attention. I absolutely courted it, without apology. I was proud of my attention-grabbing looks and outfits and confidence, and I was happy in my sexual prowess. I was stupid with power. I would be punished for it.

I feel the need to account for such things as being a kissing bandit, for dressing in high-heeled boots and short skirts during college and beyond, for smiling giddily at my professors and showing up regularly to their office hours. This cataloging feels essential.

First, because for the era in which I became a young adult—the late eighties and nineties—I was as intellectually and sexually empowered as any girl my age could hope to be. This was despite my very Catholic upbringing, which was accompanied by no formal sex education whatsoever. The closest my parents, my mother, ever got to talking to me about sex was during one summer when I was nine or ten. I'd been playing outside with the neighborhood kids and was running up the front walk to go in the house and grab a snack from the kitchen. My mother was gardening in a nearby flower bed, kneeling on the brown scratchy rug she always used, gloves on, trowel in hand, the brim of her floppy gardening hat shielding her eyes. One of the boys we'd been warring with was riding by the yard on his bike, and he yelled some taunt or other at me as I neared the front door.

I stopped and turned.

"You SUCK!" I yelled back at him.

We said this to each other all the time while playing. You suck, he sucks, they suck. I don't know when it started, but we all called upon the power of *suck* regularly. It did not seem momentous to be yelling this at one of the stupid, annoying neighborhood boys and in front of my mother. But I remember seeing out of the corner of my eye how she shot up from her gardening rug, trowel still in hand. Uh-oh.

"Donna!" she scolded, already walking toward me. "Go inside. We're going to talk."

She sat me down on the couch, it was all very serious, and my stomach knotted and reknotted while I waited to see what I could have possibly done wrong.

"Do you know what *suck* means?" she asked.

I shrugged. Then I shook my head. I had no idea where this was going.

Her eyes did not leave me. "It has to do with *sex,*" she said.

I swallowed. Why had I yelled that stupid word? What in the world was she talking about? Now I was stuck on the couch with my mother, still in her floppy gardening hat, discussing sex on this sunshine-filled summer day while the playing between the neighborhood kids went on outside without me.

"It is something a woman does to a man," my mother went on, without elaborating what sucking thing, exactly, the woman would do. "It's against the Catholic Church. *And* it's against the law."

"Okay," I said, unable to comprehend what she could be talking about or what she might mean, but I wanted out—out of this conversation, out of this house and into the fresh air, out of this sucky, sucky situation.

"We do not say that word in this family. It's a bad word about a bad thing."

"I won't say it again," I told her. "I promise."

My mother stood. "Good," she said, and that was that.

I got my snack, she went back to her gardening, and the subject of sex never came up again between us or with anyone else in my house.

That was the extent of my sex education—an impossibly vague sexual association with the word *suck*. Only years later would I realize that my mother was referring to oral sex, and by the time I figured this out, I thought the whole thing was hilarious. But in so many ways, this lesson was indicative of how the rest of my sex education was and would continue to be—a sort of learning by doing on my part, a figuring out how things worked by trying them out or thinking enough about them that I would eventually understand how and if they were something I thought I'd like, would want to try, or if they sounded appealing or unappealing. But I had no fear, no hang-ups, mostly just an insatiable curiosity and interest and excitement about the mysteries and pleasures of sex and all that went with it, much like the curiosity I had for everything in the world and history and life. Sex was just one more thing to investigate and enjoy. I experimented with glee.

So, I got to this place of sexual empowerment through sheer experience and trial and error. I came to know my limits, my own desires, through practice, and I drew and withdrew boundaries accordingly with my various partners and with respect to my own volition. I had zero anxiety about saying no to someone, and an unbending faith that my nos would be respected by my partners when I did. My expectations for sex, for pleasure, for what would and wouldn't happen, for how I was to be treated and not treated, were expressed clearly and openly and with total self-assurance on my part.

This does not mean that my life unfolded without pain, without difficulty, without heartbreak or setback or disappointment. It had all of these things, and plenty of them. But these common occurrences in the life of a young woman did not sway or shake or dismantle the sexual confidence with which I left high school and then Georgetown and went out into the world of work and graduate school. When things happened with a partner that I found I did not like, or if a partner behaved in a manner that seemed problematic or unbecoming of someone I wanted to be with, I had no qualms about ending things, about telling this person what I thought, about turning and walking in the other direction. The trial-and-error aspect of my sexual education did not harm me in any irreparable way. I had an unbreakable sense of certainty with respect to my sexual decision-making, an unshakable enthusiasm about sex and sexual experiences. I was happy and sure of myself in this regard.

This confidence I possessed, the reason I emphasize it, is not to brag or pat myself on the back. It's because I think that we believe, or we hope—I certainly have hoped—that raising young women to be empowered sexually, certain in the drawing and withdrawing of boundaries, exuberant in their yeses and nos, will somehow save them from the experience of assault and harassment. That it will shield against or at least soften such experiences, temper the force of tragedy, protect girls and women from the worst of what can happen. This didn't prove to be true in my case. No amount of sexual liberation, freedom, confidence, intellectual talent, joy, or voracity would save me from going through what I did with my mentor. When it happened to me, no amount of sexual empowerment could have prevented me from becoming the silenced, anxiety-ridden, nearly destroyed young woman that I became further on in my graduate-school years. The girl who began to blame herself for everything that happened.

It was in graduate school that my life split in two. One life continued to be one of total and utter sexual empowerment with the young men I hit on, dated, went out with, kissed, had sex with. I was studying feminist theory, eating it up and loving every second of it. I was thriving intellectually, and as usual, my professors loved me as much as I loved them. But as time went on, that second life emerged, utterly divorced from the first. It was a life of fear, uncertainty, of self-condemnation, of second-guessing and third- and fourth- and fifth-guessing and so on. In *that* life, I questioned everything I was, my decision to attend my professors' office hours, every stitch of clothing I put on my body when I went to classes.

Who did I think I was, showing up to graduate school

each day dressed like I'd stepped off a magazine page? What did I expect would happen? Did I really not know that older men might pay attention? What was I doing, going about the world kissing and dating and having sex with all the boys I wanted? What is the punishment for a young woman with sexual and intellectual confidence? Doesn't she know that the world sees this as hubris, that it will not allow her to thrive for long? That the world in fact is far better at crushing such qualities in a woman?

The more pressing questions I have now, in hindsight, are these: Why didn't feminism save me? Shouldn't it have functioned like armor, to ward off what happened? Why didn't it transfer from the pages of my books and studies into reality, like fictional characters who leap to life in a movie?

In the end, there wasn't enough feminism in the world to save me from the situation in which I eventually found myself. I maintained those two conflicting identities day in and day out: the sexually empowered young feminist among my fellow students and men my age, and the utterly sexually disempowered, shattered young woman with one man far older and more powerful than me. The second identity I hid from everyone. For a long time, even from myself.

4

One day, maybe a couple of weeks after that outing to the theater, I found a newspaper clipping in my mailbox at graduate school.

It was an article about the basketball team I grew up cheering for, about the unexpectedly successful season that they were having and that might land them an NCAA bid later that year. An article about basketball was out of place in my TA mailbox. It made me smile all the wider when I saw it, this reminder of home, of family, of nights seated next to my dad at the gym where URI played, screaming at the ref, praying for those last-minute half-court shots to go in, trying to negotiate the superstitions that haunted my family in the silliest of ways, use them to help our team make foul shots and win possessions and turnovers.

It meant a lot that when my professor saw this article in the paper, he remembered how important this team was to me, that he knew it wasn't "just" basketball, but something central and constructive to my family, something that cut to the heart of the complicated relationship I had with my father. My professor knew this so well he thought I might want to have the article and had cut it out of the paper for me as a keepsake.

I know it might sound like an insignificant gesture, but I look back on this one tiny thing, a short article about my family's basketball team, as one of the foundational acts on his part that I would come back to again and again as evidence of his innocence, of his selfless concern for my well-being. It was a gesture that won him a lot of forgiveness for other things, at least at the beginning. The way to my heart is through the heart of my father, of my family, and somehow in those early days, he already knew this to be the case.

Basketball, this team in particular, was central to my childhood. The University of Rhode Island was the place my father wanted to go to college as a young man, but couldn't, so he'd installed himself as an avid athletic supporter later in life and installed all of us around him in the venture. My mother, me, my grandmother, too.

My father is a good man, a quiet man, stoic and enduring, hardworking, so hardworking that it hurts me to think about it directly. I love him so much that it's painful to see through to his vulnerabilities. Life has been difficult for my father, as it was difficult for his immigrant Portuguese family when he was growing up. He developed a thick shell to weather such challenges, so many setbacks and disappointments. He is a small man, bald, with golden skin that turns the deep brown of the earth in summer. He doesn't talk much, except to make the occasional wry comment or observation, and he keeps his emotions in check, so much that I have feared the moment when they will surely erupt, vast and terrible, burning him down in the process because he's held them in for so long.

But basketball, URI basketball, opens my father up like nothing else I've ever encountered, and he's always taken me along with him in his excitement around it. On Christmas, gifts that were Keaney blue, URI's jersey color, were especially prized in my family, and any time we could match a pair of socks, a sweater, a T-shirt, a tie, anything to that shade of blue was a triumph. Our family's life revolved around each basketball season, from the first practice of the year until the very last loss during the tournaments. We went to every single home game and traveled in cars and on buses to some of the away games, too. URI basketball was as sacred to my family as church on Sunday. To miss a game, we needed to be on our deathbed, or perhaps receiving the Nobel Peace Prize. Luckily, proms took place in the springtime, because if a prom had conflicted with a URI game, the prom would have been the obvious sacrifice, and not the other way around.

I rarely resented this. Going to games is one of my happiest memories of growing up, of time spent with my family, with my dad especially. Being at Keaney Gym was an experience that spans the entirety of my childhood and young adulthood. I grew up there as much as I grew up at my house. When I was a little girl, the cheerleaders fascinated me so much that my mother and grandmother made me pompoms in Keaney blue and white, a painstaking process that took them weeks to complete. I dragged those things around with me for years, shaking them wildly and constantly in the stands. When I was small, games meant two hours of delightedly watching cheerleaders on the sidelines and during time-outs, learning their chants, and fantasizing about getting to be one someday. When later I fell in love with the baton twirler who did the halftime show, Santa brought me my very own baton that next Christmas. There was nothing as exciting as knowing that, just after the buzzer signaled the end of the first half, the lights would dim, a spotlight would go on at the center of the floor, and for five thrilling minutes the girl in the amazing spangled leotard and tights would twirl her baton and throw it high into the rafters, miraculously catching it without fail, while I watched her, rapt, sitting between my mother and grandmother.

Basketball itself—the action on the floor, the players— was also a great attraction. I learned to love the game; my father taught me the rules as we watched together. I witnessed my normally subdued, working-class father come alive for those two-and-a-half-hour snatches of time as he shouted his approval of the players, and yelled and swore at the refs. My parents would invite the players to our house on the weekends for a home-cooked meal, and how I loved them all, loved having these seven-foot friends. The weekly ritual was that the moment they walked through the door, one of them would pick me up, high enough that I could put my hand on the ceiling. It delighted me, how they had to duck to get through the archway between the foyer and the living room. I loved their impossibly long legs, the way they towered over the grown-ups. Every week after we ate lunch or dinner, one of them would read me a story on the couch, usually something by Dr. Seuss, because it made me laugh when they tripped over those crazy rhymes. I think they did it on purpose because they knew I found it funny. The players closest to us were so trusted by my parents that occasionally they would pick me up from school or attend my gymnastics meets. One of my most thrilling memories of childhood is leaving school and seeing my favorite seven-foot player standing there outside the building, dwarfing the other parents and children. He lifted me high into the air for a hug, then set me on the ground again, taking my hand so we could walk to the car as everyone watched, mouths gaping wide.

When my family didn't go to the away games, if they were broadcast on TV we'd watch at home, all of us, my grandmother, mother, father, and me, gathered around the television set. When it comes to sports, I am tremendously and proudly superstitious, and it was during these games that I learned this essential aspect of being a dedicated fan. In between the screaming and the yelling, the jumping up from the couch and the chairs of the living room to clap and cheer, my father would bark orders about who could do what, who could enter the room and leave, who had to remain standing or sitting, depending on when things took a turn for the worse or better during the game.

"Grandma," my father would direct, "go back into the bathroom," if my grandmother happened to have slipped out earlier when both foul shots were made. She would dutifully endure her banishment in the service of helping the team to more baskets as the clock ticked down its final seconds—as any of us would have, including my father.

Nowadays, as friends and loved ones have witnessed my behavior at a sporting event, whether at a game or at home, they've been slightly shocked to see the extent of my superstitions, and the lengths to which I will go to act them out if the game is a nail-biter. During the 2017 Super Bowl, when the Patriots were embarrassing all of us New England fans in a game against the Atlanta Falcons that seemed impossible to turn around, the very moment they began to come back, when they scored the touchdown that changed everything, I happened to have gone upstairs. Because of this, I watched the rest of the game from the bottom step, jumping up and down and cheering from there, convinced that if I placed one foot on the living room floor and the Patriots lost, it would be my fault. I didn't want that kind of responsibility on my shoulders, so I fulfilled my duty as a fan and stayed put.

My superstition around sports may be a source of amusement to friends, but it's a source of pride to me. It's something I share with my father, a fun and funny trait we both have, a sign of our devotion to and investment in a team. My father taught me to care deeply about sports, he passed this love on to me, and the expression of these superstitions is a way of expressing his influence. I looked forward to telling him the story of my personal contribution to the Patriots' 2017 Super Bowl win, because I knew how much he'd appreciate it. I knew he would recognize himself in my behavior. That he would say to himself, *Yes, that's my daughter.*

The love my father and I have for basketball and other sports is one of the central dimensions of our closeness. It is a shared truth between my dad and me, and we have relied on it to get us through some of the most difficult turns in our lives over the years.

My decision to become a philosophy major at Georgetown nearly destroyed us. My father, who had not been lucky enough to go to college himself, saw Georgetown as a means for me to avoid the economic hardships he'd faced as a young man trying to make a living without a degree. My parents had checked off the box for my major the summer before I left for college; they signed me up for accounting in the business school. Accounting was a sure thing for a life of steady work and a good salary, and this was what they cared about most. When I arrived on campus and discovered my love for philosophy, a love related to those books I'd read in my private English class during high school, I had no idea what a battle I was in for with my father over majoring in it. I thought he might never forgive me for defying him in this way.

For nearly the entirety of my undergraduate years, basketball—URI basketball, Georgetown basketball—was the only thing he and I were able to talk about. We hung on to basketball for dear life. It was all we had.

⁓

When I said earlier that I gave my professor things during my first semester of graduate school, this is one of the things I'd handed over. This knowledge of my family, of my father in particular, this method through which he and I still held on to each other, that URI basketball was our enduring tether. Bits and pieces of this story had come out during my weekly visits to my professor's office hours, including how my father had come around to the idea of my getting a PhD partly because of basketball.

Just as he'd opposed my becoming a philosophy major during my undergraduate years, my father originally argued against this new pursuit of mine. He wanted me on a path to a stable, moneymaking career, and in his mind, a PhD was not going to get me there. Once again, we were in the middle of a familiar standoff. But when I was accepted into multiple graduate programs, the departments began to outbid one another in the amount of funding they could offer me.

"It's like you're a basketball player," my father observed one day over the phone, after I'd told him about the different offers.

For him, this was a eureka moment, and the highest of compliments. Likening me to a sought-after basketball player was a sign that my father had finally understood, in his own way, that my getting a PhD was a good idea. I remember feeling teary on hearing these words from him, teary and relieved and happy that he was starting to make a shift away from dismay about the path I'd chosen toward support. Little by little, he continued this shift, and ever since he likened me to a basketball star being recruited by colleges, he's never looked back. It was a turning point in our relationship.

I don't know why I told my professor so many personal things that semester. I'm not sure if I was needy for affirmation from someone I saw as a mentor, greedy for attention, or if he was sneaky and pulled these things out of me through innocuous, seemingly innocent conversation each time I visited his office. All I know is that I told him things, and plenty of them.

It's not as though my other professors in college or teachers in high school didn't know me on a personal level. In fact, my philosophy professors knew all about my parents' resistance to my course of study at Georgetown. I went to them for help when my father threatened to pull me out of school if I pursued a philosophy major. I was traumatized at the thought I wouldn't be able to study what I loved, which was also what my parents hated. I wanted desperately to follow my intellectual desires, an experience they could not relate to, a reality that still makes me sad to remember. Like so many parents who were the children of immigrants, they'd longed to give me a college education, yet by giving it to me they'd unwittingly set me up to become a person they could no longer understand, who had hopes and dreams that were outside of anything they could imagine or conceive of as sensible. College was a means to a job and a steady salary, not a place to sit around and explore exciting ideas. If those ideas didn't make you into an accountant, or get you a job on Wall Street, they weren't worth thinking about, according to my mother and father. My parents did everything they could to set me up for the moneymaking career that no one had set them up for, and I was squandering it on a degree in philosophy.

My undergraduate professors helped me frame my philosophy major as something more practical, helped me think about how to explain this to my parents. I am grateful to those professors at Georgetown for so many things, but I will always be indebted for their help in negotiating with my family, my father especially, on this issue. He never came around to supporting my philosophy major, but he eventually got to a point where he stopped threatening to pull me out of Georgetown. We can laugh about this now, though for many years, my studying philosophy during undergrad was something we didn't speak about. Lucky for us, in addition to being a philosophy major I'd also become a basketball cheerleader, so when friends at my father's bar would ask what I was doing at Georgetown, he would answer by telling them that I was a cheerleader.

I stood there, next to the TA mailboxes in my department's office, reading the newspaper clipping in my hand. My professor had placed the article in an envelope, addressed simply, my name written across it and nothing else. I was touched that he had taken the time to give me this small thing. I thought it incredibly sweet.

Is it wrong that I told him so many things about my life? Poor judgment that I gave him such personal details about my life, my family? My fault that I spoke to him like he might be my age, telling him the kinds of details that I share with the people closest to me, stories that I would confide in a boyfriend or a best girlfriend? Why didn't I know any better? Should I have? I was in my early twenties, not a child anymore, not a teenager.

Or is it wrong that he took the things I gave to him, filed them away to use for later, as a means to get to me, as a means to *get me,* to try to make me his? I don't know who is at fault here. If he believed that I was the one trying to create intimacy between us, if he thought that these stories about my family, my history, were an attempt to entice him into something else, something other than an appropriate relationship between professor and student, mentor and mentee. Did he regard me as some kind of Lolita, showing up to his office as I showed up everywhere else, in my skirts and boots and sweaters? Someone who was asking for it, asking for him, asking for something more from him?

What I do know is that I regret it, that I wish I could take it all back. That I will blame myself forever for these initial, intimate offerings that I brought to him, like I sometimes brought the bread and wine to the altar at church. He was a priest, after all, accustomed to receiving gifts each week.

But at that early point, it never occurred to me that this professor would have cut out that newspaper article and placed it in my graduate-school mailbox for any other reason than to be kind. It never crossed my mind that maybe he was trying to impress me, like a boy who wanted to date me might want to impress me, or that he hoped to deepen the intimacy between us, to use the tether between me and my dad as a way to insert himself into that tender space I reserved for my father in my heart.

5

My professor was outside my apartment, peering through the window.

It was not quite a basement apartment, but sort of half underground, the windows level with the sidewalk. I'd gone to retrieve a pile of mail that had fallen through the slot in the front door. I jumped when I saw him, watching me from above. He wasn't smiling, didn't wave. It was a cold day in late February, or maybe it was early March, and he just stood there staring at me through the small rectangular pane of glass. He hadn't warned me that he might show up, or asked if I'd be around that day, or requested permission to say hello at my home. He just arrived.

I opened the door. Moved aside so he could descend the steps into the living room.

"I was in the neighborhood," he explained as he entered my house. He had a conference that day in Georgetown, he told me, or perhaps it was a meeting with other priests, or a visit to the library to pick up a book he needed. I can't remember exactly. Or maybe it was none of those things and he simply lied and invented a reason to be near my apartment so he could come by and visit, see where I lived, what my life was like outside school. He wore his typical all-black attire, the black shirt of a priest, black pants, but no collar. He rarely wore a collar and often had a loose black blazer of sorts that he wore over everything.

He stopped in front of the couch, looking around.

This was a first for me, to have a professor in my house.

"Would you like some tea?" I asked. "Or coffee?"

His face brightened, he said yes, he wanted tea, and I invited him to sit at the little wooden table pressed against the wall of the kitchen while I put on the kettle. The day was gray, a good day for drinking something warm.

We were alone.

My roommate worked during the week at an office, left at eight in the morning and usually didn't return until well after six. I don't remember if I'd told him about her, about our friendship, our style of living, the fact that she and I would occasionally put the music on loud and dance in the living room, how she was as obsessed with fashion as I was and we would have marathon shopping days, or how once in a while we would host a keg party and persuade one of our guy friends to go to the liquor store and bring the heavy metal barrel back for us and tap it on our back patio.

I joined him at the table while we waited for the water to boil.

We made small talk. He was very animated. I served him the tea when it was ready. I was still a bit startled that I suddenly had him in my house. But I wasn't unhappy. I came around to enjoy the conversation, as I'd always enjoyed our conversations when we met in his office. He was a smart man, enthusiastic about our shared academic interests, and it was easy to like this part of him. I don't remember how long he stayed. Maybe an hour? Eventually he went on his way again, and that was all. The visit wasn't a big deal. Short, just a cup of tea, and then he was off.

There are several mental snapshots from that visit that have stayed with me, though. Seeing his face peering at me through the window of my front door. Seeing him standing in the middle of my living room. Seeing him sitting in the blond wooden chair in my kitchen, his expression pleased.

After he left, I had my first flicker of doubt, a slight disquiet that nagged at me.

It reminded me of the moment at the theater when the man was naked onstage, and I'd felt paralyzed with awkwardness and discomfort. But that was different from what I felt now. My professor couldn't control the plot of the play or the actors within it. Yet today, this time, he'd made a decision to come over to my house, which struck me as forward. The unease it provoked was faint, like a single bead on a necklace. I barely felt its tug.

It was easy for him to justify his visit. It made total sense that he would be in my neighborhood, which was Georgetown's neighborhood—Georgetown, a Jesuit school full of Jesuit priest-professors. As a Catholic priest and a professor himself, he would surely have reason to be there on occasion. Georgetown was a place where he had plenty of his own affiliations. He was an alum, like me.

But it wasn't until much later that it occurred to me that I had never given him my address, or directions to my somewhat hidden apartment. That he must have looked up my home address in my personal files at graduate school, to which he had full access since he was my professor and also, at the time, an administrator of a department; that he would have had to write down my address on a piece of paper and go scouring the neighborhood to find it. This was the nineties, well before GPS and Google Maps.

Now, decades later, I wonder what he was thinking as he made his way to my apartment that first time, if he'd woken up that morning and made it his purpose to visit me at home, or if he'd even planned this excursion in advance. I wonder if he thought much at all about what he was doing, or if it really was a spontaneous decision on his part, as he'd told me. Back then, it wouldn't have occurred to me to wonder if he was lying.

If I had to guess the truth today, knowing what I know, I would say that he likely planned his visit, maybe even days ahead. He needed my address, and for that he had to go into my records. This required him to stop in the main office of the graduate school. This looking up of my records would become a habit of his. I would guess, too, that when he set out for Georgetown that morning, if he did indeed visit the library, or some other priests on campus, he did it only as a way of justifying his presence near my house. Maybe it was also a way to justify the letters he began to send me there.

I had two places where I collected the mail. One was in my department at school, where I received correspondence about my program, and the other was at my apartment.

I went to school pretty much every single day. I was full time, so I was often in class, plus I needed to attend the lectures of the professor for whom I was a TA, and on Fridays I ran discussion sections with my students. I was always around, and I often liked to sit in the little room where people went to get coffee and tea, or to read between classes, or sometimes to eat their bag lunches at the round table near the windows. It was called the Etc. Room and had a sign on the door naming it as such. I was a regular presence there, like many of my fellow students. I loved being at school because I loved everything about getting my PhD.

That spring, I did not have a class with this professor, though I would still swing by to see him occasionally. His office was on a different floor than my department, in a different wing of the building. I had to go there on purpose; I was never just walking down his hallway. We didn't see each other regularly anymore as we had in the fall, so when he began leaving things in my TA mailbox—that first story about the URI basketball team, then other newspaper articles that he thought I might like to read and short notes asking if I would stop by his office, followed by requests that we make time for coffee, or maybe another play—at first it seemed like a nice thing for him to do. He was making sure to stay in touch. I appreciated his effort to maintain his concern for my studies and my place in his program. I was flattered, too. I was, and I need to admit that. His attention made me feel special, though not special in a way that a boy I liked might make me feel special. Special as an aspiring intellectual, as an aspiring PhD, as an aspiring professor, like himself.

But when the first letter from him arrived at my home address, I thought: *Huh.*

I picked it up from the floor of my apartment with the rest of the mail, a letter addressed to me in a long rectangular envelope. I knew his handwriting by then because of the notes he'd been leaving in my TA mailbox and from his comments on my papers the previous semester. Plus, I recognized the return address. He'd used his abbey stationery, which had the abbey's address printed in the top left-hand corner. I don't remember the contents of the letter, just its arrival. It was the first of several he would send to me at that particular apartment, and the first of many more he would later send to my apartment on Georgetown's campus, once I began working in Residence Life there later on in the summer.

I never gave him any of my home addresses. Not the apartment I shared with my roommate, not the one I'd soon have at Georgetown, not the house where my family lived in Rhode Island. But he sent letters to all of those places. Eventually I would have three mailboxes, and he would send things to every one of them. Notes. Cards. Invitations. Articles. Sometimes, there would be a letter from him waiting for me in all three places on the very same afternoon. To this day, no single person has ever sent me that much mail. Not a friend, a boyfriend, a lover, a husband. But early on, I still thought of his letters as nice gestures.

Even today, as I recount these stories about the correspondence he began with me and that surprise visit to my house, I am still full of doubt about everything that happened. Am I making too big a deal over it? Is it really innocent after all? It's not as though he showed up in my apartment that day and grew violent, or tried to have sex with me, or even gave me the kind of line that a man who was hitting on me might at a bar. There was no "Hey, honey" or even a "You look beautiful today" or any other comment that might be considered out of place. He was perfectly cordial, perfectly gentlemanly, perfectly nice. He made the visit seem like one of my visits to his office—it was just that this time, he'd shown up where I happened to live.

I go back and forth, back and forth, as I examine each moment.

But this is the thing about what I went through—the kind of harassment that, in my case, eventually grew to be stalking, and that was complicated by his being my professor: you begin to doubt your judgment about everything. Technically, each meeting between him and me, each effort on his part to insert himself into my life, could be

considered innocent. During the first year of our relationship, I certainly gave him the benefit of the doubt, once
I'd started to have any doubts. I assumed the best about
him, presumed any nagging feeling was my own fault, that
I was just imagining things, inventing the unease that came
to reside inside me that spring, and never left me again.

It is only when I force myself to look at everything as a
whole that I realize how what he did must look to someone else, someone who is able to assess things from a safe
distance, to see the whole story at once. Or when I begin
to push beyond my original assumptions about his goodness and kindliness, his justifications that were always above
reproach in my mind, to see the layers of planning on his
part for something as simple as a visit to my house for tea,
or the sending of a letter to my home address. That he
would have already needed to cross the lines of propriety
to find himself on my street, that he would have had to
go digging into my file for personal information that was
there only in case of an emergency, that he used his access
as my professor and mentor to pry further and further into
my life, that he used his vow of celibacy, too, his role as
a Catholic priest, to mask what I now suspect were less
than innocent intentions, probably from very early on. He
used all of this like a key to enter my world, without any
express invitation on my part—though it's also true that I
did not resist. Not at first.

When I stop excusing everything that he did, each in-
dividual event and decision as most likely innocent, when
I allow myself to wonder if he knew exactly what he was
doing the entire time, if deception had always been a part
of his behavior toward me and with me, I'm able to see
my reactions at the time more clearly. If I let myself believe
for a moment that he lied to me from the beginning about
why he was in my neighborhood that day—or outside

my classroom, or standing in the stairwell the moment I arrived at school for a seminar. If I do all of this and then consider the possibility that the entire first semester of his correspondence with me, every letter and article and note, had been carefully calculated from the get-go in a collective effort to take a professor-student relationship in a very non-professorial direction, *only then* do I feel stupid and naïve to not have seen what was happening more immediately. I feel like an idiot to have been so passive in the face of all he was doing, to never have allowed myself to suspect that his intentions were anything other than appropriate.

Either way I look at it, I end up concluding that what happened is all my fault. Either I was too complacent for too long, and too participatory, or I am making a big deal out of nothing, and still, he was and has been innocent all along. And either way, I am always the one who loses, and he is always the one who wins the game.

6

That spring, it was still easy to allow him to blend into everything else. He was like camouflage, fading into the background of my life, nearly hidden.

I had a string of sort-of boyfriends during my first two semesters of graduate school. There was Max. There was Brad. There was even a boy from one of my classes, Owen.

Max I'd met on campus. He was a PhD student in another department, and he reminded me of Tom Hanks because he was just as charming and funny. He and I would get together to take long walks, to enjoy long coffees, to wander Georgetown for hours, sometimes five or six. Max and I never kissed. I wasn't sure what we were doing, exactly, but I could tell he liked me, a lot, and I could tell I liked him, too, more than a lot. Each time our long afternoon or evening was waning and one of us had to go, we would console ourselves by planning our next outing before we said goodbye. This went on for months, until one day I came home to a message on the answering machine.

"Donna, there's something I've needed to tell you."

His voice crackled through my kitchen after I'd pressed Play, the recording staticky.

"I can't get together this Friday like I told you"—there was a long pause—"because I have to fly home. For a party. An engagement party. I'm engaged and getting married. I'm sorry I didn't tell you before now. I'm sorry I'm telling you like this. Let's talk when I get back," he added.

Then there was a click.

Oh.

Lightbulbs went on in my brain even as my heart was collapsing. So *that's* why we never kissed. So *that's* why we spent hours together during the day, the afternoon, the early evening, but never went to dinner or hung out late into the night. I carried around a sadness in me about Max for a long time, but the way I'd always dealt with heartbreak was to throw myself into dating other people, going out and having fun, and there was plenty of fun to be had. There were so many boys in the world, and I rarely had trouble finding reasons to like one of them.

Plus, right around the tail end of Max, I met Brad at a friend's party.

He was handsome, he was a med student, he'd been a philosophy major in college, which I liked, of course, and he was tall with big, soft brown eyes, which I also liked, of course. I remember sitting with him in the backyard, twinkle lights strung above us, beers clutched in our hands. We hit it off right away, stood there talking by the keg. But what I most remember was the confession he made, maybe an hour into our conversation.

"So my divorce was final today." He'd dropped these words so casually.

I laughed—I thought he was kidding. "What?"

He went on to explain that he'd gotten married a couple

of weeks after graduating from college and now, barely two years later, had already separated from his wife. I listened, curious about an experience that seemed so foreign and impossible to me in that moment of my own life, trying to focus mostly on the fact that I found Brad interesting and very good-looking.

When my roommate and I were walking home that night and I told her what he'd confessed, she said, "Oh, Donna, you do *not* want to be the first person he dates after a *divorce.* He's *divorced!* At *our* age!"

I didn't listen to her and dated him anyway.

Then sometime early that spring semester, I'd met Owen in one of my classes. Meeting someone I might date in a class had seemed impossible the previous fall, but then Owen showed up and suddenly all of that changed. He had spiky blond hair that he'd dyed a bright blue, or maybe it was purple—he changed the color about once a month. He wore jeans and a gas attendant shirt with someone else's name on it. He stood out among the rest of the students for his style, his looks, his age (the same as mine). He was dynamic, he was funny, he had a voice that went up and down, slightly scratchy, theatrical. His words, the way he talked, would pull you in and hold you there—his eyes would pull you in, too.

All this, and he turned out to be a professional juggler. Like for real. Like this was how he and his juggling partner made a living. He could swallow fire, he could balance a chair on his chin, he could wow a crowd with his humor and talent within about sixty seconds. I learned this maybe on the second day we had class together. We'd stayed after everyone else had left, chatting.

"You want to come to a show next weekend?" he asked me.

"Yes," I said, without hesitation. I *did* want to.

I went, I was mesmerized by him, and this was the beginning of many months of writing each other letters, of hanging out in much the same way I'd been hanging out with Max during the fall, an enticing game of will-they-or-won't-they going on between us, a romantic courtship simmering beneath what we were calling a friendship. He taught me how to juggle, the perfect excuse for hours of hanging out and having fun together. I was on- and off-again with Brad, the divorcé–med student, whom my roommate had been right about—he definitely wasn't ready to be dating anyone—so it was easy to justify the time I spent with Owen. Besides, that time was delicious, and I had no interest in forbidding myself the pleasure.

Meanwhile, I met Xander, a boy with a tongue piercing, tall and handsome and seductive, soon followed by Christopher, short and young-looking and skinny, the person who would become my real boyfriend, the boyfriend who would stick around. All of these boys populated my first two semesters of graduate school.

I loved dating, in general, and I was unremorseful about this, about how one boy led to the next, about how they sometimes (often) overlapped, about how the next boy would help me to get over the previous one.

I still am unremorseful. And why shouldn't I be? What was wrong with having fun like I was having fun? What was wrong with dating a lot of boys? With having a lot of sex? With enjoying myself like the boys around me were enjoying themselves? The stakes were low, we weren't worried about too much of significance or anything that was overly serious at the time. I was exercising my voice, my power, letting my desires lead the way, all the things that the feminists I was reading in my classes had fought to allow women the freedom to exercise according to their will.

But there is a part of me now, a part I can't shake or

darken enough so I no longer see it, that believes I *was* eventually punished for my behavior, for exploring beyond the boundaries young women were allowed, for wandering into what was typically the territory of young men; for the way I moved through life, sexual and sensuous and playful. It is one of those suspicions that cut me into two. One woman, proud of the freedom she felt and how she used that freedom. The other, sure that punishment is always lurking just around the corner for women like her.

And my punishment happened to be him. He was the man God sent, that the world sent, that the patriarchy sent to take the giddy light that burned inside of me and snuff it out.

Every time I visited him in his office during that spring, he would ask if I was going to take another class with him. He would ask what I hoped to learn next, and then he would offer to teach whatever it was that interested me. Not only this. He offered to plan his teaching around my schedule. He kept asking me to give him my list of fall classes, so he could ensure that whatever he taught would not conflict with my required courses.

What, *exactly,* did I want him to teach? And if he taught *exactly* that, would I *promise* to sign up for the class?

Toward the beginning of that semester, back in January and February, I answered his questions directly. But around March, by April, I became evasive.

"Yes, I'll figure it out," I would tell him on one day.

"I keep meaning to get that information to you," I'd tell him on another.

I avoided promising him anything. I could tell this bothered him greatly, but still I couldn't give him the answer he so desperately wanted. At the time, I wouldn't have been able to articulate why I resisted, but I did it anyway. I felt terrible for giving him the runaround, for not just saying "Yes, I promise." I worried that I was being mean, that I should be grateful for his willingness to put himself out for me, believing that any other student in my program would have been thrilled for a professor so determined to avail himself to her.

But this hemming and hawing, my half answers that were really nonanswers, became a refrain from me to him from there on out. I couldn't bring myself to give him what he wanted, but I couldn't bring myself to say no to him either. Not outright. My non-consent was murky—a kind of half-assed non-consent. He was a leading scholar in my field, and it's also true he taught many of the courses required for me to move forward in my program. I could sense he would be very upset if I said no to him, and I didn't want him to get angry. Saying no, literally uttering "Sorry, but I'm not going to," also just seemed a bad idea. Like I was dismissing him, or even scolding him, which was not something a student did with a professor. I would need him to complete my studies, so I had to tread carefully.

He'd asked me the same thing the previous fall: Was I going to take another course from him in the spring? But back then the stakes were different. They *felt* different. In the fall, his question hadn't seemed so loaded. Just a simple, innocent inquiry. I was so wrapped up in my excitement about graduate school that if there was anything other than plain curiosity in his voice I didn't notice. My response to him of "I don't know—maybe?" wasn't fraught, it was earnest. The schedule I'd needed for that spring semester conflicted with his teaching, so I wasn't able to take his courses—though I would have happily done so if the schedule had worked. It would have been nice to have a class with him again that first spring. It would have been fine.

But there were so many professors from whom I wanted to take classes, so many exciting possibilities and topics, that I was happy with any and all courses available. It wasn't even a blip to me that in the following semester he would not be one of my professors.

What I hadn't counted on was that not taking another course from him would be such a loss to *him*. It never occurred to me that he might be disappointed or, frankly, that he would give it much thought. He had plenty of other students clamoring for seats in his classes. He was a popular professor, and someone helpful to have on your side. The kind of professor who was good to have on your dissertation committee, not only because he held such sway, but because he was important to the field beyond this graduate school. He was connected enough that he could help you get a job somewhere after you finished.

That prior January, around the time we'd gone to the theater together, he realized I wasn't taking a course with him again and confronted me about it, wanting to know why. My answer was little more than a shrug, an unworried "It just didn't work with my schedule" and a noncommittal "Hopefully next time it works out." I wasn't concerned *at all*. I didn't feel like I'd failed him, or that he'd see this as a failure to meet an expectation he held for me.

I soon learned that it was very much his expectation— and that I had let him down. That he was woefully disappointed in me and was not inclined to hide this. Maybe he thought I was ungrateful, that after all the time he'd spent with me during his office hours in the fall I should show more respect, that this respect should come in the form of seeking more of the wisdom only he could offer. Maybe my lack of concern or awareness that I'd failed him made him realize I was less invested in him than he was in me, or that I was more invested in the program as a whole than in one particular professor who was a part of it.

So that spring, he tried a new tack.

He wanted to make sure there was no reason I wouldn't be able to take a class from him. He expressed a clear desire to accommodate me in every way he could. He would even wait until I had planned my schedule to figure out his; that way we wouldn't run into the same problem again, where his courses conflicted with mine. Because for him, I soon realized, it was absolutely a problem that I was not currently taking one of his classes.

"So I was considering teaching *this* course," he would say on one occasion, handing me a paper he'd printed out with a description of a topic and a list of thinkers. "What do you think? Would you want to take it?"

"You know that I haven't taught this one in a while," he'd say on a different afternoon, opening up a flimsy booklet the department published with a list of available classes in the graduate program and short paragraphs about each one. "Maybe you'd like it?"

That's a requirement for you to graduate. What if I do that one in the fall so you can get it out of the way?

What about this? What about that?

You told me such-and-such thinker interested you. Perhaps I could develop a seminar around his work?

These questions from him, the angling to find out which course, which topics, which philosophers and theologians and thinkers I wanted to read, were never-ending. On the one hand, this was flattering. A part of me believed his pressure and maneuvering were due to the fact that I was special.

But this was also among those initial moments when I began to detect something else. Something off. Underneath his persistent questioning about my schedule, if I wanted to take another class with him, if I planned to sign up for whatever he was teaching, I could sense a need simmering. He *needed* me to be in his classes, even though he was trying to mask that need. And it wasn't just *need,* it was *neediness.* Like the kind I sometimes detected in one of those boys I'd date, a clinginess that surpassed the relationship as it stood so far, a desire to move faster and grow closer than I was ready for or closer than I wanted.

Everyone, at some point, experiences that kind of im-balance in a romantic relationship. It is a common feeling, the result of a difference in power, sometimes barely there or sometimes fairly great. One person is more excited about things than the other, and this tips the balance. It was something I often dealt with in the ups and downs of flirting, of entangling myself in a fleeting romance, where one person pulls back suddenly or wants out. But I'd never before experienced this imbalance with an adult, and by *adult* I mean someone far older, someone I regarded like a parent or a grandparent, an authority figure, a professor, a mentor, a priest. To detect a new boyfriendlike clinginess, a desperation of sorts, in the attentions of my professor seemed wrong, it didn't make any sense, or at least I couldn't make sense of it. Why would someone so much older and more powerful act as though I held power over him? It was clear to me that, because of his position and professional stature in my field, he held all the power and, as a grad student, I held none. He was not my equal, he was far above me, so what, really, could he need from me? I had nothing to offer.

This made it easier for me to dismiss whatever seemed off. I chalked it up to my imagination. To my overblown self-esteem. I thought I must be mistaken.

But it's also true that I developed an allergy.

I became allergic to this aspect of our interactions. His

inquiries about my schedule, what classes I hoped to take, and what I wanted to read. It became a kind of pollen floating in the air at school, especially concentrated in his office. I began to defend myself against it, to anticipate it before I walked through his office door, make sure I wouldn't be there so long that I would begin to suffer a reaction. I would stop by, say hello to him, then try to get out before I was affected. Soon, I visited him less and less. By the end of the semester, I would stop going entirely.

It was easier to lose myself in the boy-dramas and friend-dramas in my life outside graduate school, things other than him and his persistence, his ever-intensifying need. More and more I allowed myself to be swept up in these welcome distractions, I held out my hand to them freely and hopefully, let them pull me along like a current, happy to go wherever they led. And I began to build a wall between the good parts of my life and this man, though I didn't realize I was doing this at the time—but it was a wall that would eventually become impermeable, like steel or iron, so strong I was incapable of taking it down myself. Decades later I would still be taking a hammer to it, trying to break it enough that I could see through it to the other side, so I could try to become whole again, one woman, not two.

Somewhere in those conversations between us that spring he also began to raise the subject of my dissertation, and how he absolutely planned to be my dissertation director. He assumed this would be the case, and of this he had no doubts. He didn't ask if this was what I wanted; he just talked about this future where we would work together on this pivotal part of my PhD as though it were a given.

In mid-April, registration for fall came and went. Despite his constant pleas and the fact that he did actually arrange his schedule around mine, I didn't sign up for anything with him. It wasn't long before he figured out that I wasn't on any of his class lists. I remember how perplexed and dismayed he was when he realized this and how he confronted me about this stunning failure.

After all he'd done for me, I'd ignored his efforts. Maybe I had forgotten? Maybe it was a mistake?

I remember not knowing what to say or how to handle his upset.

Why didn't I just add in, then? I still could, if I wanted, he told me.

I didn't want. I definitely didn't want.

This I knew for certain, but I also didn't tell him as much. And I didn't know what to do with the helplessness I sensed that he felt. That, no matter the things he'd done and all of the maneuverings on my behalf, he still couldn't sign me up for one of his classes himself. That was my job and I had failed to do it. By then he'd already gone into my file several times to retrieve information about me, my home address, my phone number, which now, looking back, makes me wonder if it crossed his mind to do just that, to go into my file and change my schedule of classes so at least one of them would be with him that next fall.

But I also didn't quite grasp why so much resistance to him was building inside of me—resistance growing by the day. I wasn't sure how to articulate it or what, exactly, was causing it. On the surface, everything he did was a kindness, was benign, seemed to be about helping me or investing himself in my intellectual future. So, what was my problem? Why was I beginning to turn my back on him? He was so much older than me, and not only my professor but a celibate priest. What was wrong with me, to be so unkind toward someone who obviously had my best interest at heart, someone who was, by definition, safe?

It wasn't a conscious decision to begin to avoid him, it's just what I found myself doing. It's not that I suddenly disliked him or wanted him gone from my life for good. But by May of that spring semester, I began to remain at a distance. The enthusiasm I once felt about his interest in my life, my studies, the attention he paid me, had dissipated. It was no longer something I was excited about. It had become something I tolerated. *He* became something I tolerated. I found myself dodging him.

This bothered me.

I wanted to go back to that happy place where I was eager to have his advice, his knowledge, to learn from him. I wanted to fix whatever was happening inside of me that made me dread seeing him, even for five minutes, dread anything to do with him. I wanted to make things better again, but I didn't know how, couldn't seem to make myself want to see this man, talk to him, as I had only a couple of months before.

This bothered him even more.

He must have sensed I was treating him differently, holding him at a distance, even though if I agreed to see him outside school I acted like nothing had changed, that I was as happy to spend time with him now as I had been early on. Just as my resistance to him was growing, his dismay at my resistance was also growing. The fact that I was going to his office less and less really upset him, and he pressed me as to why.

"I'm really busy," I'd say.

"I stopped by the other day," I'd lie. "You just weren't around."

He tried to make sure I knew exactly when he would be there so I wouldn't miss him, so I'd *never* miss him. It became an obsession with him, making sure he was available to me at the right times.

My allergy grew worse. But as with the fall and spring seasons, when the leaves turn and all the flowers begin to bloom and the pollen is thick and floating in the air, what else is a person supposed to do but endure?

I never did take another class from him. And he never forgave me for it.

7

A t the end of May, he asked me to go away with him. I'd just finished my second semester of graduate school and I was flying. I'd done well, I was full of ideas, I was one step closer to my dream of a PhD and becoming a professor.

What's more, I landed a job in Residence Life at Georgetown, and I was thrilled. The position was designed for people who were in school. I could make my own schedule, work closely with the students who were my RAs, and help with programming in my hall, all while prioritizing my classes. Better still, I would have no living expenses. My resident director apartment was free, electricity, gas, everything included, and it was mine and only mine. I'd even have a partial meal plan, and the position came with a decent monthly stipend. Between my RD job and my TA work, which also came with a stipend, I'd be able to graduate with my PhD debt-free.

Life was good. My new apartment was perfect. It was

big and beautiful and full of light. One entire wall was lined with windows. The building was next to a gigantic parking lot, but my place was high enough that when I sat on the couch I couldn't see any cars. Only endless sky and the trees that stood between Georgetown, the parkway, and the Potomac River beyond it. Those first weeks after I moved in, I would sometimes just sit there, staring out the windows.

But by then, my professor had taken to calling me at home. He'd called a few times at the apartment I'd shared with my roommate, and now he called at my new one as well. The shift of his calls from one place to the other was seamless. I never gave him my number. After he started calling me once I'd moved, this knowledge registered somewhere in my mind. But I buried it deep with the rest of my unease, with the related knowledge that he also had my new address and my fall schedule and I hadn't given him those either.

When he called and I would pick up, he began using his first name to tell me who it was.

"Hello, Donna, it's L.," he'd say.

I remember feeling immediately uncomfortable. My parents had raised me to use *Mr.* and *Mrs.* and *Ms.* with my elders, *Dr.* and *Professor* and *Father*. Not only was this man my elder, but he could claim two honorary titles, *Professor* and *Father*. I wasn't about to call him by his first name. It was improper.

But it became his new norm with me.

"Hi, Professor," I'd say in return—always.

In my new apartment, I had two phones, each with its own line. One was in the first room you stepped into on entering the apartment, which served as my office. The office was separated by a door from the living space, the area I considered my real home, which was where the second phone was. The office phone and the home phone had different numbers. Both of them were those old-school, clunky, ugly beige phones with push-button dialing. They had enormous, heavy receivers, and those awkward spiral cords attached. These were not state-of-the-art phones, and there was no caller ID. They rang, you had no idea who was calling, and if you wanted to know, you had to pick up and say hello.

In the Office of Residence Life, where I now worked, the expectation was that you always answered—both phones. While the first-year students in my hall did not and would never have my home number, my colleagues had it, and so did my RAs. It was normal that work-related people called you on your personal line. In the beginning, I didn't care, this seemed fine. The perks of the job and the apartment were so fabulous that even the fire alarms pulled by drunken students at 3 a.m. seemed a reasonable price for my new living situation.

And early on that summer, I was absorbed by moving and settling in, by setting up my apartment the way I wanted it to look, with arranging the university furniture the way I liked it, making it appear prettier than it actually was. There were trips to Ikea and Bed Bath & Beyond, and invitations to friends to come over and check out my new place. I was busy, busy, busy.

Maybe my professor was annoyed by this. Maybe he felt I was slipping away from him. Maybe he was daunted by the long stretch of summer ahead, which he would have to endure without the assurance that I would be walking the halls near his office before class or stopping by to say hello when I had a break. Maybe he'd noticed that I was stopping by to see him less and less, that by the end of the semester I'd stopped stopping by altogether. Maybe he didn't like my having gotten a job that would take me away from graduate school, that would divide my time between my work and my studies, that would erode my ability to be around the department as much as I had been the first year. Maybe my preoccupation with moving and showing off my place to friends reminded him how young I was, how fickle I was, compelled by the shiny new toy that was my first real apartment. Maybe he became envious.

Regardless of his reasons, he called me on my new home phone one day, I picked up, we said hello. It's L., he told me, using his first name yet again.

"My abbey owns a retreat house," he began.

I remember standing near the square table I'd set up by the windows, the cord stretched as far as it could from the base of the phone, as I listened to him propose what he did next.

His abbey had a modest house, in a beautiful, remote place, where he and his fellow monastics could go to be away, to pray, to work. He had reserved it for a week in mid-June and he thought I should join him there, that it would be a lovely time, a chance to do some writing, to discuss my studies, to begin to think about my dissertation.

"Who else is going?" I asked.

Just him. It would be the two of us and no one else.

I listened as he talked, the way he made everything sound perfectly reasonable, the way this invitation seemed a totally understandable one to extend. I wanted to give him the benefit of the doubt, and I did give it to him as I had so often already, and would continue doing for many more months, or try to. I reminded myself that he was a celibate priest, and I reminded myself of this fact several additional times during the phone call. He was older, he was kindly, he was investing himself in my graduate work. I told myself how lucky I was to have a professor who cared so much that he would want to spend an entire week with only me, helping me consider my future and what would get me there. These justifications fought to the surface of my thinking, creating a hard shell over the other, less appropriate things that roiled in my gut, keeping them out.

Despite all of my rationalizations, I knew, clearly and acutely and immediately, that there was no way I was going on a retreat with this man. Absolutely not.

"That sounds great," I told him. "But I'll have to get back to you."

The disappointment in his voice on hearing my answer was evident.

He began to pressure me. When would I know? I didn't have to go for the whole time. If I didn't go for the whole time, would that make the trip more feasible? He would drive. Would that make it easier? It was a wonderful place, a wonderful house, I would be missing out if I said no. It was a great opportunity that he'd been able to reserve the house. It was in high demand, especially in summer. What luck that he could get it for us. He went on and on, trying to talk me into going, trying every possible angle to make me say yes.

A war began inside of me.

It was fine that he'd invited me, right? No, it was weird that he had, wasn't it? He was a priest, so I had nothing to worry about, right? No, it was odd for a professor to invite a student to go away with him, even if he was a priest. I should be more adult about this, shouldn't I? I was acting like a child, feeling strange about going on a retreat with someone old enough to be my father, even my grand-father. He didn't mean anything untoward. Of course not! He was celibate! He was a respected professor! Any unease that I felt was my problem. I was the one making this invitation weird and strange and off. He was just being nice. I should be grateful and let it go at that.

"I'm really not sure I can go," I lied. "But I'll do my best to try to make it work."

We ended the call. He would phone several more times before he left, asking about the trip. He would write to me, too, explaining the same things that he had when we'd talked. It reminded me of his maneuverings about my schedule. But while initially I'd found his interest in my classes flattering, now, for the first time, I moved straight into outright avoidance of him. I became evasive, I resisted his pleas and arguments as to why I needed to do something with him, go somewhere with him. I knew with total certainty from the first moment he suggested going away that I would never say yes, that there was no argument or concession in the world that would change my mind or make it feasible that I would go.

I did *not* consent. No way.

But I kept my non-consent to myself.

I was still too afraid to express my resistance openly. I was afraid I would hurt his feelings. I was also afraid that my saying no, unequivocally and without hesitation, would convey to him that I thought his invitation stemmed from ulterior motives. The possibility that he might realize I was thinking this shamed me.

And I felt so ashamed.

I felt many kinds of ashamed. Shame that a professor had thought to invite me to go away for a week. (What had I done to plant this desire in him? Was it the way I smiled? The way I carried myself at school?) Shame about what this might mean. (Had I led him on somehow? Had I said something that made him think I was hitting on him?) Shame that it might be because of the outfits I wore to school. (Had it been my boots? Or was it my short skirts? My tight jeans?). Shame that I even wondered whether he'd taken my outfits the wrong way. (How could I be that arrogant, to think I was *so* attractive that he couldn't help noticing me this way?) Shame that I was having thoughts that disrespected his vow of celibacy. (A priest would never cross that line, right? Or think about one of his students in a sexual way?) Shame that whatever it was that made him invite me to go away, just the two of us, was all my fault. (Obviously I *had* led him on, like sometimes I led on the boys I dated. And I *was* guilty of leading people on occasionally. I *could* be a shameless flirt, so maybe I was flirting with him and didn't even realize it?)

My answer to him came only in the form of time running out on the trip. The deadline of his departure approached, then it arrived, and still he hadn't been able to persuade me to go. Every time he asked me about the retreat house, I hemmed and hawed and said, "Maybe, maybe, maybe?" None of his concessions—to make the trip shorter, to drive, to offer to take two cars instead of going together, to help me think about my dissertation proposal—had gotten a straight yes. Only more avoidance. As a last resort, exasperated with me, he suggested I could invite another friend if I wanted. But nothing worked, not even this. "Maybe?" I told him. The reality settled in that I really was not going because it had come time for him to leave and I still hadn't told him one way or the other if I could make it. My no came from inaction, from halfhearted excuses, from lies of indecision. My no was indirect in that it was expressed by my failure to make the trip work on my end. By my doing nothing to make it happen.

He went alone.

I breathed a sigh of relief once the possibility of going was off my plate. I'd successfully avoided doing something there was no way I was going to do, and I'd done it without actually having to say no outright, as if my professor were an annoying friend or, worse, an annoying guy who was trying to date me. I hadn't exactly been subtle or skilled in my excuses and avoidance tactics, but at least the decision was behind me. I could now enjoy the rest of the summer in my new apartment.

But then he called from the retreat house to tell me I could still change my mind and get in the car, drive out there, and meet him. He called again to tell me what I was missing by not doing this, how wonderful it was to be there, how much I would love it if I joined him at the house. How much we could accomplish, how we could cook meals, how we could take walks.

My relief evaporated. The desperation in his voice was unmistakable. And as his calls mounted, it became evident that even though the departure date for the retreat had come and gone, even though he was actually on the retreat right now, he still thought there was a chance he could convince me I should go. He would continue to offer me the chance until the opportunity had passed and he returned from the trip. But then a new opportunity to go on *another* retreat arose immediately following, and the back-and-forth about my going started all over again.

This would become a pattern.

It might have been those calls from the retreat house that struck the first real blow at my knees, crippling me from there on out. Those calls made it clear that there would be no end to his need. That his requests would never stop. That there was no number of excuses or avoidance tactics that would reach him. That he simply could not be reached in this way. If it wasn't this retreat, it would be the next one, which he planned to go on only a couple of weeks later, or the next one after that. Or it would be an event at the theater, or a museum, or the Kennedy Center, or a dinner, or a coffee, or a visit to my house, or the possibility that I could *still sign up* for one of his fall courses, because didn't

I realize it was only summer and the semester hadn't even started yet? There was plenty of time for me to change my mind, for me to fix this failing on my part, for me to fix all the things I'd begun to fail at, a list that grew longer by the day, because by now he was contacting me by the day. According to him, I soon learned, there would always be time for me to say yes. That yes was the only answer he was willing to hear.

Most people would have understood my behavior for what it was—the politest, most appropriate manner I could find to say no to an elder, a professor, a priest, without actually saying no to him. Most people with social and relationship skills, someone with the capacity to pay attention to the signals and feelings of someone else, would have gotten the picture and realized I was declining their attention in the nicest way I could manage. Then again, most people wouldn't have been so persistent, so insistent, really, so unable to hear or perceive that my excuses were really nos, that my avoiding answering was really a "Sorry, but no, no thank you." Most people would have been willing to see my behavior for what it was. But what do you do when someone is unwilling? When they refuse to see? I still don't know. I wish I did.

I want to talk about my inability to say no.

When we talk about consent, especially with high school and college students, we make it seem like it is as simple as uttering the word *no* or *yes*. We encourage young adults to speak these words *enthusiastically*. Determinedly. With resolve. That is actually the word we call on when we teach about it—*enthusiasm*. Enthusiastic yeses as the mark of consent, and firm nos the mark of its absence.

When I consider these words in my situation, *yes* and *no*, it just makes me laugh and think, *Are you kidding?* How in the world does a student give a firm no to a professor? To someone so far her senior? To someone who could determine her future? To someone on whom her future depends? How in the world does a young woman give a decided no to a Catholic priest?

For me to give someone a firm and enthusiastic yes or no is to presume the person I am saying yes or no to is my equal, or at least someone I feel equal to saying yes or no to, as though they are a partner, a friend, someone with whom I am on the same footing. It presumes I am in possession of some power in the situation. It presumes that the other person sees me as an equal, or something like a peer, and is waiting to see if they are going to get a yes or no before proceeding with whatever they'd like to happen next. It presumes the other person can see me at all, or cares to; that they have respect for me as though we are both the same.

For me to have given this professor a firm no, for me to have said no outright, would have sounded like a scolding. It would have involved me acting as though my professor were just another boy my age who was hitting on me and I was rejecting him. The young woman student I was could not wrap her brain around the notion that a professor was hitting on her, never mind rise to a place where she would treat him like he might be just another guy making a move on her at a bar. Not only was there too much at stake, but a student's regard for a professor doesn't simply vanish if his behavior makes her uneasy or seems off in some way.

Using the word *no* was too tall an order in my situation. The only thing that seemed feasible was for me to go along with just about everything this professor suggested as best I could, and to demur and put off situations when I didn't want to comply with his wishes. While my very early yeses to him may have indeed been enthusiastic, because early on I *was* enthusiastic about this professor, eventually they grew fainter and fainter until they were less like yeses and more like tolerance of whatever he needed at the time. Or, they became a putting off of my no, a deferring as long as I could, so that the issue passed and an actual no was never necessary.

But saying no, really saying it firmly, was out of the question for a long, long time—until his behavior grew so intolerable and so out of control and so obsessive and unyielding that I no longer cared about my future or what might happen if I offended him. Until I was so desperate and broken that I didn't want a future anymore at all.

The power dynamics between the old and the young, between a big man and a small woman, between someone famous and important in your profession and you, when you are just starting out, between someone whom everyone loves and admires and you, who are still a nobody, between someone you aspire to become and the person you are now can seem insurmountable. To name their behavior as unacceptable, to do so explicitly and forcefully, may seem impossible. You know that to name it outright will more likely destroy you and your future than his.

And that has been the pattern in our culture, hasn't it? The woman pays the price with her future, and the man keeps his present *and* his future as though he did nothing wrong. That is the deal we strike when we come forward, isn't it?

So you don't name it. You say nothing. You just stay still and hope that nothing too terrible happens. That whatever does happen, you'll learn to live with the consequences somehow. And most of all and above everything, you hope and pray that no one else will ever find out.

★ ★ ★

Everything with him happened so fast after that.

In one semester, his attention had gone from a kind invitation to take me to the theater to inviting me to go away with him, just him, the two of us alone. In January, I had been happy to spend time with him, in February, happy to have him leaving me notes and newspaper clippings, but by March, the sheer amount of attention he began to heap on me happened too fast for me to get my bearings. I was just suddenly *in it,* buried in it. I don't even know what the tipping point was, if it was as simple as him peering through the window of my front door that day at my Georgetown apartment, having arrived uninvited, or the maneuverings about my schedule, or the obsession with the retreat house, or if it was all of these things together. But the dread inside me, the revulsion I had for him, grew until it became monstrous. He became monstrous. And like that of any poor soul in a terrible, ugly fairy tale, my life became about learning to trick the monster.

8

The letters he sent piled up.

My summer was busy. I was in training for my new position. Working in Student Affairs is all-consuming, it's often around-the-clock. Also, by now I was dating Christopher and I was really into him. We spent all of our time together when I wasn't working. He made me laugh like no one else I'd ever known.

But he was so not my type. Christopher had a Southern drawl so strong sometimes I could barely understand him, and he drove everywhere in a giant red truck, gunning the engine. He was from Tennessee, and I made a million assumptions about his politics when we first met, all of which turned out to be wrong. He was a teacher, an excellent one, and I admired him for this from the beginning. He was also the hugest flirt, but when we met, I marked him boldly and clearly in my mind: *Nope. Not gonna go there.* Christopher worked hard to get me to give him a chance—and once I did, I fell in love, and soon it was me driving around the city with Christopher in that big red truck, sometimes taking long road trips to Tennessee to see his family.

Christopher also happened to be roommates with Dan, my closest friend at graduate school. Dan was a few years ahead of me in his PhD. He and I were fast friends, though he always felt more like a brother. The two of us would go out for drinks after classes, talk about what we were working on, about ideas and books we loved and our respective relationship dramas. He and Christopher played on a soccer team together and got along so well they'd decided to become roommates. That I'd ended up dating Christopher was totally unrelated to his friendship with Dan and was a serendipitous, convenient accident for all of us. I'd go to their soccer games, we'd hang out afterward at their place, go to dinner, the movies, play video games. Spending time with Christopher and Dan was the perfect antidote to the parts of my life that were growing increasingly worrisome.

Meanwhile, my professor wrote to me. He was going on trip after trip that summer. He was a sought-after speaker, a scholar who'd grown popular in certain circles for his wisdom. He wanted to make sure I knew all of these things, so he'd write to tell me about every single one of them. He signed his letters with his first name and only his first name.

Letters from him arrived at my new address, a mailbox in the Student Affairs office. I grew used to the steady stream of them. At first, I opened them, read them. They were always so benign, just updates on whatever he was doing, where he was traveling, conferences where he was speaking, interesting people he'd met. Maybe a copy of a talk he gave, or an article he thought I should read. I received them, saw what was inside, set them aside in a pile on the windowsill of my new office.

He called, too. Sometimes every day, if he wanted something from me. Sometimes more than once a day.

I tried not to think about it much. Tried to tell myself it was nice that he wanted to stay in touch. I was determined to see it that way. I had a lot going on that was good, so it was easy for me to be consumed with things other than him that summer, and I let them consume me. As the summer progressed, I pushed his invitations to go away to the retreat house into the back of my mind, until they began to seem far away, almost like they hadn't happened. I loved the intensity of my Student Affairs job, my RA staff, the constant activity, my new colleagues, some of whom would become friends. My residents would be arriving soon, and my hall would open and be full of life.

His letters increased. Sometimes there would be three in one day.

I would collect them in my purse with the rest of the mail and walk them across campus to my apartment. I no longer opened them immediately. Most of them I didn't open at all. Instead, I'd add them to the pile on the windowsill in my office. The pile grew.

It's difficult for me not to wonder what I might have done differently if he hadn't been a priest. Would I have said something about his behavior sooner? Would I have been far less forgiving? Would I have justified and rationalized everything much less than I actually did?

Sometimes I think it's the celibacy issue that tripped me up most, made it seem impossible to tell anyone anything. Even as I began to worry that his behavior was something other than a benign and selfless interest in my intellect, the vow of celibacy he'd taken muted all of these concerns.

This was the nineties, before news of the Catholic abuse scandal broke. No one knew, or no one was talking openly—not Catholic laypeople or regular people—about priests who were abusing children, who were assaulting people. Nobody knew the Catholic hierarchy was covering everything up, that it had an established MO for doing this. When I was in graduate school, priests were still sacred figures, untarnished role models who did only good in the community, who offered up their lives to take care of others. Priests were representatives of God, and you didn't question this if you were Catholic. Likewise, you didn't question them or their authority.

Catholicism, Catholic people, even Catholic stories, had filled my childhood. My father went to public school, but my mother went to Catholic school and regularly plied me with funny anecdotes about the nuns of her youth, how they measured her skirts, how they made her wear paper "doilies" on her head at daily mass if she forgot her hair covering. She spoke of years of learning Latin, of the saints who populated her days and with whom she populated my youth, placing mass cards and statues all over our house. My mother was also a Catholic schoolteacher. She had two best friends, one a nun, the other an ex-nun who had taken her vows young and then left, gotten married, and had a family. In the summers they sat on the beach together, these formidable, complicated Catholic ladies, and I played with the children of the ex-nun throughout my childhood. During the school year my life was filled with nuns and priests, too, especially my mother's nun best friend, who came to the house, drank coffee, socialized with my mother, while I sat in the living room watching television or joined them at the kitchen table. I loved the sisters who taught at my mother's school and who taught at mine, too.

We went to mass on Sundays, and we thanked God on Sunday afternoons at our weekly Sunday dinner, which my mother and grandmother spent hours cooking. I went to Sunday school every week when I was little and catechism classes when I got older. Eventually, I helped my mother teach Sunday school, which she did every week for years. I did my first communion, the rite of penance, and I was confirmed in the church as a young teenager. I went to Catholic nursery school and kindergarten, Catholic elementary school, middle school, and high school. I went to a Catholic university for college. My life, everything about my existence, was steeped in Catholicism. Being Catholic was synonymous with being a part of my family, with being half-Italian, half-Portuguese. Going to school, all school, every kind of school, was an extension of this, since every school I attended was Catholic.

Like a million other kids raised this way, I hated plenty of things about growing up Catholic, and I rebelled against those things I hated. While I'd loved Sunday school, I loathed catechism classes. When I was old enough to hate getting dragged to mass on Sunday mornings, I would feign sickness whenever I could get away with it, which was not often. I lobbied my parents to go to one mass and not the other, since there were two priests in our parish and one was known to drone on with his endless homily, trapping all of us there for more than an hour, whereas the other was famous for being lightning quick and getting us in and out sometimes in under thirty minutes. (On one deadly hot and humid summer day, instead of delivering a homily, he smiled, looked out across all of us, sweating in the pews, and said, "Well, God has given us a wonderful beach day! Let's thank him for it and that will be enough for this morning!" and sent us on our way.)

At Georgetown, when I began to meet the Jesuits, I developed a newfound respect for the priest who is also a professor. Unlike the two parish priests in my hometown, these Jesuits had PhDs; many of them had two. I was surrounded by priests who challenged me academically. I began to talk to Jesuits about theology, about the existence or nonexistence of God, and I grew to love the ways they pushed me about my ideas, my beliefs, my opinions about the Catholic tradition. My experiences with the Jesuits elevated my attitude toward the priesthood. Priests were an integral part of what made Georgetown a wonderful experience, an integral part of my intellectual awakening there.

So by the time I arrived at graduate school, having a priest who was also a professor was not only a norm, it was something I looked forward to, that I relished, even.

Someone who is not Catholic, who has never been Catholic, someone standing on the outside of the Catholic tradition, might have a difficult time understanding why it was so hard for me to get around the priest part of my professor's identity. You may already see him for who he is and was, which is a man acting inappropriately with a young woman in his program. But I could not see this, refused to see it. It was a betrayal of everything I'd ever known, and I, like so many Catholics of the pre-scandal era, was overly prone to giving representatives of the Church the benefit of the doubt—completely.

His vow of celibacy acted as a wall I could not breach, that I could never dream of scaling. It had always been the thing, the one special thing, that turned an ordinary man into a man of God; it is what defines a Catholic priest on an ontological level. It never occurred to me that a priest would break this vow. Perhaps that makes me stupid. But even the thought that a priest might do this was so sacrilegious, so egregious, that it made me nauseated to consider it. I hated myself for allowing the possibility to enter my brain. It made me ashamed and it made me fearful. To articulate it even to myself, never mind to someone else, was to tug on the essential brick that kept the entire Catholic Church standing, like sliding out the one piece in a Jenga tower that causes the whole building to come crashing down, my family trapped inside.

To question this professor's intentions toward me was to question the priesthood itself, and I was not up to the task. I had no idea that I was not alone in this, far from it, that American priests had been behaving like this for decades, that priests all over the world had been behaving like this for decades, knowing they could lean on the hierarchy to cover up what they'd done if anyone dared come forward. I thought I must be the only person in the universe with whom a priest was behaving this way. The more this man paid me attention, attention that was beginning to make me desperately uncomfortable, the more alone I was. The more I became mute. The thoughts I was having about him were ugly and unspeakable, so I didn't dare speak them to anyone.

I told absolutely no one about him. Not Christopher, not Dan, not any of my other friends.

Not a soul. Not a peep. Not the letters, not the calls, not any of it.

The abuse I suffered was mental, it was emotional, it was not physical, like most of the crimes in the abuse scandal. Though, to me, it *was* also physical, the way he began to encroach on all the spaces *surrounding* my body, so much that eventually it was hard for me to walk through the world without also having to wade through his presence, submit myself to his ever-watchful eyes.

I don't know if he stopped just short of crossing a physical, sexual line with me on purpose. If he thought that by falling just shy of the physical, he was continuing to honor his Catholic vows and that he could, in good conscience, claim that he never did a thing to hurt me.

To this day I don't know what is worse, the sustained unwanted attention I suffered, silently, until I could endure no more, until I didn't care about anything, not even my life, or instead, the possibility that he might decide one day to cross that line into physical abuse. There were moments when I longed for him to do just this, because—however vile I sound—physical abuse might leave a mark on my body, a mark I could point to, that I could show to the police. As it stood, I had nothing to show anyone. A pile of letters didn't seem like something that would raise any alarms. So silent I stayed. And soon I grew sick with it.

It wasn't long before he realized that I wasn't reading my mail.

I had no idea what was in his letters or even what he'd sent me. He'd talk about their contents, assuming I'd seen whatever they were. I'd grow confused, and this would confirm I hadn't bothered to open what he'd sent. This prompted him to begin telling me ahead of time what he would be sending me, something I should make sure to open.

When he pressed me about what was on its way, told me how essential it was that I read it, I would tell him I would. But as the summer marched forward, I became less and less worried about complying with his wishes or offending him. He could tell me a thousand times to open a letter and I would just toss it on the windowsill of my office with the rest of the pile.

His frustration about this grew, his anger about this grew, his dismay about this grew, until they were so big and tangled he began to seem larger and more grotesque, even though he was a small man. Small and meek. But to me, his features became distorted, his innocent eyes became menacing, his elfin frame—not muscular, not strong but rather frail—became intimidating. His thick salt-and-pepper hair was ever grayer, as though he were aging quickly, before my eyes, the distance in years between us expanding by the day.

The pile of letters in my office swelled to maybe a hundred, nearly all of them unopened. They spilled every which way across my windowsill. I hated seeing them there. They produced a cocktail of guilt and revulsion and fear. I did my best to push these feelings away, to beat them back, to ignore the nauseating worry they provoked every time my eyes traveled to the place where they sat. It seemed like they were taunting me. Eventually there were so many and the mountain so unruly that one day I picked up the garbage can in my office, carried it over to the windowsill, and with one arm swiped every single one of them into the trash.

9

I tried to tell him about my boyfriend.

It was July, smack in the middle of summer. I was sitting with him in the basement of his abbey, drinking tea. There was a kind of accounting going on between us. He had taken to complaining about the things I no longer did or readily agreed to on his behalf, listing my failures. I had taken to making all kinds of excuses as to why I no longer did these things and was desperate to make him believe my lies. At no point did I stop needing this professor's approval and support for my graduate work.

My ability to finish my PhD depended on his willingness to get behind my candidacy, get through comprehensive exams, my dissertation proposal, and the dissertation itself. There was still so much of him that lay ahead of me. He would sit on the committee that judged both sets of my exams, and he would likely have to be on my dissertation committee, if not actually be my director. To turn this man's approval into disapproval would be disastrous to my program. I had to make sure I didn't do anything to jeopardize this.

So, I tried to appease him now and then by agreeing to see him. I would pick and choose among his constant invitations, try to pick wisely and sparingly, as a way to limit the time we spent together. I became aware that avoiding *everything* was starting to make him crazy, would only make his need to see me spike all the more, and I was trying to keep it at a low simmer. It was almost as if he were acting like my boyfriend and, like a jealous boyfriend, getting upset when I wasn't making enough of an effort to see him, to attend to him, hang out with him. I worked so hard to hold back this comparison. It felt so wrong—but wrong on my part, not his.

The accounting between us was an accounting of effort. He felt he was making a constant effort to reach out to me, write to me, be a part of my life, be present and available, yet for the last couple of months I'd made virtually no effort to do the same in return. It upset him that he could look back on the previous school year and remember when I was making a big and obvious effort to spend time with him. He could see very clearly that something had shifted since early May, or even as far back as April. It was making him desperate, and his desperation was making me desperate to fix things.

I wanted to calm him down. I learned that a single, solid yes to one of his requests would reset the balance again for a while. He would seem to be at peace again with things, with me, would forget for a few days the growing list of my failings that plagued him.

This was how I coped.

This was also how I ended up driving my sad little Mazda Protegé across the city to the abbey where he lived with his fellow priests so we could have tea in the basement. Like all of his previous suggestions, it seemed a benign request, or one of the more benign requests compared with the invitations to go away together that kept on coming that summer. It wasn't as if I'd be driving him anywhere in my car. I would go there alone and leave alone. I would be in a building full of priests and monks. It would be fine.

There are moments I remember that I now realize were turning points—things he did that shifted everything, or things that occurred that I could not banish from my mind afterward. Tea in the basement of his abbey is one of those moments.

By the time I arrived at the abbey and got out of my car, I was almost excited to see him. I headed up the front walk with a kind of eagerness. I had a plan for today, and it was a good one. I wanted to enact it, get it over with. When I left later that afternoon I would feel a world of relief. I would be happy to have him in my life again. Everything was going to be okay.

The plan was to tell him about Christopher.

I'd thought about doing this when I agreed to the visit, and I'd thought about it on the drive over to see him as I listened to the radio, air-conditioning blasting, convincing myself that this was going to work. Telling him about my boyfriend seemed like it might right the listing ship we were on. It would introduce something into our relationship that would make everything safe again, like it had felt in the beginning. It was going to disarm the strange tension that had settled between us like a houseguest who refused to leave.

I knocked on the front door, and another priest answered. He didn't seem surprised to see me, or surprised that I was a young woman there to see another priest in his community. This encouraged me. It had been a good choice to meet my professor at his residence, where plenty of other priests were around, all of whom were celibate. I was going to be surrounded by people who had vowed to make themselves safe.

I was led to a place where I could wait for my professor to appear. I sat down, folded my hands in my lap, tapped my foot. I was ready to get this over with, ready to cross the distance between living with constant unease and living with the cool relief that everything was good again.

He appeared, he led me down into the abbey basement, which was arranged as a kind of sitting room where the monks could host guests for coffee and tea and snacks. There was a small table with chairs. He made us tea and filled a small plate with cookies. We sat nearly next to each other, the little table alongside us. We began to talk. I have no idea what about. Fifteen minutes passed. Thirty. Forty-five.

I kept thinking to myself, *Now, Donna. Do it. This is the moment. Say it.*

But I couldn't quite figure out when or how to interject a comment about my boyfriend into the conversation. It's not the kind of thing I openly discussed with my family, not the kind of thing I'd bring up with my own father, since in my family we didn't talk about boyfriends or my current romantic feelings for someone. But I knew I had to take a deep breath and dive in. I was convinced the reward would be worth it. The reward was going to be my liberation from dread.

"So," I began, after around an hour had passed. I kept my eyes on the half-eaten plate of cookies. "I have something exciting to tell you!" My voice was overly enthusiastic, shrill, nervous.

I looked up.

He was smiling as he sipped his tea.

He seemed happy as he awaited whatever news I was

about to tell him. He was always pleased when I told him something important, something personal, especially lately. Those gifts of information I so freely offered my first semester of graduate school had become few and far between. He now dug for them, pressed for them, and here I was about to hand one over without any prodding on his part.

"What is it?" he asked.

"I'm in love! I have a boyfriend and he's wonderful! His name is Christopher!"

Even now I cringe as I write this, cringe as I remember it, cheeks burning with the shame I still feel about the stilted, naïve way I brought this up, like a little excited girl more than a young woman; like a teenager.

I watched him. Waited for him to say something, for him to tell me how wonderful this news was, to ask me about this boyfriend like a doting parent, ask how I'd met this young man, where he'd gone to college, what he'd studied, if he had a job or was in graduate school, too. I imagined we would have a bit of gossipy conversation, like I might with a girlfriend curious to know everything about this delightful turn in my life. I was such an idiot to imagine that any of these things might happen.

His smile faltered. His happy expression crumbled. There was a moment where he seemed to have stopped breathing, the silence stretching far longer than was comfortable. Then, finally, he spoke.

He changed the subject.

I don't even know to what. I don't remember what he said, but him changing the subject is one of the clearest memories I have in my life.

He moved the conversation onto a new topic as though he hadn't heard anything, as though I hadn't just confessed to him that I'd met someone, that I was dating this person, that I'd fallen in love with him. It had felt like such a big deal to reveal this to him, an effort at a certain kind of familial or filial intimacy. But instead of being congratulated, I'd been slapped.

I'd truly believed he was going to respond by telling me he was happy for me, that he'd even like to meet this young man. At my most delusional point on the drive over to the abbey I'd fantasized about how soon the three of us would be getting together for coffee, my boyfriend, my professor, and me. How he would grill my boyfriend like a father might, to make sure his interest in me was genuine, albeit playfully. How the three of us would laugh and have such a good time. How later on I'd realize how ridiculous I'd been to feel any unease with this kind, grandfatherly man, whom I'd eventually invite to my wedding, who might even *preside* over my wedding.

He talked on and on between sips of his tea.

I sat there, stunned. My plan had backfired in the worst possible way. Not only had it failed, but the possibility of relief receded so far in the distance that it disappeared. In fact, my plan had made everything worse. Now I was the one who was crushed. I wanted to weep.

Somewhere I knew that his changing the subject, his refusal even to acknowledge my words about a boyfriend and being in love, was a kind of confession in its own right—that it meant he couldn't bear to hear this information from my lips. That it was so unbearable that he pretended not to hear it. That he literally acted as though it hadn't been uttered out loud. His reply was to erase it. I knew what this behavior revealed, but as with everything else to do with him, I piled up so many excuses for why he reacted this way that the knowledge was soon buried.

And I blamed myself for what happened that afternoon.

I doubted everything about my decision to bring the subject up. Maybe it was my fault that things had grown awkward. Maybe it was inappropriate to talk about a boy-friend with a celibate Catholic priest. It's not like I had much experience befriending priests from the parish where I'd grown up, not enough that I would tell them about my love life. Though it was also true that I'd enjoyed eating with the Jesuits at their on-campus residence with my fellow Georgetown students, and I *could* imagine bringing up the topic of a new boyfriend at their dinner table and having them quiz me jovially about him. But this had never actually happened, and it wouldn't have occurred to me to tell a Jesuit about my boyfriend.

I stared at my professor as he rambled on, fingers gripped around the handle of his mug, his overly sweet voice filling the abbey basement like too much sugar, the perpetual hunch in his shoulders curving him forward, always forward, always toward me, closer. I plastered a smile on my face. I stopped drinking my tea, eating the cookies. Eventually, I left the abbey and drove home.

I had a secret.

He was my secret.

"Where were you all afternoon?" Christopher asked, later that night.

He'd come over to my apartment to stay with me. I was busying myself with anything and everything I could get my hands on. Doing the dirty dishes, cleaning surfaces, arranging books on my shelves.

"I went shopping," I told him.

"You didn't get anything?"

"No."

Christopher laughed—a good-natured, happy laugh. "That's not like you."

I tried to laugh in reply. "Sure it is. I can go shopping and not buy anything!"

Now I was lying to my boyfriend about my where-
abouts. Some of the things my professor did I couldn't
hide. If someone went to look at the mail on my windowsill, for example, they would notice it was all from one
person. The phone calls to my apartment would come at
all hours, including when Christopher was over or when
other friends were visiting. The invitations were largely
invisible, unless I accepted them and went somewhere,
which I was no longer doing—at least not much. But
before this I had not actively hid what I was doing, where
I was going. I had not told outright lies to people I cared
about—I'd only told lies of omission.

But my afternoon of tea and cookies with my professor
felt sordid.

Like *I* had done something wrong.

Like *I* was the one who had crossed a line.

So I didn't tell Christopher where I'd been. I found that
I couldn't. I was too ashamed.

The wall I'd been building between my professor and
everything else in my life grew taller, wider, more opaque.
My brain worked tirelessly at this construction job, like a
contractor facing a deadline.

"Are you hungry?" I asked him, opening the fridge.

"Always," Christopher said.

It wasn't long after my visit to the abbey that my professor
sent me that dull yellow manila envelope with his article
inside it, demanded that I read it, informed me that we
would discuss it when he returned from his trip. Informed
me that it was imperative we do this.

Carrying the weight of two people is exhausting.

Being two people is exhausting. Having two brains.

That August, while he was away, I tried to pretend he
didn't exist. But the energy I would get from my new job at

Georgetown, all the dynamic people I was meeting because of it, all the busy distractions of the work and the schedule, all the fun my boyfriend offered, that Christopher and Dan offered because they lived together, would drain away the moment I spied that manila envelope on my coffee table. I would have to start all over again, from scratch, erasing its existence, his existence, from my brain and the life I was living, or trying to live.

I've tried to abolish my memories of him, especially the strongest ones, like the ones from the day I finally read that article. They are the most vivid of snapshots, the color overly saturated and bright, glaring images that are fire resistant, indestructible.

The light was yellow, nearly orange at the edges, the humidity smudging the air.

The coffee table was rectangular, long, nearly the length of the couch, the color of milky coffee, smooth with faint fake lines across it, to make it seem like real wood.

The envelope was jagged in places, from having been through the mail. It was set on the top-left corner of the table, about three inches from the edge on two sides. It was facedown so I didn't have to see my address in his handwriting, my name written by him, the address of his abbey, the place where I'd recently failed to fix things.

The television was at an angle, in the corner by the wall of windows, just beyond the coffee table. I had the furniture set as close to those windows as I could get it, because I loved those windows, the sky beyond them, the warm breezes they invited, all that sunlight. I would sit on the couch, feet propped on the edge of the table, turned toward the windows and the television, angling myself away—always away—from the envelope.

In hindsight, it would have been so easy to throw that envelope away without opening it. I'd done this already with so many other things he'd sent me. But he would know if I did it this time. He would find out that I had because he was so obsessed with this one particular thing, and I would get in trouble once it became clear it had gone into the garbage. I guess because the article inside was a confession of love, he needed me to read it, wanted to gauge my reaction to it, was desperate to know what I would say to him in response.

I remember so clearly how my heart sank and sped, how I heard the blood rushing in my ears, how I had my bare feet propped on the edge of the coffee table, my back curved into the cushions on the couch, the article propped on my knees, my bare thighs, as I turned one page after the other. I remember so clearly the phone ringing later on, how loud it was in my apartment, how I dreaded answering it, and how, though it was not him as I'd feared, it was my father introducing a new form of dread into my life—into our lives.

"Your mother has cancer."

But *that* pain—of facing the imminence of my mother's death, the likelihood of it—was delayed because of the horror layered over it, numbing it. The article, its talk of love, of priests in love with women decades their junior, how lovely and wonderful such an occurrence was, how it was a gift from God, truly, to fulfill that love sexually, with kisses and embraces, roiled in my gut so strongly, so forcefully, that it took precedence over this other news my father had given me.

It shames me to remember how my father's call had produced a new energy in me, a new sense of purpose, a righteousness in my step, each of which would take me away, away, away from this professor and his stupid need for a discussion about his essay. By then I wore a cloak of shame everywhere I went—I still wear it, sometimes—invisible to the naked eye, but as evident to me as the high-heeled boots I clomped around in during the school year, the sound of their *clack, clack, clack* informing everyone around me of my approach.

I made two calls after I hung up with my father.

The first was to Christopher.

"My mother has ovarian cancer. I need to go to Rhode Island. Like, right now."

"Give me thirty minutes," Christopher said, the usual playfulness gone from his voice. "I'll be right there."

The next was to *him*.

I left a message at his abbey.

"I won't be around when you get back. I'm going home. My mother has ovarian cancer. She's having surgery tomorrow. She might *die*," I added, repeating my father's words to me.

I hung up.

Within the span of five minutes I'd already practiced my new refrain twice.

My mother has ovarian cancer. She might die.

It was the grandfather of all excuses and I would pull it out, wield it in my defense against him, against the strain on my life because of him, so often in the coming months, so much it makes my entire body flush to remember.

I began to hate myself.

The worst part is that I thought—I really believed—that the fact of my mother's cancer would be enough to end the issue, to close the conversation about the article for good with him, disarm his advances, because who advances on a young woman, vulnerable, grieving, watching cancer break her mother bit by bit? Who does a thing like that?

He does. He did.

Like I said at the very start, I thought I was saved. But I wasn't saved, not at all. The worst was just beginning.

PART TWO

10

When I got home to Rhode Island it was dark. My mother was in the bedroom, wailing. My mother who never cried.

The drive had been long and silent. Christopher and I couldn't find much to say even over the eight hours we'd spent in the car. What could be said after receiving news of a possible death sentence for one's mother the very next day?

My father was sitting in the living room, collapsed into one of the squashy brown pleather chairs that had furnished our house for as long as I could remember. His elbows dug into the armrests, his hands covered his face as he listened to my mother sob.

We barely said hello.

"Go and see your mother" was all he said.

I dreaded this, I was scared to confront her, to face the fact of her cancer. Her room was dark, my mother in a fetal position on the bed, a shadowy lump. When she heard me come in, she began saying, over and over, between wails, the same thing.

"I thought I would see you get your PhD! I wanted to see you graduate and become a doctor!"

I stood there listening, just inside the doorway, despairing about everything happening, about the fear and anguish so clear in my typically strong mother's voice, my mother who was the rock in our family. It was unbearable to witness. I began to calculate in my mind what it would take for her to see me get my PhD. I wanted to give her this thing she kept crying about, I wanted to give it to her with everything in me.

In all the horrors of this night, that the one thing my mother was mourning was the possibility of not seeing me get my PhD caught me off guard. She wasn't wailing about seeing me get married or have children, but about watching me walk across a stage to receive my diploma, the moment I would become Professor Freitas. This touched my heart and broke it. It meant my mother had finally realized what made me tick, that she'd seen the thing I cherished most about myself and had chosen to cherish it, too. She wanted to share in my PhD because she knew it was the thing that would make me proudest of myself. It was the first time my mother revealed that she'd figured this thing out about her daughter, that she'd come to care as deeply about it as I did. This was the same woman who, like my father, had threatened to take me out of Georgetown a few years before because of my desire to study philosophy. She had come around completely. I was moved by this and I was also shattered.

The chances of her seeing me do this one thing were minuscule. It would require a miracle, pretty much. I had at least four years remaining in graduate school. And then, only if things went flawlessly. My mother would have to survive fourth-stage ovarian cancer for me to give her this wish, and at the moment this seemed impossible.

But I would do my best. I would try to make it happen. I would have to do everything perfectly, finish everything on time, even early, I would have to persuade my professors to help, and God would have to do his part and let my mother get through the next day. I didn't have much faith in God, but my mother did, and more than God, I had faith in her. If she could survive this surgery, she would come around to be the rock she'd always been and fight this cancer like the formidable Italian lady she was.

"Please stop saying that, Mom," I told her when she wailed about my PhD again. I finally approached the bed, climbed onto it, and put my arms around her. "You never know what's going to happen. That's what you've always told me."

The day of my mother's surgery was the longest day of my life, and probably the longest of my father's, at least until that date. Her doctors made it crystal clear there was a good chance she wouldn't survive, and that if she did, there was so much cancer the surgery might not do any good. My father and I left Christopher at the house, watching my confused grandmother, making sure she was taken care of, while we spent the day at the hospital. My grandmother was showing signs of Alzheimer's by then, and my mother had been looking after her.

The waiting room was narrow, sunlight flooding over our backs from the windows along the wall behind us. Friends stopped by to see us during the morning, then around lunch, then in the afternoon. They brought food and company. Mostly, though, my father and I sat in silence as the hours stretched on and on. The morning turned to afternoon turned to early evening, and we grew desperate for news, any little bit of it. I went in search of the nurses to see if they could tell me anything about my mother's condition. My father and I began to fear the worst, that the surgery must be going poorly for it to take so much time. We were approaching twelve hours. The nurses were kind, they listened, they did their best to get information for us even though I began to ask for updates at fifteen-minute intervals.

I no longer sat in the waiting-room chairs. I couldn't sit at all. I paced the hospital corridors, passing the nurses' station again and again. We'd been there since 4 a.m.

Well after five o'clock in the evening, approaching six, my mother's doctor came out to see us.

"Your mother made it through surgery," he told us.

My father is a stoic man who, like my mother, never cries. He is a pillar of reserve. He wept like he'd been holding in all the tears of his life until that moment. He and I sat there, hugging each other, as the doctor gave us the less than good news. They'd gotten a lot of the cancer out, but there was plenty left. They couldn't touch it because it was all over her diaphragm; they couldn't risk perforating this important muscle, because she would die. Her prognosis was about six months, maybe a year if she was lucky. Ovarian cancer is a virulent form of cancer. It had metastasized, and her chances of survival were slim. But they would try to fight it with chemo and radiation. It would be a long road ahead for my mother. For all of us.

All throughout the conversation I asked him "what if" questions—about the cancer, about making it disappear, about what would happen if it did disappear. He was patient, but at one point, after yet another of my inquiries, he stopped, took a deep breath, and told me something I already knew, that everyone knows, that I'd heard a million times, but this was the first time its meaning truly sank into my academic brain.

"There is no cure for cancer," the surgeon said. "Your mother will always have cancer. And even if we get it all out now, it will come back. Ovarian cancer always does."

My father and I waited another hour before we were allowed to see her, just for a few minutes because she was exhausted and needed rest. She was barely awake but moaned a little when she saw us there. Her mouth was completely dry, her skin cracked and nearly bleeding, her lips white. We fed her ice chips from a little Dixie cup one of the nurses gave to us.

On the drive home, my father and I were a little more talkative, a little more hopeful. Her prognosis wasn't good, but we knew that my mother, who often drove us crazy with her constant activity and ideas and projects, would surely drive her cancer crazy, too, perhaps sending it into hiding. My mother was larger than life, always laughing and cooking sauces and pastas and Italian cookies from recipes she refused to write down. She talked too loudly, so that you could hear her from far away, so that you always knew she was there. She had more energy than all of us put together and taught her nursery-school students with a vibrancy few of their own parents could muster. She was a force. She would gather the strength of a hurricane to tear through the cancer that remained in her body.

By the time my father and I pulled into the garage and walked in the door of the house, we realized we were starving and decided to order pizza.

Poor Christopher was sitting on the ugly pleather couch, watching television, looking relieved to see us. My grandmother was sitting in one of the nearby chairs, half-asleep. He jumped up and took the two stairs that led into the kitchen. We updated him on my mother's condition. I'm sure he could tell that, despite her prognosis, some hope had sprouted within my father and me. The mood was decidedly different from the oppressive despair that filled the house the previous night and that morning before we'd left for the hospital.

"How did it go today?" we asked him, referring to my grandmother.

"Well," Christopher said, "she kept asking who I was, and if something was the matter with Concetta. I kept telling her that Concetta was at the hospital having surgery, but then she'd forget and ask again. That, and your grandmother vacuumed the house about fifteen times."

Yeah, she does that, we explained to him, chuckling. When my father picked up the phone to order the pizza, this jogged my boyfriend's memory about something else.

He turned to me. "Oh, your professor called. Father L.?"

I remember how my insides tightened on hearing this, my empty stomach aching, my throat constricting. I remember the darkness from the night outside contrasting with the bright lights of the kitchen. I remember how Christopher was standing on one side of the wooden cutting-board island and I on the other. "He called me *here?*"

Christopher nodded.

Everything was collapsing. My lungs, the muscles in my legs. I gripped the edge of the island, leaned into it to hold myself up. "What did he want?"

"He was concerned about your mother and wanted to know how the surgery went. He wanted me to tell you he's back from his trip and needs to talk to you. He wants you to call him right away."

"Okay." I turned to my father. "How long until the pizza's ready?" I asked, and the conversation shifted to other things.

For the second time, I was panicked, truly panicked.

The first was when I had opened that manila envelope on my coffee table and read his article. It was only the day before, but it felt like a year ago, given all I'd gone through during the twenty-four hours since. But his phone call to my family's house in Rhode Island seemed to indicate a new level of decision, an escalation of his attention, of his desperation. When I'd left him that message at his abbey, I'd truly believed my mother's cancer and surgery would buy me a lot of time with him, a lot of relief. Who would interfere with someone dealing with such terrible news? Who would bother someone when they were with their family, trying to cope with this awful new reality? Who wouldn't give that person space?

Never, ever had it occurred to me that he'd call the house in Rhode Island where I'd grown up, the house of my family. Never, ever had it occurred to me that it might occur to him to do this. I hadn't given him the phone number there, of course. But of course, he went and found it. Like all the other numbers and addresses he'd found, my family's address in Rhode Island was also in my file at graduate school.

I was enraged—at him, at myself—but to speak this out loud to someone else, even to Christopher, would cause me to lose control of it, would calcify it in my body like a new bone. To remain silent about it, to never speak my fears aloud, was to permit the situation to remain a figment of my imagination. Not quite real and, therefore, possibly just a fiction that had taken root in my mind. If it lived only inside me, if I never let it out into the open, I could still retain power over it, distort it, bend it to my will, and my will was to refuse its truth.

So, like with everything else that he'd done and continued to do, I did my best to bury this newest act. I didn't have time to deal with him and his stupid needs. I didn't have it in me to deal with him, to divulge any of what he was doing to Christopher or to my friends, and I certainly wasn't about to share it with my father. My mother had barely come through surgery and she still might die. My grandmother had Alzheimer's, my father couldn't make a bowl of spaghetti, and I had to make sure my family got through this horrible situation. That was my number one priority. My only priority.

But I also remember thinking, as the fact of his phone call kept rising to dominate everything else on my mind, that nowhere, not anywhere at all, was safe.

I was home for four, maybe five days.

Each morning my father and I would get up and go to the hospital to see my mother. Each day she was a little more awake, a little brighter, a little more talkative. She delighted the nurses with her humor, with her positive attitude, with her determination to get better—and fast. She wanted to be up and walking already, even though it would be a while before that was realistic. She was driving the nurses crazy, just like she always drove us crazy, but in a way that made them laugh.

"Your mother has a will on her," one of them said during a visit, with a big smile on her face, shaking her head. "And that bodes well for her recovery."

"Your mother's faith is strong," her surgeon told us one afternoon. He would continue to be the oncologist who treated her throughout her chemo. "It's going to help her. Praying to God and her belief that God is listening have given her hope and a good attitude. That goes a long way in fighting cancer."

I was surprised that a doctor, a cancer surgeon, would speak about prayer and God at all, that he would speak about these things with my mother and take her Catholic faith seriously. But he did, and that meant the world to her, which meant the world to my father and me. I suddenly felt so guilty about the ways I'd spoken to her as a college student, so harshly about her God and how I didn't believe in him. In college I'd become an avowed and outspoken atheist, I no longer kept my suspicions that God didn't exist to myself, and I hadn't cared how much this upset my mother. She would call me on the phone sometimes, asking me what I believed, why I didn't believe, what I might be willing to believe.

"What if God was a she?" she asked in the car one day when I was home for a visit. "I think God could be a woman," she offered—a comment to which I replied, at the time, "Whatever, Mom."

But now I was grateful for her God and the ways this God was going to help her survive cancer. I would pray to that God and any other if it might give my mother another day of life, if it would set her on the road to recovery. Whatever worked, I would do it.

Meanwhile, the Catholic Church, the parish of my childhood and my mother's Catholic school, swooped in to take care of my family. People left food and more food. Some of it we ate and some of it went into the freezer for later. I remember taking a lasagna that someone made for us and cutting the entire thing into large squares. I wrapped each one individually in tin foil so that all my father had to do was heat it up in the oven, then put it on a plate. I was worried about what he and my grandmother would eat, if he would eat, when I wasn't around.

Neighbors, parishioners we knew well and some we didn't, came by the house to say hello, to ask how we were doing, to offer to help us take care of my grandmother, who continued to ask us daily, nearly hourly, where my mother was and what had happened to her. We answered each time and then she'd forget.

The parish priests came by, the nuns did, too, especially

my mother's best friend. When my mother returned home from the hospital, one of them would come to the house every day to give my mother communion. They would do this for the entirety of her chemo and radiation, which was nearly a year. The teachers at my mother's Catholic school, where she'd been head of the nursery for over a decade, pooled their vacation days and donated them to her so she could get through chemo without quitting her job or taking leave without pay. They wanted to make sure she received her full salary during this difficult time, wanted to make sure that her health insurance didn't lapse. This, and they wanted her back the next year, were determined that she would survive to teach again, despite her gloomy prognosis. That extraordinary act of kindness still makes me teary when I think about it.

Our Catholic community, the priests and nuns, the schoolteachers and the parishioners, and their willingness to help were everywhere we turned. My father and I were so grateful. I still am and always will be grateful to those people. I still am and always will be grateful for the intensity of my mother's faith and the way it became a life raft for all of us.

Even my new boss and my staff at Georgetown wanted to do what they could to help.

"Stay at home as long as you need," the head of Residence Life told me when I'd explained that I had to go home immediately for my mother's surgery, that I'd probably keep having to go home that semester to help.

She said this despite the fact that my going home meant I would miss the opening of my residence hall, hundreds of first-years moving into the building with their parents in tow, one of the biggest responsibilities of my position. She arranged to have everything covered that day and every other day I would need. She told me there were more important things than work, that my mother was the most important thing of all. She brushed off this gesture as if it were nothing, when I knew exactly what a tremendous something it was. She and the rest of the staff would continue to help me however they could, whenever I needed them, for the remainder of that school year. Catholics everywhere I turned were being so good to me, were offering their hands to help me across this difficult stretch of life, even at my place of employment.

My father and I discussed graduate school and what I should do for the semester, if I should return to my classes or move home. I was conflicted. I talked about moving home, but he wouldn't have it. Privately, I was relieved. How was I going to give my mother that wish of seeing me get my PhD if I dropped out? My father argued that she would be horrified if I gave up grad school because she was sick, and I knew this was true. We agreed I'd come home as much as I could, every weekend if possible, and as long as my professors and boss were okay with my absence. They were, and soon I began to commute between Georgetown and Rhode Island, between TAing and classes and my job in Residence Life, and my father who couldn't cook and my grandmother who couldn't remember and my mother who was literally in for the battle of her life.

My professor called again, once, during those first few days after my mother's surgery.

After Christopher gave me that first message, I'd stopped answering our home phone because I was afraid I'd hear his voice on the other end after I said hello. I happened to be out the second time he rang, too. I was at the supermarket. When I got home, grocery bags in hand, my father looked up from the newspaper he'd spread across the kitchen table.

"One of your professors called? A Father L.?" My father's tone inclined upward, turning the information into two separate questions.

I set the bags on the counter and thought I might vomit. "Okay, thanks, Dad."

"He wants you to call him back immediately. It sounded important."

"All right."

My father pointed to the notepad we kept by the phone. He'd carefully written out my professor's name and his number and had underlined the request that I call him back, *immediately,* which he'd written in caps.

He went back to reading his paper.

I began to unpack the food and put it into the cabinets and the fridge.

My grandmother shuffled by, wanting to know where my mother was, if I'd bought milk and juice, even though we had three cartons of each already because it was her favorite thing to get at the market.

My father didn't seem to think much about the fact that a priest-professor from graduate school was calling me at the house. He knew that I'd always been close to all of my teachers, knew they were a regular part of my life, so it must not have seemed too out of the ordinary. Teachers calling the house, coming to visit us, was a normal thing, teachers of all types—my teachers from growing up, who were also my mother's colleagues. I was a dedicated student and my mother was a dedicated teacher who knew every other teacher in our town. There were all kinds of priests and nuns and Catholic people calling on us in every way they could, at the door, on the phone, in my mother's hospital room.

What was one more priest to add to the mix?

★ ★ ★

Christopher and I drove back to Georgetown. He didn't remark on the calls either, probably because, like my father, he knew I kept in close touch with my professors at Georgetown, especially since I lived on campus. He would joke about me being a teacher's pet, and we'd laugh about this, since Christopher was also a teacher.

I got home, I unpacked my clothes, I breathed, I tried to have a quiet night at my apartment. I didn't call my professor while I was in Rhode Island and I didn't call him now, either.

11

He wouldn't let up.

He used my mother's cancer as a new excuse to be in touch. He called my apartment, wanting to know how she was, would she be all right, what was her diagnosis? He would use these questions as a pretense for the real reason he'd rung my apartment:

When were we going to talk about his article?

Had I read it? When would we get together for a conversation about it?

I certainly hadn't forgotten about his article, though I wished I had. I pushed it as far away from consciousness as I could during those days I was in Rhode Island, but no matter what I did, it would emerge again, like a buoy that refused to stay under water. Each time it popped up in my mind, I would renew my internal debate about whether the article was trying to tell me something—that it was a confession of love, however indirect—or if it was simply coincidence that he'd written an essay justifying the love of an older, celibate priest for a much younger woman. A woman with whom he would meet, clandestinely, in the woods, so they could have sex.

Depending on the day, or the hour, I would come down on one side or the other. Obviously, it was a confession of love. Obviously, it was an overture. Obviously, I was letting my imagination run wild and the article was really nothing. It was a clear declaration, who was I kidding to think otherwise? I was undoubtedly a horrible person to suspect a priest of such inappropriate behavior, of breaking his vows or, at least, insinuating that he'd like to.

Then again, wasn't the article itself a justification of this—the breaking of the vow of celibacy to experience the love between humans? Hadn't he argued that it was actually a good thing for a priest to break that vow, because human love pointed to divine love? Wasn't it right there on the article's pages, his claim that love between a man and a woman could help a priest know God's love in a better, more intimate light?

Yes, I'd read the article, but I wasn't about to give him this information.

So, I lied and lied again. I told him I hadn't had time, that I was about to read it when I'd gotten the call about my mother, that because of going home and the chaos that followed I just hadn't gotten to it. He demurred: But didn't I have nearly a month before her diagnosis to read it? Hadn't he made sure I had plenty of time? Hadn't her diagnosis come at the very end of his long August trip?

Yes, but. Yes, but. Yes, but, I told him, my excuses mounting. My new job. My new job training. My new RA staff training. Only I never mentioned Christopher, my boyfriend, because when I'd tried that before, it was a disaster. I pulled up everything else I could think of to fend off his questions, his pressing me about why and when and why not and how come.

Well, could I read it now? Soon? When?

He really needed me to. He *really* wanted to discuss it.

No, um, I don't think so. Classes are starting. I have a lot on my plate. Staying in school. Getting my PhD was important to my mother, and I didn't want to let her down, especially now. Besides, I would be going home on the weekends to Rhode Island, making that long eight-hour drive back and forth each week. When would I have extra time to read something on top of everything else I was reading for classes? It just wasn't realistic. No, I'm sorry, but I can't read it now. It's too bad, I would have liked to very much. I'm so sorry. I really am. Maybe when things slow down, I'll get to it. But that won't be for a long time.

Nope. No. No. I can't. No. Sorry, but no. There isn't time. No.

I'd finally made the shift. I went from silent tolerance, from quiet avoidance, to outright denial of his requests.

I do not consent.

I. Do. Not.

I was articulating my nos out loud, but only because I felt I had no other choice. He was forcing those nos out of me, squeezing me until they emerged from my mouth, dislodged from my throat. He was pressuring me so much, so often, he was so persistent, that I didn't know what else to do.

Could I get together with him for coffee?

For a play?

To grab dinner?

Could he come over and visit my apartment?

Did I want to meet anywhere, anyplace, anytime?

We should just get together, he said, regardless of the article. As my good friend, he was worried about me. He wanted to make sure I was all right. I had a lot going on. And friends made sure their friends were all right. Friends checked in with friends who were going through a difficult time. Friends do this. Friends do that. Friends, friends, friends.

This became his new favorite word.

As your friend, I want to . . . I am . . . we should . . . He would call my apartment and preface whatever he was about to invite me to do with these words. When, inevitably, I said no to his newest idea for getting together, he took to scolding me with this very same word.

"Don-*na,*" he'd say, always pronouncing my name the same way, pressing down on that second syllable like he had a hand on my head and was trying to push me to the floor. The word *friend* always followed, like an out-of-tune piano key that clanged through my insides. "*Friends* spend time together. *Friends* do things for each other. You're being a bad *friend.*"

I was being a bad friend.

He began to tell me this over and over. To make this claim.

Was I? Was I being a bad friend?

I began to ask myself this, too. I began to wonder if I was.

Again, debate roiled within me. Maybe he really was a friend, and here I was, treating him terribly. Worse still, I was treating a professor terribly. A *priest* terribly. One who was also the head of my graduate program. What was I thinking, upsetting him like this? This was not good. Not good at all. What a mess I was making of everything.

But then, I had so many friends, and I knew I was a good one. I was. I swear.

Revulsion. Disgust. Fear. Rage. Helplessness.

Hatred.

So much hatred.

I began to hate him.

I began to wish him ill, wish that some horrible thing would befall him, like getting hit by a bus. I wished him dead. Anything that would make him stop contacting me. I began to fear that only something dire, like major illness or death, would be enough to make him go away.

I was a trapped animal in a corner, arms crossed in front of me, trying to fend off this foe who kept coming at me no matter what I did. He refused to stop. He just refused. It didn't matter how I said the word *no,* or how many times I said it, he would try again. My consent or non-consent was completely beside the point. Or maybe it was more that he simply couldn't hear my *no* because he didn't want to hear it. The only word he wanted to hear from my lips was *yes.* And until I said what pleased him, he would remain deaf.

My mother was home for about a month before they started her on chemo. Her doctor wanted her as strong as possible because the chemo was going to be beyond tough. She was happy to be at the house, to be alive, to be with my father and her mother, my grandmother, to have some peace before facing everything else that lay ahead.

We talked every day on the phone when I wasn't there to visit.

It was during one of these conversations that she informed me, around the end of September, in that lilting, singsong tone she always used as though I, too, were one of her nursery-school children, that she'd received a nice letter from my priest friend.

"What do you mean?" I asked her.

I honestly didn't know what she could be talking about. Not at first.

"Your professor from graduate school," she clarified. "You gave him my address?"

Nausea. Fear. Dismay. Shock. All of these hit me at once.

I know it must be difficult to believe—looking back now, with the perspective that decades of distance have given me, it's difficult for even me to believe—but I did not see this coming. His cleverness at inserting himself into every corner of my life still came as a surprise each time he found a new method of doing so. He was an octopus of a stalker, in each hand a letter, or a phone, or an invitation, using all his arms at once, and me caught in the blur of them.

In that moment I gave up. I surrendered to the impossibility of defeating such an enemy.

"Oh, yes," I lied to my mother. "That's right," I lied some more. "He asked me for your address and I gave it to him!" Lies, lies, lies. "He wanted to send you get-well wishes!"

My insides were sinking as I told her these things.

He was writing my mother now?

He was writing my mother now.

12

I stopped going to see him in his office, so he started coming to see me instead.

I didn't have any classes with him, which meant I didn't have a reason to see him when I went to school. Not having to see him was freeing. Unlike the prior year, this fall semester I had no plan to make the extra effort to go to the wing where his office was, to descend the stairs to his hallway and see if his door was open for visitors. I wanted to steer clear of any space where he might be breathing. He had all of my numbers and my addresses, and I couldn't prevent him from calling my apartment, from inviting me places over the phone, from sending me letters or sending my mother letters, or from calling me if I went to visit my family in Rhode Island. But this much I felt I could do.

I was wrong.

Now he went into my file to consult my current schedule, the location of my classes, so he knew where I was at all times, what hallways I'd have to walk and when I'd have to walk them. He took to waiting outside the classroom until my professor, his colleague, let us out.

I would leave and there he'd be, standing in the hallway. Hovering. Acting as though he were doing something else. Or he would happen to be in the stairwell when I was going from one class to another, looking at a book or a list of students or even a paper he was grading. When he saw me, he would always act surprised.

I would act just as surprised. At first, I *was* surprised.

But as these chance meetings in hallways and stairwells grew more frequent, they seemed far less a matter of chance and far more the result of his knowing my schedule and positioning himself in the building accordingly. I began to hurry everywhere, or pretend that I didn't see him in the hall, refuse to turn his way. When this was impossible and I ended up face-to-face with this man, I acted as if I were thrilled to see him, even though each new time I saw him waiting for me, my stomach sank like it was attached to an anchor.

"Oh, hi!" I would say, as though I couldn't be happier. "It's so good to see you!"

"Your mother seems to be doing better," he would say in return, or something like this, something to indicate that he and my mother were in touch. He loved telling me things about my mother.

Yes, she was writing him back.

I knew this, and I hated it. I hated hearing this confirmed by him. But what was I going to do? How could I possibly stop her from writing him? The Catholic Church, its priests and nuns and its God, were helping to save my mother from cancer, helping my family survive this situation. I wasn't about to destroy my mother's faith in one of its authority figures by telling her she couldn't return the correspondence, that I didn't want her to. And I *didn't* want her to, of course I didn't, but if I communicated this she would ask why, and I'd either have to tell her the truth, which I felt I could not do, or I would have to come up with another reason, and I couldn't think of an excuse that would make any sense.

So, after my mother began receiving letters from one of my professors who was also a priest, like any good Catholic woman she dutifully wrote him back. And he wrote her again, she wrote him, and so on. This was how their correspondence began.

He was incredibly pleased by it, and not shy about letting me know how good a letter writer my mother was, what a kind person she was, what a good Catholic even while she was suffering so terribly.

Unlike me, the bad friend.

"Don-*na*," he'd call my name through the hall. And when I tried to pretend I didn't hear him, "Don-*na!*" he'd say again, only louder.

His voice followed me everywhere.

I was failing at so many things now, and he continually reminded me of this. I didn't go to his office, I didn't open his letters, I didn't want to stay on the phone long when he called, and I was no longer accepting his invitations—not any of them. When he complained, I did my best to assuage him, to make him believe that everything was okay between us, to make him feel better. I wanted everything to be okay with every molecule of my being. I felt I could make things okay by sheer force of will, through the brightness of my smiles and the enthusiasm in my tone of voice. The alternative was unthinkable, so I refused to consider it. I had too many other things to juggle.

I didn't want to see him, I really, really didn't.

I would sit there in my classes as the clock ticked away their final minutes, hoping that this time when I left the room, he wouldn't be outside waiting. But there he'd be, no matter how hard I hoped or how much I prayed. Good days became the ones when he wasn't there, and they grew fewer and fewer. I began to hate leaving class. I began to dread the moment when I'd have to. Sometimes I would stall by talking to the professor as the other students filed out. Sometimes everyone else would file out and I'd be alone, the last person left in the room, thinking that maybe if I waited just a little bit longer he'd think I was home sick that day and leave.

I began to think I must be crazy, that I was going crazy. I told myself again and again that I must be imagining things, that it was just coincidence he was so often outside my classes or in the stairwells between floors, that there was nothing wrong with a professor standing in the hallway or traveling the stairs, that he had every right to stand wherever he wanted. It was his place of employment. It was normal for him to be in the building.

The more terrible and upset and crazy I felt, the more I turned on the smiles when I walked through the halls at school and ran into my fellow students. I needed to prove to everyone around me that everything was fine. I was afraid of what other people might start to think if I didn't, if I failed at this duty. I was afraid of rumors getting started, of getting kicked out of graduate school for whatever I'd done to make this man do whatever it was that he was doing.

It was a lesson in pretend. I got so good at it. I became an excellent actress.

One night, after having sex with Christopher, I realized the condom had broken.

I called my friend Hannah, in a panic. Hannah was obsessed with women's reproductive health, was a font of information about it, so I knew she'd have an answer that could help.

"You need the morning-after pill," she told me.

First thing the next day, I went to Planned Parenthood to get one. This was the late nineties, a time well before such things were available at the drugstore.

"You're probably going to get very sick," the woman at Planned Parenthood said. "But you have to take all of these pills—*all* of them—no matter what."

I agreed, I would take them, since pregnancy seemed like a far worse problem than a little vomiting. Christopher came over and vowed to take care of me, stay with me, no matter how sick I became.

At first, I felt fine.

I thought, *Well, maybe I'm one of the few people who can stomach this sort of thing.*

I'd dodged a bullet, I thought.

Then the first wave of nausea hit, and once it did, it kept on coming. I remember the world swaying and swimming like I was on a boat, I remember being slumped over the toilet for hours, heaving, forbidding Christopher from seeing me there, from helping me. I remember being splayed on the floor of my university apartment bathroom, my head, my hair, my cheek, swaths of exposed skin, lying across the floor of my bathroom, lying right against the grime that had worked itself into the grooves between the tiles after years of occupants, that I knew no amount of cleaning could remove, because I'd tried a million times to do just this. I remember not caring how dirty that floor was, because the tile was cold and the cold was soothing.

But more than this, I remember thinking:

This is my punishment.

For having sex, for being a sexual being.

For attracting people, boys, men.

Him.

For attracting *him*.

The God who was helping my mother was hurting me, the same God I didn't believe in—though I was discovering I *did* believe in this God, but only when I thought I was being punished, when I felt ashamed, when I believed I had done something bad. Then, God would show himself to me. He would swoop down from the sky above and appear before me, finger wagging, scolding, judging.

"Don-*na*," he'd say.

I started dressing differently.

Gone were the fashionable outfits, the high-heeled boots, the short skirts, the tight tops, replaced by baggy jeans and baggy sweatshirts. Baggy everything. I stopped wearing my hair long and loose and instead put it up in a ponytail or a knot. Sometimes I didn't even shower before school.

I wondered if this might help, if somehow he'd gotten the idea that I'd been dressing like that for him. That maybe if he saw me disheveled, he'd realize I wasn't interested in looking good for him. Not at all. Not one bit.

I survived on the hope that eventually he would get the picture, that he would hear the pleas of *No* and *I can't* underneath my false smiles, that he would grasp the fact that everything I was now doing at school involved an effort to unattract him. To make him stop turning my way, following me around, writing me letters. His only crime was paying me attention, but there was such an onslaught of it.

Why me? What had I done to draw him in? What could I do to stop it?

I tried everything, but nothing was working.

He began to watch the entrance of the building from his office windows. Sometimes, after I parked my car in the school lot and was heading inside, walking up the stairs and toward the door, I'd see him there, peeking out from between the blinds, watching me. He'd started to guess when I would have to arrive for my classes. So I stopped parking in the university lot and tried parking down the street as a way to avoid this new behavior on his part.

My dread about leaving class became a dread about being at school in general, about everything to do with that building and my classes. I still went, but I hated knowing I would probably see him no matter what I did or how hard I tried to elude him.

My life had firmly divided into two, and I lived both versions at the same time.

In one life, I loved my classes, my professors, my fellow students, everything about getting my PhD, which was still my dream. In the other, I hated everything about my classes, my studies, and getting my PhD. It was the reason that I was beholden to this man, that I would continue to be beholden to him. It was why I had no choice but to put myself in his vicinity on a daily basis. I was at his mercy and though I had so far avoided taking another class from him, I would be hard-pressed to continue this tack and would likely be forced to do so the very next semester. He was the main person who taught courses in my field.

One side of my life was expansive, was normal, was populated with friends and family and my boyfriend and work and responsibilities. One side held the possibility of the future I'd always longed for.

The other was windowless, airless, dark.

Populated only by him and me.

I could see no future there; I had no dreams.

My love for graduate school, for my studies, for ideas, for my professors and my classes, were the very same things that were trapping me, that were allowing him to trap me. And he was so very good at trapping me.

13

"Was that your other boyfriend?"

Christopher was sitting in my bed, grinning, when he asked me this.

I'd just gotten off the phone with *my professor.*

He'd called, and I went into the living room to answer. It was late, maybe 10 p.m., on a school night. As usual, he wanted to have a conversation, tried to persuade me to get together with him. We spoke for maybe ten minutes. I stood there, listening to him, fending him off—I never sat down when we were on the phone. Never. When you sit down to talk to someone on the phone, you are settling in for a long chat, for something you think you are going to enjoy, or for a serious conversation. You are making yourself comfortable. Talking to him was not relaxing, was not comfortable at all, it was a game of How Quickly Can I Get Out of This? I wanted anything other than a serious conversation, especially since that stupid article was still hanging over my head. So, sitting was out of the question, seemed incongruous with the experience of having to deal with him, and all my memories of our conversations involve me standing somewhere in my living room.

"What do you mean, my other boyfriend?" I asked Christopher back.

"You know," he said, "the professor that's always calling you."

My face burned, my body burned. I felt *caught*. Caught doing something *wrong*.

"What—no! That's ridiculous! Don't say things like that! He's a *priest!*"

Christopher had been smiling, chuckling, *joking* as he said these things to me. His voice was lighthearted, as it usually was. I was used to this, loved it, his constant kidding around. It was one of the things I cherished most about him, his ability to make me laugh, especially given what was going on with my mother. I loved how Christopher could break through the gloom, the fear, the uncertainty about her, make the sun shine again, even if it was just for a few minutes.

But his words that night had the effect of a hammer to my head, pounding me into the ground. It wasn't the first time Christopher became aware that a professor was calling me at home—he'd answered the phone in Rhode Island, after all, and taken a message from this man. It wasn't the first time my professor had called me at Georgetown when Christopher was over. That had already happened plenty—this was inevitable because Christopher spent a lot of time at my apartment, and my professor called daily. The nights when I could stay at his place, hanging out with him and Dan, playing video games, eating pizza, felt like vacations from my life because my professor could not reach me there—happily, universities didn't require students to register their boyfriends' addresses in their files.

Plus, I didn't have a cell phone yet, no one did. I would have gone to Christopher's more, done it all the time, but because of my Residence Life job I was required to be present on campus most nights. Moving to his place was out of the question.

So Christopher was around my apartment enough that by now it was a fairly ordinary occurrence, my professor calling me, though we'd never before discussed this. I would answer the phone, talk, get off as quickly as possible, then act like it hadn't happened. This was the opposite of what would happen after I got calls from a friend or my family, when I would tell Christopher afterward what had been discussed—my mother is going for chemo tomorrow, Hannah said hi and she wants us to go to dinner with her on Friday, Dan doesn't want you to forget you guys have soccer practice tomorrow. When it was my professor on the phone, he never got the post-call summary.

Christopher rolled onto his side in the bed, still smiling. "Yeah, but he calls you practically more than *I* call you!"

"He does *not*," I protested.

Though in truth, Christopher was right, and my professor did call me more—more than anyone else in my life, more than Christopher, and more, even, than my mother.

I made myself laugh—and laugh hard. I wanted in on this joke.

I needed to *ensure* the joking.

That night was the first time someone in my life, a *witness* to my daily comings and goings, an observer of *me*, took what I still wanted to regard as benign, as innocent, as No Big Deal, and named it as something potentially romantic—using the term *boyfriend* to encapsulate my professor's behavior—even though Christopher had done so kiddingly. He'd made the link, out loud, that I'd forbidden myself to make.

My entire being revolted. Refused the connection. Worse, I was caught off guard by Christopher doing this. I was amazed at the cavalier way that he could toss a statement like that out into the open, draw it into the air and give it sound and form.

It was like he was trying to fuse together two halves of a girl that repelled each other, weld them, but they would not fit, they were wildly mismatched, unjoinable. I could not allow this connecting of my two selves because if I did, the fragile bubble I was living in with Christopher, with my friends, with my life apart from this professor, would burst and my ugly side would soil the other, this professor would dirty the clean, happier parts of me. And I needed those parts of my life to remain pristine and pure.

"He's just a dedicated professor," I went on. "He was only checking in—he knows I have a lot going on! He wanted to ask about my mother. Isn't that so nice of him? *You're* a teacher." My voice turned teasing—I forced the teasing into it. "You should be as concerned about your own students as he is with his!"

I was still standing at the threshold of my bedroom. This conversation with Christopher, his questions, his comments, had halted me, had frozen me there. I hadn't moved an inch since those first words about my professor as "my other boyfriend" had left his mouth. I couldn't seem to budge. It was as if taking a step closer to Christopher, joining him on the bed while we were talking about my professor, would bring this man smack into one of my favorite places, where I found rest and joy, and smack into the person I most regularly found it with. I could not allow this, so I stayed where I was.

"Come to bed," Christopher said.

I hesitated, then I changed the subject. "Do you and Dan have a game tomorrow night?"

Only when he answered, only when he allowed the topic to turn to soccer, was I able to climb under the covers and join him.

I began to concoct a story.

A tall tale I would tell others to explain the ever-presence of this professor in my life. A story to excuse his behavior. To make it seem okay. I would not be caught off guard again, like I was that night with Christopher. My story would spill from me whenever people inquired about this man. Because they definitely began to inquire—people beyond my boyfriend.

"Isn't he wonderful, to be so invested in his students? In me?"

I would say this, voice high-pitched, eyes wide and blinking, trying to act as though everything were fine. It was usually a friend or an RA who asked. On one occasion he showed up at the end of an RA meeting and waited by the guard desk just beyond the door to my apartment. One of the RAs noticed him as they headed out. Or sometimes one of my friends would wonder why a priest was calling on my home phone, asking to hang out with me. Or someone would get curious about the growing pile of unopened letters on the windowsill of my office. Who were they from? Why were there so many? Didn't I ever open my mail?

Despite my attempts to avoid talking about him, he became a regular source of making fun with Christopher, who continued to joke about this professor as the other boyfriend in my life, joking that would make me wince inside even though I always went along with it on the outside, laughing as hard as he did, working diligently to effect a casual, nonchalant demeanor every time Christopher said something about him. Eventually, when he found out the truth, he felt terrible for laughing, for all those remarks about my professor-boyfriend, for not knowing instinctively that something was terribly wrong and had been that way for a long time; for not realizing how much his joking had deepened my suffering and shame.

"He's a *priest*," I learned to say at the outset, then would go on to use the title liberally, believing that conjuring this word immediately dispelled any untoward thoughts, that it would prevent people from wondering if something inappropriate was going on; as though this word, *priest*, would protect me the more I said it. "A priest who is also a professor. He treats his students as though they're his children? I think he decides to help the ones he thinks have promising academic futures? Aren't I lucky he picked me? That he chose me out of everyone else?"

There was always a series of rhetorical questions in my story. I needed whomever I was speaking with to collude in my effort to cover up his behavior. I needed the person to affirm that yes, everything was okay, it was even more than okay, it was *lucky*. Just as in high school and my undergraduate years, my luck in finding wonderful teachers, professors, mentors, had continued. Continued and expanded. Whichever person had drawn this story from me held the subsequent job of helping smooth over the unease their question provoked; it was their turn to answer with nods and smiles, to participate in disarming this loaded situation on my behalf.

"Donna, I got another letter from your professor," my mother would inform me happily during one of my visits home to Rhode Island or over the phone.

"Oh, how nice of him!" I would affirm, my excitement plain. I wanted my mother to continue to feel good about this correspondence, so I worked hard to ensure she knew I was okay with it. I think she truly believed the effort my

professor made to be in touch with her was not only something he did out of his duty as a priest, but also because he
saw her daughter as extra special, with a promising future
as a professor. I helped her continue to believe this.

I had a number of versions of the story I told people,
but all of them contained certain features. The mention of
my professor's status as a Catholic *priest*. My describing his
behavior as *kindly* and *selfless* and for my obvious *benefit*.
My sincere *gratitude* for his attention and time, and for his
investment in my future. My evident *enthusiasm* in tone
and body language as I told the story.

I would smile, I would laugh, I would gesture with my
hands and arms, wave them around in a way that suggested
dismissal of any cause for alarm or suspicion that this
professor might be extending himself for any reason other
than his selfless interest in my academic career and promise.
I've always talked with my hands, and when I talked about
him my hands were exaggerated, as though I could swat at
the problem like it was a fly, smashing it dead with a good-
natured expression on my face, everyone's innocence still
intact, his most of all. If he lost his innocence, I would lose
mine, too. Of this I was certain.

Why did I try so hard to protect him? Why did I work so
hard to justify his behavior? Wasn't I only prolonging my
own suffering? Doesn't my story, this effort at excusing
his behavior, undermine my claims that something was
wrong? Doesn't it mark me as a liar?

I know that, at least for a while, I made everyone outside
of my own situation believe that all was well between me
and my professor, that his behavior was entirely welcome.
I colluded with my stalker's behavior, as a way of preserv-
ing my own sanity. I did this because the potential cost of
telling the truth was *everything:* my professional future, my

reputation, their credibility, my general well-being. Lying to shield him was a form of self-preservation for *me*.

There is a liminal space created between the powerful person and the person who is the target of unwanted attention, a liminal space between outright yes and outright no. That space is not a compromise—not a maybe-yes or maybe-no—but more of a hovering, a being caught and not knowing where else to go or how to move without making things much worse. So you stay put. You hold the person off as best you can without causing them to retaliate too terribly, and because you know they can retaliate if they want to, that they have the power to do this, that they could decide to ruin you for displeasing them or rejecting them too forcefully. On the outside you continue to exist as though nothing is wrong, you perpetuate everything as though it is normal. You maintain the status quo with the abuser and with everyone around the abuser. Yet inside you are at war, you are shrinking, you are wishing you could die rather than continue much longer as though everything were fine. You become exhausted with the responsibility of making a situation okay that is not at all okay.

Part of the problem with any relationship that begins with a tremendous power differential is that the younger, less powerful party has everything to lose in this equation. That younger, less powerful party is in a dependent role so total that in the beginning, she likely doesn't recognize exactly how dependent she is. She has no idea what she is getting herself into. She thinks she is more capable, more mature, more secure, in her own position than she actually is in reality—because we all think this when we are young, and don't figure out until we are much older that we were in over our heads. Only after we are in the situation, only after the abuse and harassment start, do we realize how wrong our assessment was. Yet by then, it's too late.

For relationships like these to remain consensual depends entirely on the more powerful party to maintain them this way—and this is the problem. The older, more profession-ally accomplished person holds the reins. There is no getting around this. The younger, less powerful person is dependent on the willingness and ability of the other person to choose *not* to abuse his power. It is the older person's job to see this imbalance of power from the outset, to see that the younger person is too callow and inexperienced to realize this for herself. Yet the older person might refuse to see his respon-sibility, might not care, might be entering the relationship exactly because the other person is naïve and he likes it that way. Or, he might be so unself-aware, so inflated with his own power, that he believes himself to be truly benign.

I *did* want the attention from my professor that I got in the beginning. I wanted it and thought it was a good thing. That was my crime. But I was in way over my head before I realized my initial consent to his behavior could not be ungiven, that this man would continue to see how I was in the beginning and refuse to see how I soon became once my feelings about his behavior shifted. He was either emotionally and mentally incapable of seeing the shift, or he couldn't bear it. He drowned it out, replaced it with his own ideas, which were hallucinations, and in the process he drowned out the real me that existed in front of him. I will never forget what it felt like to realize one day that it didn't matter what I said or how many signals I sent, because this man simply *could not see me.* He'd erased the real me entirely. In place of me in reality, he substituted the me he wanted to see. He projected a Donna who didn't exist, a young woman student who adored him and wanted all of his attention, who loved it, was desperate for it.

And all throughout this time, I was trying to right the sinking ship I was on by acting like everything was all right. I really did not believe that coming forward was a possibility, so my only option was making things look okay. That fall, after my mother was diagnosed with cancer, this became my full-time job.

We doom ourselves, of course, when we do such a thing. We doom ourselves in the eyes of everyone around us. We undermine ourselves and our ability to seek justice later on. We create the materials that will be used against us, that will become the proof that yes, we consented to all of what happened. I, myself, created the fiction that told everyone who asked me how wonderful, caring, and concerned my professor was on my behalf, the lie that explained how I welcomed his attention, was grateful for it, how it was a *kindness*. I willingly participated in the charade of it, created the materials to keep the charade going. I was their author.

Accused harassers and assaulters will often justify whatever transpired by pointing to the existence of "friendly" correspondence and interactions, before, during, and after the alleged behavior. They will argue that the accusers visited their houses, sent them kind, even flattering emails, accepted invitations and professional opportunities proffered by them. Such evidence is offered to make the accuser appear the liar, to make the woman the one who has been taking advantage of him. But what else are women supposed to do when the powerful men in charge of our careers and futures behave in this way? When women are convinced that no one else will believe our accusations? When we, ourselves, can scarcely believe what happened or is continuing to happen?

This can account for why there is often such a delayed reaction to harassment, to assault, a keeping it to oneself for days, months, even many, many years.

At the heart of being harassed by a person with a great

deal of power is secret-keeping. From your friends, from your family, but especially *from yourself.* This secret-keeping may appear to others as collusion with the behavior. But you collude with *yourself* by not naming what is really happening, because naming it requires you to face it and you simply cannot. It may look a lot like consent, but it isn't. It's the way you survive.

I remember, clear as day, the moment I realized my story was a lie. That my story was a cover-up. I remember the exact spot where I was standing, just outside the inner door to my apartment. The door between my office and my living room was wide open at the time. Several people were gathered there with me, a few friends, Christopher and Hannah among them. We were about to go out somewhere.

The phone rang before we left, and I picked it up. It was him.

Everyone overheard my side of the conversation.

They heard me say no to his latest invitation. They heard how many times I had to say no, because he kept pressuring me to say yes, kept trying to persuade me to change my answer from no to yes, or at least from no to maybe. Everyone overheard how difficult he made it for me to get off the phone, the way he tried to keep me on the line even though I kept telling him I had to go, that friends were waiting for me, that they were waiting right there that very moment, in my apartment, while I talked to him. They heard me avoid telling him where we were going, and they knew he must be asking about this, since I was floundering around, trying to answer him without answering him.

Finally, I hung up. When I turned around to rejoin my friends so we could head out, they were staring at me, silent.

"What was that all about?" Hannah asked, with a weird, hesitant tone.

I put on my happiest smile and then, like so many times before, I launched into *the story*. But on this telling, unlike every other, I heard myself rehearsing it as if from far away, outside my own body. I could see my own face as I spoke those tired lines, the one about this man's kindliness and his concern, the repetition of the word *priest* over and over. And in that moment I finally sensed something different as the words emerged from my mouth. They rang hollow, they were off. There was a sickly sweetness to them, and I could taste it on my tongue.

Everything I was saying was a lie. But I was not lying for him, or even for them, I was lying for me. I was lying to myself, as a way of avoiding the truth. I wanted to avoid the truth so badly because the alternative was not an option. This I believed was still true. I had no options. And now my cover was gone. Reality lay there before me like an exposed wire, live and dangerous.

And that was when I knew I'd lost everything, because I'd lost my own lie, too.

14

He wanted me to see *Wit* with him.

It was playing in New York City. I was driving back and forth to Rhode Island, passing by on a regular basis. Obviously, he told me, I should meet up with him there so we could go to the theater together.

Wit is a one-act play by Margaret Edson about a woman who is dying of ovarian cancer. Emma Thompson would eventually do a version of it that aired on HBO to great fanfare. It would go on to win the Pulitzer Prize in 1999. By the time he wanted to see it with me it had already been heaped with critical acclaim and deemed a masterpiece. I knew all about it and not just because of him. Other people had mentioned this play to me, its existence, because of my mother, informed me that it was supposed to be wonderful, riveting, heart-wrenching.

Plenty of people process tragedy and loss by reading books that have to do with these same topics, books about how to get through grief, that help a person face whatever it is they need to endure. There are people who steep themselves in the stuff of their tragedy, who prefer to swim in it for a while before emerging, cleansed and whole, onto the dry sand of the shore. I am not one of them. I received a number of well-meant gifts in the form of such books shortly after my mother was diagnosed and given a death sentence. I said thank you, and I put them somewhere and never looked at them again.

I needed to keep walking on dry land to get through what my family was facing. I was tired from making the sixteen-hour round-trip every other week or sometimes every week to cook for my father and grandmother, to take care of my mother. I was witnessing her suffering close-up. In the month between her surgery and her first round of chemo, she'd lost fifty pounds. It was shocking.

My mother had always been this big Italian lady, nourished on daily bowls of pasta with homemade sauces, on Italian fried chicken, which we loved in my house and which she and my grandmother cooked weekly. My mother would often joke that she didn't know whose genes I had, since I certainly hadn't gotten hers. My mother and grandmother were robust and round in all the places I was skinny and flat. Her voluptuous figure was part and parcel of her larger-than-life presence, the big, loud Italian personality she possessed to go along with everything else that was big and loud about her. She shopped at Lane Bryant to get the sizes she needed, but she resented this. She spent her entire life intermittently dieting, going through every fad out there for women, going on and off Weight Watchers, and eventually tuning in as Oprah's weight went up and down alongside her own. For years, my mother did aerobics every morning at 6 a.m. with Joanie Greggains, a thin, tall, muscular blonde on television who was always jumping and bouncing, encouraging women to keep going, to not give up, barking her orders as I ate breakfast before school. But Richard Simmons is the dieting guru I remember most from childhood. My mother loved him, loved his television program, his advice. She watched him every day, diligently, doing her best to follow his health and exercise plan. But no matter what my mother did, she never lost weight, or if she did, it was negligible.

Now she'd shed fifty pounds in a few weeks. I almost didn't recognize her. Her face had grown sunken. It was as though someone had let all the air out of her body. None of her clothes fit. They hung off her frame like collapsed tents. On one of my visits home, the moment I was about to walk inside the house my mother flung open the door before I could grasp the knob.

"I'm a size ten!" She wore a big smile on her gaunt face. "I bought new clothes!"

This was the one and only benefit, according to my mother, of cancer. She finally lost the weight she'd dreamed of losing. She went from a size sixteen to a size ten practically overnight, and soon she'd be down to a size eight. When her clothes stopped fitting, her friends took her shopping. They'd gone on quite a spree. She was thrilled by her new size. She modeled her new outfits for me, and I oohed and aahed over her new figure.

"Who knew that cancer was the best diet of all?" she told me, laughing.

I remember feeling happy that my mother could find this sliver of joy in the middle of her tragedy, that she had friends who wanted to help her take advantage of this faintly silver lining. I remember being in awe of my mother's ability to look on the bright side of things, to find that bright side even when everything seemed shrouded in an impenetrable darkness from where I sat. She needed that pleasure, however perverse the source of it might seem. When she had her rounds of chemo, the darkness would eclipse all the light, every glimmer of it.

Ovarian cancer is a terrible, virulent cancer, and her doctors were treating it with an equally terrible chemo. There have been so many advances in cancer treatment over the last two decades, but this was the late nineties. My mother would go to the hospital for her treatment and be there the entire day. It would take about six hours of sitting there, her arm stuck with a needle. One of us would try to be with her for it, to keep her company. She took her medicine with a smile, always in good spirits, her positive attitude coursing through her along with that poison dripping from the bags the nurses would change and change again, with an occasional cup of ice cream they would bring her in between.

But the days following each round of chemo were miserable, and my mother suffered from that poison. It nearly hurts too much to think about it all these years later. I'd always thought her spirit unbreakable. Even with all she'd been through, her massive surgery, all that weight loss, a prognosis of certain death within six months to a year, she took cancer in stride and found bits and pieces of joy within it. But when the chemo really hit her, those four or five days when it was at its worst in her system, the mother I knew disappeared, replaced by someone living an agony so terrible there was no bright side to be found, not even for her. My father and I were forced to watch chemo do the one thing that seemed impossible, which was to break my unbreakable mother. She would eventually bounce back once she began to feel better, but I think he and I came to dread this triweekly ordeal nearly as much as she did.

My mother had lived in my mind as an immortal for so long, and now her mortality, its imminence, was in front of all of us and we were unable to turn away from it.

★ ★ ★

I didn't want to see *Wit*.

I didn't ever want to see it. Seeing *Wit* was pretty much at the top of the list of things I had no desire to do. Going to a several-hour play about a woman suffering and dying from ovarian cancer was the last thing I wanted to do, the last way I wanted to spend my precious free time. Why would I want to put myself through the fictional performance of death by ovarian cancer, when I was already living it in reality? When I was forced to witness it happening to my family and my mother?

No. No, I would not go. Not with anyone, but especially not with him.

What I wanted to do in my free time was hang out with Christopher. I wanted to hang out with Dan, too, who by now was my best friend from graduate school. I wanted to spend time with my girlfriends and I wanted to watch *Felicity* with my RAs, which we loved to do after our weekly meetings because Felicity was also an RA and we delighted in this. I wanted to cook, and I wanted to see disaster movies with ridiculous plots involving volcanoes and asteroids, or watch silly romantic comedies where everyone gets their happy ending. I wanted to go to chain restaurants like the Olive Garden where everything was a known quantity and where even the food was safe because I'd tasted it before. I wanted to drink Coffee Coolattas from Dunkin' Donuts as often as possible because my mother and I had gotten addicted to them over the summer before her diagnosis, when they were the new "it" drink, and even though now, twenty years later, I think they are disgusting.

The only thing that could top *Wit* on the list of things I did not want to do was going to see *Wit* with this man whose attention I had grown to hate with everything in me. I could not think of a more loathsome combination of things I did not want to do. And the only thing that could match my desperation to avoid such an outing with him was his desperation to make that outing happen with me. He wanted to go to see *Wit* with me as badly as I did not want to go.

As usual, he called and he invited, he showed up in the hallway and he asked. He called again and he pushed. He gave his reasons and made his arguments as he badgered. He thought it was a good idea, he thought it would be cathartic, he thought it would help me understand my mother's suffering, he thought it would assist me in processing her cancer. He offered a million reasons that I should go, why I needed to go, how it was imperative that I go.

It didn't seem to occur to him that even if I did want to put myself through this play, maybe I would want to endure this emotionally wrenching experience in the company of someone other than him. Someone with whom I had an intimate relationship, like a best girlfriend, or perhaps Christopher. Someone who would hold my hand, who would feel comfortable putting their arm around me, letting me lean on them, hugging me if I so desired. Someone who would be able to dry my tears, which I would inevitably cry, given the subject matter.

But, was this his plan all along? His hope for the outing?

Did he want to be this person for me? Become him by means of this play? Had he foreseen that there would be a need to console? Did he hope to provoke the need to console, and become my chosen consoler?

I would have no other choice but to lean on him if we went together, because he would be the only person with me. Perhaps this was his fantasy, to escort me to a critically acclaimed play about the tragedy my family was living, knowing full well that it would shake me and dredge up all the fears and emotions over what was happening with my mother, so that he could be the person I turned to, that I leaned on, that I needed to help soothe the pain I would inevitably feel. Perhaps he wanted to be the person to rescue me after my certain collapse by the end of the play.

"Don-*na*," he pressed. "You *really* need to go."

"Maybe," I would tell him. "Maybe next week."

As usual, I hemmed and I hawed. I used my busy schedule as an excuse for why I could not go on this trip or the next one. I used my mother's cancer, her schedule of doctor's appointments, taking care of my grandmother, to explain why this weekend wouldn't work or that weekend either. I used papers that were due, my midterm exams that were coming up. As his invitations continued, I eventually explained that I had no desire to see this particular play, that I felt I couldn't handle it emotionally. I flat out told him no, that I was not going, that I couldn't bear to go, that I would see anything else in the world over this particular play, but that this play, my going to it, was just not happening.

He finally gave up on getting me to see *Wit*.

He had to, because the play had closed.

I was relieved. Once again, I'd avoided a close call, a situation that felt much like the one with the retreat house. But he took my suggestion that I'd rather see anything other than *Wit* to heart and proposed something other.

"The symphony is playing at the Kennedy Center," he began.

It was some special performance he was dying to see. Obviously, I should accompany him.

I remember, once again, where I was standing in my

apartment when he suggested this latest outing. I was facing the back wall, the cinder blocks shadowed, the light from my kitchen just barely spilling over them. We were on the phone, as usual, because he was calling my house nearly constantly. Avoiding seeing him in person had become a skill of mine, and also a full-time job. But I could not figure out how to dodge his calls. I had to answer my phone because of my mother, because of my job, so answer it I did, but I dreaded its ring. More likely than not, it would be him on the other end.

I wanted to collapse. I wanted to scream, I wanted to cry, I wanted to throw that clunky old push-button telephone across the room so that it smashed against my shadowy cinder-block wall. Hadn't I just narrowly avoided seeing *Wit* with this man? And now I was already facing another situation? Another invitation to avoid, to reject, to out-maneuver, was sitting before me, hovering, pressing into me, threatening me.

I knew, then, that there would be no end to this.

No end to the invitations, no end to the attempts to get me to spend time with him, to go places, to do anything and everything he could possibly think of. If it wasn't *Wit* it would be the symphony, and if it wasn't the symphony it would be some other play, and if it wasn't a play it would be a musical, and if it wasn't a musical it would be dinner or coffee or tea or breakfast or lunch or a snack in the afternoon and so on and so forth until the day of my death.

I was so tired. So very tired.

But I told him no. No, I could not go.

The cycle was triggered once again, his pushing me about why I could not go, and my reiterating, for one reason or another, that I was not going. As usual, he told me I was being a bad friend, that friends spent time together, yet I was not spending time with him. I don't remember the excuse I gave him as to why I could not go, but I now asserted my nos with little remorse or fear.

My will was cracking straight down the middle. My capacity to see a future, my beloved future as a PhD who became a professor, was fading. I was losing my ability to care about anything other than my mother's survival and making this man stop being in my life. If it cost me my future, so be it. What was this future, anyway, if I had to have him in it? Why would I want a future that included him? He was in my field, after all, and always would be, so there was no form of my being a professor that would not involve him.

He refused my no.

Refused to acknowledge it, hear it, accept it. He willed it out of existence. He would only hear my yes, and he would continue to badger me until I gave it to him. Even though I told him no a million times, he bought two tickets for the performance anyway.

The difference between this symphony outing and *Wit* was that the symphony was playing on a specific date, a date that was marching toward us. He knew that I would not be in Rhode Island on that date. He made sure of this. He would call my mother and check these things, since they were occasionally talking on the phone now in addition to writing letters. He knew I didn't have classes because he had access to my schedule and was friends with all of my professors. He knew that I didn't have an RA meeting because he knew what night I held those weekly meetings. He felt I had no excuse but to go, that no excuse I offered was good enough, made sense, was legitimate. But I said no anyway, kept saying it. He asked every single day all the way up until the afternoon of the performance. When that day finally arrived, I was so relieved. I was crossing the finish line of successful avoidance once again.

The phone rang.

I picked up.

It was him.

"I'm at the Kennedy Center," he said.

He was calling from a pay phone. There was still time for me to change my mind, to come down there and meet him. He still had my ticket, had it with him. He'd gone alone, still hoping I would join him.

No, I told him. I'm sorry, but no.

15

A pear sat on my kitchen counter, rotting.

It was a gift from him, brought back from a trip. I don't remember where he went, though I feel like it might have been Japan. I no longer cared about his comings and goings. I'd stopped listening closely when he talked. My only desire was to get away, my only thinking about how to make my escape, which began the second he approached, the moment I noticed him out of the corner of my eye.

He'd presented the pear to me like a special offering, a delectable gift. I took it from him because I felt I had to, but when I got home I'd tossed it onto the counter and there it sat for days.

It became an eyesore in my kitchen. I hadn't even placed it on a dish or in a basket. It sat directly on the counter, a black stain now pooling around it. I don't like pears, I never have. I don't eat them. I don't like their faintly sweet taste, a blander version of the tart, bright apples that I love. I don't like the pear's yellow-green color, the way tiny brown dots often mark its skin. I've never liked anything about pears, and now that he had given me one I liked them even less. I hated that pear in particular. I hated it on my counter, I hated its perfect pear shape, wide and round on the bottom, sloping and so very female as it curved upward toward its stem. I resented its existence, that it had decided to grow from a pretty flower on a lovely tree, big and bursting until someone decided to pick it, so that it would make its way into his hands, and eventually from his hands into mine. I wanted nothing that had touched his hands. I was not about to ingest something that had touched his skin. I would rather have starved.

So I left it there. It began to sink into the rotting flesh at its base, becoming shorter.

I refused to touch it.

Meanwhile, I cooked Italian sauces and pastas, homemade raviolis, and everything else in my culinary repertoire. I had my RAs over for the occasional dinner and my friends and of course Christopher, too. He never commented on the pear, but he was used to mess, his room in his apartment always a disaster. I wonder if anyone noticed there was a pear grown putrid in my kitchen, that it sat directly on the countertop in a pool of brown mush, whereas everything else nearby was spotless. I cleaned around it, ignored its existence, acted as though I couldn't see it. I wonder if the people who visited my apartment saw it and thought it was disgusting.

It wasn't the first gift he'd given me.

Aside from the letters, he'd been giving me books he thought I should read. Books from his very own collection, or the occasional one he bought just for me. I had them in a stack in the corner of my office, by the windows. While I was getting good at tossing his letters into the garbage without remorse, I could not bring myself to do the same with the books. How could I? How could anyone? I was a graduate student. Books were something I saved up for, objects I cherished. I spent entire afternoons wandering bookstores, especially used ones, scouring them for out-of-print volumes by my favorite philosophers and theologians, treasuring the experience of triumph when I managed to locate one on a dusty shelf. Some of the books he gave me were the out-of-print kind, books I needed to read for my PhD and my comprehensive exams. I seemed to have no other choice but to keep them. It was against sanity and defied logic to throw away books, it was a sin of unimaginable proportions. It was beyond my capacity.

As with the pear, once I put those books down somewhere, I didn't touch them again. That allergy I felt in the vicinity of this professor extended to them, too. They were books I was supposed to read, that I needed to read to do well in my program, but I couldn't bear the thought of doing so. My aversion grew to encompass the authors themselves. I now associated those writers with him, so I avoided them by extension. I found myself unable to go near anything they'd written, in addition to the books of theirs that he'd given me. These authors provoked the same dread, the same unease, the same nausea that he provoked. I knew this was a problem, that I could not erase these thinkers from my graduate program, because they were too central, that my other professors would not allow me to do this. But my sickness had become so constant that I didn't care. By turning these books and these thinkers into special gifts, he'd ruined them, much like this ruined pear I couldn't seem to throw away.

Most of the time I tried not to see the pear when I wandered into my pink kitchen, which was constantly. But there were times when I would consider the pear, its presence, the fact that I knew I would never eat it. Yet I still wasn't doing anything to get it out of my house. I was allowing it to invade my consciousness, much like that article of his had invaded my consciousness in August.

What had he been thinking when he decided to carry this pear back from his travels? Did he think it was romantic, to give a female student a piece of fruit? To give me something so symbolic within religion? Was he playing the serpent, tempting me from the tree of the knowledge of good and evil, albeit with a pear and not an apple? Did he know it would make me think of Saint Augustine and his *Confessions*? Was he certain that it would, since we'd read Augustine together in my first semester of graduate school, when I was in his class? Was he hoping this pear would transport me back to happier times, when I would waltz into his office on a weekly basis, ready to discuss whatever was on the syllabus, eager for his wisdom?

I've had a long love-hate relationship with Saint Augustine, ever since my first year as an undergraduate at Georgetown. He knew this about me. We'd talked about it endlessly during those office hours. The pear confession is one of my favorite moments in that famous autobiography by Augustine, a book I've taught many times now in my on-again, off-again life as a professor. It's a moment that makes me roll my eyes at Augustine, makes me love-hate him all the more.

During his youth, many years before he converted to Catholicism and later became a bishop, Augustine was a champion sinner, a champion in that he was masterful at cataloging each and every sin he believed he had committed, down to his cries as an infant. One night Augustine wandered into an orchard with a group of boys and they decided to steal some pears. For most people this would turn into a funny story later in life, or an event that would fade until it was forgotten, but not for Augustine. For him it was a moment he could never let go, that he refused to let go.

Stealing the pear was symbolic. It tortured him. It was so basic, so minor, so like the boy he was at the time, goofing off with other boys his age. But to Augustine it meant everything that he took that pear. For him it was the sin that began it all, the formative sin that led to his life as a sinner on a far more serious and condemning scale.

Now, sitting in my kitchen, I had a pear.

A pear given to me as a gift, from a priest who'd also sent me his article about the virtues of celibates who fall in love.

Did he think of Augustine's first sin when he offered me this pear? Did he mean it to symbolize for me something similar? Was the pear intended to represent that first venial sin of Augustine's, but as a parallel to him, in relation to me? Did he want me to understand this particular pear as his venial sin, the first of many, the sin that would lead to other, mortal sins he would commit with me on a far greater scale? Was this his fantasy?

I didn't know, couldn't know for sure, which was always the case with him. He would always do startling things, things that chilled me, like sending me that article, yet these things were never straightforward. They always left room for doubt, so doubt and doubt and doubt I would. One day when I walked into my kitchen and was confronted, yet again, by the pear, I would be sure he'd meant the world with it, that it was symbolic of the many other sins he wanted to commit with me, sins on the same grand scale as Saint Augustine, who kept a mistress for years and fathered a child with her.

On those days I believed that pear to be on par with his article, sure he'd meant it as a romantic gesture, certain he believed it to be the ultimate of literary, romantic overtures, and that I would appreciate its theological symbolism, that I would grasp its intellectual cleverness, and perhaps fall for him because of it. Yet on others I would laugh at myself for having these suspicions, convince myself I was crazy to think such things, to assume them. It was just a pear, after all.

A shift occurred on the night that my cover story had fallen apart.

I'd gone from a state of pretending to not know the truth, of beating it back, to knowing the ugly truth and having to live with it. Having to carry it around with me constantly. It was so heavy it was breaking my back. I was dragging myself from one place to the next, dragging myself through all of my duties, my responsibilities, the work required for my classes. I was becoming a zombie, driving to and from Rhode Island to help my father, to help with my grandmother, to be with my sick mother, who seemed to grow only sicker each time I saw her. On the outside I wore my typical smile, made sure everyone around me believed I was all right, but on the inside, like the pear, I was rotting.

I began to submit to his attention.

There's no other word for it. I submitted. I accepted it as my reality. I accepted that there was no other reality for me to accept.

I endured his phone calls, and he called me everywhere: my apartment at Georgetown, my family home. I endured the onslaught of his letters, his growing relationship with my mother. I came to expect his presence in the hall-ways and stairwells and occasionally outside my apartment door. I let the constancy of his invitations, his need, his ever-escalating desperation to see me, spend time with me, crash over me like a giant wave. I just stood there, silently, unmoving, while it did. I did my best to keep breathing through the constant nausea, the despair, the exhaustion. I did my best not to drown.

I submitted to the reality that the attention would not stop, that I could not stop it, that it was not within my power to make it stop. I accepted that I could not change this. I believed I had no options, that no one would believe me if I told them what was going on. Or that the only thing they would be willing to believe was that I was crazy to suspect this man of wrongdoing, this beloved priest-professor of a man. They would see only the innocent side of his actions, because there was always an innocent side to see. They would dismiss my feelings of desperation, of rage, of fear and disgust, as overreactions.

Unless.

Unless he attacked me.

I began to pray that he would try. I wanted him to try to rape me.

I know how horrible that sounds, how utterly vile.

But I need to explain why. His behavior was so complex; he never stepped over a line. It was always just this side of excusable, technically. What's a few letters? They're not hurting anyone. What's wrong with a professor looking out the window of his office? Absolutely nothing. How can you accuse a professor of being in the hallway and the stairwell of the building where he teaches? You can't. What's a pear, a few books, a few coffees in the abbey where he lives with his fellow monks? Not much to go on. What's one article about a famous author and priest written by a similarly renowned author and priest? It's fulfilling one's obligations as a professor at a university. How about his calls and letters to my Catholic mother with cancer? A kindness, proof of his generosity.

The only argument that would ever withstand scrutiny, I reasoned, was the one that would include violence against my person. If he got violent, if he left marks and bruises on my body, if I had to push him off me, if I had to just as violently react to fend him off, only then could I tell someone what was going on. Only then would I have proof, real proof, indisputable proof. The kind you could tell the police about. The kind of thing that would allow you to say, "That man attacked me. That man tried to rape me."

This sort of behavior is the clear kind, the kind that leaves behind no doubts, no lingering suspicion of innocence. The kind that crosses a line, firmly and obviously, a line that other people do not dispute.

I never got so far in my reasoning that I hoped he would succeed. In my mind, he would never succeed, because I would not allow him to. I was confident I could physically overpower him. He seemed so weak. Perhaps I was deceiving myself, but this was my belief.

There's more. And this "more" provokes an even greater degree of shame in me than what I've already admitted. There was a part of me that wanted, *needed* him to step clear across the boundaries of that vow of celibacy. I needed him to do it *for me.*

I wanted him to try to hurt me, to attack me, so I could finally believe *myself.* About what I was going through, what was happening to me, what I was enduring, what my life had become. I couldn't stop doubting myself and my own experiences of his attention. I not only felt tortured by his behavior, but I tortured myself on top of it. I couldn't allow myself to trust in myself, even as I swam in a sea of despair. To trust myself required me to overthrow all of the trust I'd grown up to have in the authority figures that populated my life. It required me to overthrow the trust I had in my beloved professors and the kindly priests trekking daily to my family's house to give my mother communion. It required me to overthrow the trust I had, that *we all had,* in the vow of celibacy that a priest makes not only to the Catholic Church, but to God. It required me to be willing to put myself between him and that vow, between him and God, and accuse him of breaking the most holy of promises.

To break through that amount of trust, a lifetime of it, a world of it, an entire church built on it, was too much. It was too heavy. I couldn't do it on my own.

I simply did not have that amount of trust in myself. How could I, at that young an age, have the trust, the certainty, the righteousness in myself and my own experiences, feelings, and suspicions, necessary to topple that much authority? The trust that universities expect us to have in our professors? That the Church expected of its Catholics?

And then, I *wanted* to be wrong about everything. I wanted my doubts to be right. I wanted this with all of my heart.

This man was going to have to be the one who broke through all those barriers. He was going to have to do the heavy lifting for me. He was going to have to throw all that trust off because I didn't have the strength to do it myself. He was going to have to take his prestige as a professor, as the head of my concentration, as an important academic, as my mentor, and climb all of those walls to get to me on the other side. He was going to have to be the one to take his vow of celibacy, the vow that marked him as a Catholic priest, and smash it to the ground.

What a pathetic feminist I was. What a weak little girl. What low self-esteem I must have had to be unable to take care of myself, to believe in myself. How Catholic and obedient of me. How polite. How utterly stupid and naïve. I failed myself for so long. I fail myself even now as I confess these things. Aren't the things we feel most ashamed of always confessions of a sort?

The pear began to stink. It sank lower and lower into its rot, like an old man growing shorter with age. I finally threw it out.

When he asked me if I'd eaten the pear, I lied and said yes, it was delicious.

16

I agreed to drive him home from the airport.

It was mid-November, only a few weeks before I finally told, though at the time, I still didn't know I was going to tell. It was a calculated decision to pick him up and take him to the abbey where he lived.

"Don-*na*," he was constantly saying in that soft voice of his, every time I picked up the phone, "you're being a *bad friend*." He was perpetually disappointed in me, angry at me, desperate with the need to see me, talk to me, spend time with me, pressuring me, pestering me, admonishing me. I could picture him, too, even if I couldn't see him when he was scolding me, eyes wide, facial expression open, innocent, vulnerable, his hands pressed together, fingertips touching as though in prayer, the black shirt of a priest stark behind them; everything about his body and posture perfectly humble, perfectly at peace, confident he was exactly right to let me know of his displeasure.

By now, my response was always no, a no that grew louder and louder. As soon as I heard his voice on the other end of the line, I began my effort to end the call, to reject his proposals for outings, for getting together, for any conversation whatsoever. It was a seesaw existence, a series of yeses (answering phones, greeting him in hallways, submitting to his presence) followed by immediate nos (getting off the phone, inventing a reason to leave, averting my eyes), a constant and sickening tipping from one way to the other, back and forth, my legs tired from the need to be pushing upward, then immediately absorbing that downward swing. His maneuverings ceased to chill me. I grew used to the clever ways he found new avenues into my life and my world.

But the airport favor felt like a quick fix to the ever-present onslaught of invitations, and his growing frustration that he could no longer get a yes from me. It seemed a good bet as my one, rare appeasement because it was so concrete, so finite. He would arrive on a plane, I would be at the curb waiting, and I would drive him straight home. It would be fast and easy.

At the time, I also thought: *This will make him stop.* Stop saying I'm a bad friend, stop saying I never do anything with him anymore, that I don't have time for him anymore. This will prove to him that I'm not a bad person, a bad student. I was always in search of the magic fix that would make things okay again. I couldn't let go of the possibility that there existed some way to remedy all that was going wrong, and I hung on to this chance like it was the edge of a cliff and I was dangling over the side, certain death beneath me. Maybe the airport trip would be the answer, I reasoned.

As soon as I said yes, he suggested we go for coffee, that we stop for dinner on the way to his abbey, that we do anything, really, to prolong our time together. With each additional request I said no, and no again. I had papers to write, RAs who needed me, books to read, studying to do, a mother to call. All the old, now-tired excuses fell from my mouth once, twice, a third time, and then a fourth. I didn't care that I was repeating myself. He continued to push that this airport pickup become more than just an airport pickup, and I continued to dodge his maneuverings.

I began to regret my yes almost as much as I regretted having saddled myself with this favor, with having to spend any time alone with him at all. I dreaded it but consoled myself that it should be fairly painless. I could probably make it from the airport to his abbey in twenty minutes without traffic.

The evening of the pickup I got in my car to drive to the airport. I remember it was dark, it was nearly winter, so the sun was gone by 5 p.m. His flight was on time; he got in the passenger side. He suggested we stop somewhere for a bite to eat, and once again I demurred. Was I sure I couldn't? Yes, I was sure. I have no idea what we talked about on the ride, probably something about his trip. I vaguely recall that he was animated. Mostly, I concentrated on getting this favor done, on getting to his abbey as fast as I could without a speeding ticket, so that I could get him out of my car again.

I kept both hands on the wheel, facing forward, trying to make myself smaller and smaller. His presence, his being, seemed so large in that confined space, it seemed to expand, with all of his robes and his coat on top. He was unconcerned with taking up room, whereas I had become very concerned with taking up as little room as possible. The miles between the airport and the abbey dwindled. I was almost there, we'd almost made it. Soon he would be walking away from my car and I would be driving back to Georgetown, breathing a sigh of relief.

★ ★ ★

He continued to insist that I call him by his first name.

I continued to insist on not doing this.

He wanted me to call him by his name so badly. He had been using it with me for nearly a year by now, ever since he wrote me that note on my last paper of the semester with an invitation to the theater. He'd signed it *L.* at the very end. He always said his first name when I picked up the phone, and it appeared on all of his letters. He pleaded with me to use it when I spoke to him.

I refused to do it and would continue to refuse. I would never use his first name, not once, not in all the time I knew him.

Father. Professor. Father-Professor.

I put these titles between us constantly, the formality of them. I used them like a shield. I used them like bricks to build a wall, which he would constantly be tearing down. I used them as a reminder, most of all.

Father this, and *Father that,* and *Father, I can't, I'm sorry, Father.*

Father was my greatest weapon. Each time I used it, I was forcing him to remember who he was, who he was to me, who he was to everyone, who he was to himself, to the Church. He was a priest, not a man. He would always be a priest and not a man, not like the boys I dated, never like them. The priests' vow of celibacy transforms them into non-men, men who do not have romantic relationships, sexual relationships, men who do not shower inappropriate attention on their female students, men who do not follow their female students everywhere or call them constantly. This was what I believed at the time, and what I needed to be true.

The other priest-professors I'd had at Georgetown and

now in graduate school—I never called them *Father*. They were always and still are *Professor* to me or, in one instance, *Dr.* The academic title trumped the religious one, because I was always more interested in their intellectual authority than their Catholic authority. In many ways I could care less that these men were also priests. I was their student, and they were my teachers. Period. But not with him. With him I learned to say *Father*, even though for the first few months I'd called him *Professor* as with the others. Over the summer I'd made the shift.

I would lay the word *Father* down between us.

Then he would remove it again.

He would peel it away from my hands, try to forbid it from rolling off my tongue. I would take a deep breath whenever I ran into him in the halls, readying to speak this greeting. Before I could say *Father* he would supply his first name in its place, reminding me that this was what he wanted me to call him.

"'Bye, Father," I would say moments later, as I hurried away.

"We're here, Father," I said when I turned up the driveway of his abbey.

I didn't shut off the car, didn't even put the car in park. I didn't look at him, I stayed facing front, staring out the windshield into the darkness, hands gripping the wheel firmly, at ten o'clock and two o'clock, foot pressed hard on the brake. I remember feeling bundled up, a scarf wrapped around my neck, a bulky coat covering my body. My skin felt prickly in the heat.

He didn't move to get out. He just sat there, silently.

Out of the corner of my eye I could see that he was watching me.

I didn't turn my head.

"See you later, Father," I tried again.

I could hear him breathing.

Everything seemed so dark, darker than usual. Dark in the car and dark in the driveway of the abbey, which didn't have any lights on, not that I remember.

I waited for him to leave. The engine of the car rumbled as it idled.

What was going on? Why wasn't he getting out?

He inhaled deeply and leaned toward me.

He planted a big, wet kiss on the side of my face.

"Don-*na*," he said, his lips still close to my skin. "I *like* you!"

He said this with such force, such loudness, the downbeat heavy on the *like*, then he fumbled for the handle of the door, opened it, and ran away. He literally ran away, ran up to the abbey entrance, without looking back.

I sat there, stunned, disgusted, repulsed, car engine still rumbling, hands still gripping the steering wheel at ten and two o'clock, foot still pressed hard on the brake, trying to figure out what just happened, what in the world he'd meant by it. He'd finally crossed the line into something physical, yet it was so minor, just a kiss on the cheek. It was almost worse that he did this than something more serious. It left room for doubt to creep in, as it always did with him.

What was I supposed to take away from that kiss? Was I supposed to understand it as romantic, as friendly? As fatherly or grandfatherly? I'd never received kisses from a teacher before, and certainly not from a priest. In all my years of growing up Catholic I'd never even hugged a priest, and it was rare that I hugged a teacher or a professor, maybe only at graduation.

I like you, he'd said, in that lilting voice of his.

It echoed around me in the car.

I could still feel the wetness of his lips on my cheek,

how he'd pressed his face there for a moment, the heat of his breath, the slickness of my skin after he pulled away, the sliminess of his saliva. He was like some middle-school boy with a crush who'd confessed his feelings and run off across the playground. I thought I might be sick. I made myself sick. I wanted to wash off what just happened, get it out of my hair like it was lice.

I drove home.

I moved through the world on autopilot.

Going through the motions of living, of work, of graduate school, of hanging out with my boyfriend and friends, my senses dulled, not quite hearing people's voices or seeing colors and shapes. I was numb. But on the outside I continued to act like nothing was wrong, that everything was peachy and perfect, except for the one glaring, decidedly unpeachy fact that my mother had cancer and might die.

Registration for the spring semester came and went. I didn't sign up for any of his courses, which meant that I was in trouble, academically. I needed to take his classes for my program and I wasn't doing it. I was in trouble with him again, too, of course, because he wanted me there. Other students began to ask me questions about why. Why was I in their program but not in any of their courses? Was I switching concentrations? Was I thinking of dropping out?

I don't know. Maybe?

I no longer cared.

I spouted my story about him when people wondered, even though I knew it was a lie.

I was tired, I was afraid. I was alone. I've never been so alone in my life.

I'd been carrying this secret around for months, keeping this secret so tightly wound that it was a knot in the center of my chest, a hard ball of angst and fear. I could barely breathe around it. Each day it expanded, taking up more space, suffocating me.

One day in early December, I was in Rhode Island, studying for finals.

I was sitting at the kitchen table. My mother was lying on the couch. The living room and the kitchen were one big open space in my house. She was watching television, resting, and I was keeping her company as I worked. During a commercial, my mother called out to me.

"Isn't it nice that Father L. is going to visit us in January?"

My heart skidded.

I turned to her. "What?"

"He didn't tell you?"

"I don't know what you're talking about, Mom."

"Father L.? He's coming to visit Narragansett over the holiday break. He's coming to the house first, and then we planned to have lunch at the Coast Guard House. You, me, him, and Grandma—the four of us. As long as I'm feeling up for it."

I wanted to lie down on the floor and curl into a ball. "Oh, yeah, I forgot. He did tell me, Mom."

"He thought it would be fun for all of us to get together. To spend the day here in Narragansett."

I couldn't breathe. "Sure. It'll be great. We'll have a wonderful time."

The commercials ended. The show came back on.

I knew in that moment that this was it. I was done.

17

There were three pages left, then two, then, finally, only one.

It was mid-December. I printed out the last paper of my semester, and I got in the car to drive it over to school and hand it in to my professor. This final, my last of the calendar year, was highly significant. It meant that I had made it one step further in my graduate-school efforts, that Christmas break had arrived and that I could stop working for a few weeks. But it also meant something far more important. I'd made a deal with myself that day in my Rhode Island kitchen.

Get through this exam period. Get through this semester. Get through this period of complete hell because of my mother's cancer and chemo and the fear and the thought that her death was waiting, always, just around the corner. Get through it and then...

I was going to tell.

That was the deal: get all my work done, down to the

last word of the last paper I owed someone, and my reward would be to speak. I was going to tell someone the truth. I was going to try to put what was happening to me into words and say them out loud. The real truth. Not the false story I'd been peddling for months. Not the cover-up.

I drove across the city, swathed in darkness, pressing hard on the gas pedal. I sped through yellow lights verging on red.

I'd made the trip to my graduate campus so many times I'd memorized the precise timing of the stoplight on each block, knew exactly how many seconds I had to zip across the intersection. I couldn't get there fast enough. I wanted this paper out of my hands. If I didn't tell someone soon I would die. I needed to cross the finish line I'd set for myself, because on the other side of it I might find hope. I also might find shame and humiliation. But maybe there would be hope. Maybe there would be relief. Maybe, just maybe, there would be me, not being alone anymore with my secret.

When I got to school I didn't even bother to park in a spot. I left my car alongside the curb, ran inside, ran upstairs, found my professor in his office, held out my paper to him.

This professor, one of my favorites, also a priest, was elderly, but stately in his age. He had this amazing head of white wavy hair and often wore a wry smile. He moved slowly, unhurriedly, not in a passive-aggressive way, but more as though he were a turtle, steady and consistent. It felt like forever before that last paper moved from my hands to his.

"Have a great Christmas," I told him, to make clear I wasn't staying long, as I huffed and puffed, lungs heaving from taking the stairs so quickly, from the anxiety roiling inside me, from the knowledge of what I was about to do, from the need to get it over with ballooning past the confines of my body.

He asked after my mother, after my family, if I was going home to see her, wanted to know how she was doing. I answered perfunctorily and then, when it seemed acceptable for me to leave without being rude, I ran back to my car and dug for my cell phone in my purse.

Cell phones were new at the time. Well, cell phones that the average person could afford were new. I'd gotten one earlier that same week and now I took it in my hands, ready to dial the number of the person I'd decided to tell. All those months of silence and secrets, and now, suddenly, I couldn't get to the part where I would speak fast enough. It became urgent to speak the real story to someone immediately.

I'd put a lot of thought into who it would be. I needed someone I could trust, obviously, someone with whom I had a close friendship, someone I hung out with, with whom I had intimacy. But I also wanted someone I thought would be a good judge of the situation, someone I respected. Someone who wouldn't automatically side with me because they were my friend, but who would feel sympathy toward this man, a kind of kinship for who he was. I wanted the truth, I didn't want someone to humor me. I wanted a fair and impartial jury. I wanted to know if I was being crazy, if I was inventing things, if what was happening was my fault, if I was making a big deal over what was really and truly nothing.

The person I chose was a friend unlike any other. He was a fellow graduate student in my program, which was important because he knew this man. He knew of his stature and reputation as a professor, of his brilliance and importance as a scholar in my field, of the love and admiration our fellow students had for him. He knew this person as kindly and sweet, as above reproach. He liked this man, just as everyone else around me liked him. I'd chosen this friend because he was exactly the kind of person I always feared wouldn't believe me, someone who would be likely to give this man the benefit of the doubt, someone who would find it very difficult to believe that this man had done anything wrong.

I'd chosen Dan, Christopher's roommate.

There was something else that made Dan uniquely suited to the task. As long as I'd known him, Dan had debated becoming a priest himself. He had the utmost respect for the office of the Catholic priesthood, for priests in general, for the vows they took and the complicated roles they navigated throughout their lives, as men both human and divine. He understood what they gave up for this office— namely, love, human love, romantic love. Part of Dan's own struggle revolved around a woman he'd been dating off and on for several years. They were currently on a break, but she was always on his mind and in his heart. I chose Dan because I trusted him, because he was honest and fair and kind, but most of all because of his connection to the priesthood and because I was stacking the odds against myself.

I'd doubted myself for so long, felt like I must be the person at fault, and I needed someone who was going to have to climb all the walls that I had climbed to get to the place where I'd arrived. I wanted to make it hard for me to be believed. If the person I told agreed that something was wrong, this meant there *really* must be something wrong. Since Dan was predisposed to think well of this man, if he, too, saw what I saw, I'd be able to finally trust that my gut was right. That my gut had been right all along.

I punched in Dan's number as I sat there in my unreliable Mazda, in the same seat where, just weeks before, I'd

received that wet kiss on the cheek from my professor. Dan
picked up right away. I told him I had to talk to him, like
now, like that same night, like within the next hour, that
there was no waiting until tomorrow, that it was urgent,
that this was an emergency. I told him not to tell anyone
else about this call and my request.

He told me he'd see me in thirty minutes.

I drove straight there.

We met at a coffee shop in Georgetown.

"I'm probably being crazy," I started. "I know I'm probably making a big deal over nothing, that it's probably my
imagination, but I think there might be something wrong
with Father L."

Caveat, caveat, caveat, and more caveats followed. I gave
Dan so many.

But then, after a year of silence, the entire story came
spilling out. Every last detail, from start to finish. I was
careful, very careful, to hold myself accountable for every
bit of my own responsibility. I was determined not to
let myself off the hook, even a little, for the situation in
which I found myself. I gave all the benefit of the doubt
to my priest-professor and left none of it for myself. I was
hard on myself for everything I felt I'd done to create this
situation, to worsen it, to perpetuate it. It was imperative
that I confess to all of it, that I admit to every last thing.
This was a confession, that is the only word for it. I was
laying every bit of shame and doubt on the table in front
of my friend. I exposed it from every angle. I shined the
harshest light on it that I could find. I lit it up so we could
both see it for what it was.

But as the hours passed, our coffees growing cold, this
version of the story was the honest one. It was a relief to say
it out loud, even though I was afraid of the consequences.

I was peeling it off myself and handing it over to someone else to hold for a while, to look at and study, to help me carry it, to determine what it meant, if anything, or to judge if it meant nothing at all.

Dan listened, without interruption, to my monologue.

When I finished, when I finally got to the part about the kiss in the car and this man's planned trip to Rhode Island to meet my mother, to see my house, to go to lunch with her and me and my grandmother, I bookended my monologue with the same insecurity and doubt I'd started with.

"Am I crazy? I'm probably being crazy, right? Nothing is wrong. I'm just imagining things, right? Right?"

I was panting, nervous, depleted from getting so much out at once. I was suddenly aware of the glare of the café's lights overhead, the round white table where we were sitting, the cars and the people going by on M Street on the other side of the windows. I'd stopped seeing them while I talked, as though they'd vanished and only just now reappeared.

Dan asked me only a single question. His voice was quiet and steady. "What do you want to happen with Father L.?" He told me to be honest.

My heart was pounding. The truth bubbled up and I blurted it with a low, seething rage. "I don't ever want to see him again. I never ever want to lay eyes on him or hear his judgmental little voice. I don't care if he dies. I've never hated anyone so much in my life. I hate him, and I want him gone. I want him gone."

Dan nodded. "Then let's figure out how to make that happen."

I stared at him. "So you think something is wrong?" I asked this in a whisper.

"Donna," he began. "You work in Residence Life. If one of your RAs or a student in your hall told you the story you just told me, would you think something was wrong?"

"Yes," I said without hesitation.

"That's because something *is* wrong," he said. "It's beyond wrong. I'm so angry, I'm angry at him, but angry for you. I'm sorry this has been happening to you. I'm so sorry you've felt you couldn't tell anyone until now. Thank you for telling me."

Dan never stopped looking at me while he spoke. I think he wanted me to see how certain he was about what he was saying, that while I might have doubts and fears about my story, he had no doubts or fears about his conclusions regarding it. The strength of his certainty was like a balm I didn't know I needed until right then.

"Donna," he went on, "this isn't just inappropriate, it's obsession. It's stalking. Father is stalking you."

I couldn't breathe.

"We'll figure this out together," Dan said. "Okay?"

I nodded. "Okay."

And just like that, I wasn't alone.

PART THREE

18

Dan helped me to make a plan.

My world, my life, my everyday existence, was transformed. I wasn't alone, and Dan was adamant that I become even less alone, that we tell someone at school, just one person, but someone with authority we felt we could trust. I was still adamant about things, too. Mostly that we not make too big a deal out of the situation. Even though telling Dan and having him believe me made the ground a bit steadier, I was still terrified of people finding out what was going on, of getting in trouble for causing what was happening, of not being believed, of being judged. I still didn't want Christopher to know, so I made Dan promise not to tell him—which he did, though reluctantly. Also, I was worried about hurting this man. I was afraid of what would happen to him if I made an official complaint. I was scared of becoming responsible for doing something that would jeopardize his job, his life, his stature.

You would think I would want something terrible to happen to him, for him to lose his job. You would think that I would be a bit more confident that he had done something wrong, now that I had someone standing with me, a friend I trusted and respected, my impartial judge and jury who did not doubt for a second that something was very wrong. Dan was as certain that this professor's behavior was inappropriate, abusive, even, as I was uncertain. He had no problem naming it, but still I could not.

Naming it made it real. Naming it made it undeniable, and I still wanted the right to deny it. I wanted to be able to deny it for myself, to myself.

Denial is a powerful thing. It's a powerful tool, a powerful survival mechanism. I still wanted everything to be okay. In a way, I still wanted to find out that I had been making things up because then I wouldn't have to go through any of what I was about to go through. A part of me, a big part, was still hoping I would wake from this like it had been a bad dream, that with the snap of someone's fingers it would disappear, and all would be well again.

Since the beginning of graduate school, I'd been reading about the power of naming in the feminist theory in my courses. I was talking about, learning about, reading about, and writing papers about naming as a tool of empowerment and voice and transformation for women at the very same time that I was resisting this act in my own life.

But to me, naming had consequences I was not ready to confront, that I never in my life wanted to have to confront. Naming abuse, naming sexual harassment, naming something like stalking committed by a professor, my mentor, a priest, was the kind of thing that happened to someone else, not to me. It was the stuff of gossip, hushed whispers, scandalized talk. It was something you knew happened to people, but those people are never you or the people you know. If I named this thing it would stick to me, sink into me, become me. Not only would it rot me from the inside but now the rot would be visible. It would cling to me, mark me, become my scarlet letter. I would have to walk around the world wearing it, and the world would see it on me and reject me for it. I would be ruined because of it.

Naming meant loss. It meant the loss of a fantasy I'd held, that I still wanted to hold, about me and my intellectual promise, my academic talents, my appeal as a young woman and aspiring PhD. Because of his interest in me—well, let's be honest, his devotion—at first I believed it meant I was special. Exceptional. But now naming this for what it really was seemed like agreeing to label myself *sex object*. I would be canceling out my brain and my intellect, trading them in exclusively for an empty female body. I would be allowing myself to become a shell. I would be announcing my sex-object status to the rest of the world. It meant agreeing to reduce myself to an essence, and this essence turned out to be *sexual plaything*. I was of no real value in the eyes of this professor, not an equal or a future colleague, just a little girl to be watched and admired but never to be heard or listened to. Only to be seen.

Naming meant I would have to acknowledge that I was younger than I'd believed. Less mature, less adult, less woman and more girl. Naming what happened, what was still happening, meant that I had no control, that I had lost control, and maybe it involved admitting that I'd never had it in the first place—I'd only thought so. Naming meant saying out loud to myself and to others that all this time I'd been preyed upon. That I'd been gullible. Naïve in the worst of ways.

Naming this, this *thing,* made me uncomfortable. It felt like agreeing to wear the shame I felt about my role in all of it like a bright shade of lipstick on my face for the rest of my life. It felt like becoming shame, embodying it, agreeing to accept this as a permanent, ontological shift in my being. It meant being willing to tattoo this shame all over my body.

I was in a man's world. Academia always has been and still is a man's world, and my place in it, philosophy and religious studies, is particularly male. If the men in power found out who I was, if they saw what I had done, if they saw what I had done to *him,* I would never find my place in that world I so longed to be a part of.

They wouldn't hold him accountable for what he'd done to me, they would hold me accountable for what I'd done to him. To name things would be to doom myself in the eyes of the men who would inevitably control my professional fate, because it was men who still control the professional fate of all of us in these fields.

So, naming in my case, in that moment, didn't feel empowering at all. It felt more like defeat. Once again, I was failing at feminism. Or worse, once again, feminism was failing me.

We decided to tell a woman professor we both knew well.

She was Dan's dissertation director, and I had also taken her courses and loved them. She was one of the women who introduced me to feminist theory, who helped me to become a feminist myself. We decided we would tell her in confidence, ensure that she would tell no one else, but she would be another custodian of this situation I found myself in, possessing the knowledge but never speaking it out loud to others—unless it became absolutely necessary. She was our fail-safe, "just in case" things went sideways.

Dan thought it was important that someone at the graduate school know what was happening because if things got worse, we could say we'd notified a professor in the program, someone who worked there but was not an "official" official. If I could settle this outside official channels, I might emerge from the situation unscathed—or relatively so. I still hoped I might come through this to the other side as still-me, still-Donna, the Donna I had always been, the idealistic grad student who felt only joy with respect to her studies and her professors. I didn't yet realize, or I refused to realize, that this Donna was already gone.

When my friend and I decided to talk to this professor, it was a different time, back before there was such a thing as mandatory reporting at universities across the nation—and thank God for this. Mandatory reporting, a recent by-product of Title IX, requires faculty, staff, and administrators to make an official report if they hear of instances of sexual assault or harassment, even if the person who suffered the abuse doesn't want them to report it, isn't ready to, begs them not to. Mandatory reporting wrests the power of naming from the victim's hands and places it in the hands of others. It yanks it, forcefully, violently from the victim and, in my opinion, threatens to victimize the person yet again.

If I'd known that talking to someone about my situation risked my triggering official, legal action at my institution, I might never have told a soul, maybe not even Dan. I would have continued to suffer in silence, and secrecy.

Mandatory reporting has been controversial from its inception for these exact reasons. It can discourage victims from ever reporting anything, from even trying to get help for what they've gone through, because reaching out could start a process they cannot stop. In theory, it's supposed to hold institutions accountable, to keep them from sweeping claims of harassment or assault under the rug. It's supposed to force schools to count these claims, to register them, officially. But sometimes I wonder if it's yet another move on the part of institutions to make it harder, scarier, for people to report assault or harassment, because the effect of it is to do just this.

It asks too much too soon for too many victims.

It makes the consequences of speaking up that much more real, and immediate.

I needed baby steps to get through this. I needed a process, a coming-to-terms-with. First, telling one of my most trusted friends. Then, the two of us telling one of our most trusted professors. Next, trying to handle the situation outside official channels and hoping for the best, hoping that things would end there. My own survival depended on my still being able to call the shots, to make the decisions, to say yes or no to the people who now shared the knowledge of my situation. I needed to retain control, at least some control—or *regain* it, really—since for the last year my primary experience was to have no control at all. I wanted some of that control back.

The ability of Dan and this woman professor to hear my yeses or nos about what I did and did not want, to respect my wishes, to honor them, to listen and respond to them, even if they did not agree with them, was part of the healing I needed. I needed the experience of saying "I want this, but not this" and "This is okay, but this is not," needed to see that the person I was telling could take it in and respond accordingly. I needed to know that they would not run right over me, act as though I had said nothing, disrespect what I wanted—because that was the experience I'd already lived for a year. I needed to be reminded that though my nos might have meant nothing to him, that he was an isolated case, that other people could and would hear my consent and my non-consent, that they would honor it because it meant something to *them*.

I think this is the crux of it—mandatory reporting is like being violated all over again. It violates our very own teachings about consent, what it is and how it is supposed to operate. Mandatory reporting tells a victim: Once again, you don't get a no or a yes, here your nos and yeses don't matter to us, we care not whether you consent or do not consent. Once again, your agency is taken from you, forcefully. You are reduced to an object, a number, a potential lawsuit, someone who has no will or say about what happens to you. Once again, your voice is not heard or respected. You can say no, no, no all you want, as many times as you possibly can, but mandatory reporting shouts over your nos, until you learn to shut up and take whatever it is you've accidentally caused to happen to yourself again. Mandatory reporting reinforces the powerlessness of victims, and likewise reinforces the shame they feel about their own powerlessness. It perpetuates a state of helplessness and isolation. It encourages the perpetuation of their silence and secrecy.

I needed the right to decide my own fate to be restored, to be placed back into my hands. I needed my own voice, when it spoke yes and no, to become meaningful to someone else again, to carry weight with that person, to have an effect. I needed to see that someone could hear me and comply with my wishes. I needed these things like my life depended on them. I think it did depend on them. Sometimes I think it still does.

We went to see her in person, in her office.

We told her the bare bones of the story. I held out a plastic grocery bag full of letters he'd written to me. Her eyes got big when she looked inside. She was calm and patient, concerned about me more than anything else.

"What do you want to happen?" she asked, just like Dan had the night before.

"I never want to see him again," I repeated.

"Okay," she said, and then she began to talk about options, one of which was for me to come forward to the school.

"No way" was my response.

"I just want him to stop," I said.

Dan and our professor helped to come up with a step in between doing nothing and doing something official.

I would write up a list of every single thing he'd ever done, a list of all of his unwanted behaviors, all of his unwanted attention. I would put it down on paper, making sure I was specific, that I was particular, that I was comprehensive. I would write it down so I could have it in my hands, so I could hold it, so I could see it before me. Then I would pick a time that was convenient, I would call him on the phone, and I would read the letter to him word for word, making sure to leave nothing out. If he tried to protest or interrupt, I would read over him and repeat certain lines if I needed to, making sure he heard every single thing on my list. This was not to be a conversation, or a back-and-forth. This was not an invitation to hear his side of the story after I finished reading. This was a notice, it was a cease and desist, an official communication on my part, informing him that from this moment forward, there was to be no contact between us ever again. Whatever had been going on, whatever he was doing, was to end immediately, and there was to be no further discussion about it. This was to be a one-sided conversation, with the only side being mine.

This I agreed to do, not because I wanted to, but because

I knew I had no other choice. I had to get over the fact that he was my professor and also a priest so that I could talk to him like he was a pest and, even worse, a predator. A man who was hitting on me like someone in a bar, who refused to give up. I had to scale that mountain, like it or not. I was filled with dread.

I made the call on December 22. Merry Christmas to me.

I'd spent hours writing up that list, carefully penning it letter by letter, word by word, until my hand ached. Some of the words I wrote were in all caps, as though I were screaming. It spanned several pages, not only because there were so many things on my list, but because the lines got bigger, wider, taller, as they went on, as though their size might increase the chances he'd hear what they said. I'd written everything on blank white copy paper. Dan reviewed it, our professor reviewed it, and then I got ready to get this over with.

I decided to call him during the afternoon, from my apartment. We'd decided it was important I do this under circumstances where I felt at my safest, my most comfortable. We'd decided that the reading of my list should not occur if he happened to have called me, that it had to be the reverse, that I had to choose the time of the call, so that I was controlling the situation from the beginning. I chose to do it during the afternoon because I wanted there to be light outside my window. I wanted the safety of the day to reassure me.

I dragged the clunky, ancient phone to my coffee table, picked up the receiver, and punched in his number. As always, I was standing, my script clutched in my free hand. He answered right away. At first, he was happy. It had been ages, months, since I'd called him. It had been him calling me, him calling me again and again, calling me nonstop, and me scrambling to get off the phone. I think he was surprised to suddenly have this long-craved-for attention from me.

Quickly, very quickly, before that initial happiness could settle into him with any depth, I informed him that this was not a social call, that I had some things to tell him, and that I needed him to listen until I was finished.

And then I did it, I read him my list.

I don't know how long it took me, but it felt like we were on the phone forever. I read through every single one of those lines I'd written, dropping the finished pages onto the floor. I could hear him breathing as he listened. My hands were shaking, and my voice was shaking, too.

Do not call me on my phone in Georgetown.
Do not call me on my phone in Rhode Island.
Do not call my mother ever again.
Do not write letters to my TA mailbox.
Do not write letters to my Georgetown mailbox.
Do not write letters to the mailbox at my family's
   house in Rhode Island.
Do not invite me to a play.
Do not invite me to a symphony.
Do not invite me to go for coffee.

The list went on and on, and it was very specific. When I finally got to the end, he was silent at first, but then he wanted to respond.

"Do you understand everything I've said?" I interrupted, talking over him.

He began to protest again.

"Do you understand everything I've said?" I repeated, forcing my voice over his.

There was a pause.

Then, "Yes."

"Good," I said. "I'm going to hang up now."

I set the receiver back into the cradle. I thought I might pass out. But I'd done it. After all this time, it was over. Finally, *finally*, I was free.

19

Between Christmas and New Year's, he sent me an unmarked card.

I'd just come home from seeing my friend Hannah for
dinner and had gone to collect my mail in the Residence
Life Office. Hannah and I met up as soon as I returned
from Rhode Island after spending the holidays with my
family.

"So," she said, the moment we sat down across from each
other, big blue eyes smiling. Hannah is very blond, with a
wide-open, round face, and looks like she could play the part
of Goldilocks in a show, which was probably why she was
always getting cast as the ingenue in every musical she tried
out for. "Tell me what is going on with you!"

Hannah was, and still is, one of my best friends. From
the moment we met, we fell into a shared intimacy that
has never left us. She is one of the people I have turned to
in my darkest of moments. She has an extraordinary voice,
and in the years ahead she would become the person who

sang at my wedding and also at my mother's funeral. I told Hannah everything, always.

"Oh, you know," I said. "It was good to see my family. My mother is hanging in there, but it's hard. Things with Christopher are good. Tell me what is going on with *you*."

Hannah began to give me her update, and the conversation moved on from there.

I could have told Hannah that same night about what was happening to me, about what had been happening for a year already. I could have told her months before and she would have been the amazing friend she's always been. I *should have* told Hannah that night. What would one more person be on the list of people who knew?

I would tell her, soon, but not yet. Silence and denial were still my reality, my norm, my strategy, really. The fewer people who knew, the better, because then the less true it would be as a defining part of my life. Besides, I'd reasoned numerous times since my phone call on December 22, this man, this situation, was all behind me now, so maybe I wouldn't have to tell a single other person about what had gone on, not even someone like Hannah. The shame would be mine and mine alone in the vast majority of my relationships, which meant it would disappear all the quicker. Soon, "all that" would feel far away, and life would be back to normal, as though it never happened.

This hope of mine was about to vanish because of the letter I held in my hand.

Being at home on break had been up and down, but we'd managed to make Christmas happen in our house. My mother loved Christmas, and by extension, we all did, too. Christmas meant hours of cooking, of baking the Italian cookies my father loved and the neighbors also loved, since each year we made special plates that my mother would wrap with clear plastic and tie with shiny bows to give out to everyone. Christmastime meant making pasta from scratch, making sauces and Italian meats, and eating nearly constantly.

Before my grandmother had gotten Alzheimer's she was a magician in the kitchen; both she and my mother knew the family recipes by memory, whipping them up easily as though they were following detailed directions. But this year, between Grandma struggling and my mother often unable to get out of bed, it fell to me to oversee the Christmas cooking. My mother helped when she could, but for the most part I did all the food, with my father taking orders now and then, watching something on the stove or pulling something out of the oven under my direction. Somehow my mother made her cookies, so the neighbors got theirs as well. Making those cookies felt like my mother defying her death sentence. Everything had felt that way since her diagnosis, which meant that every day she endured felt like cheating it.

On Christmas, people in our neighborhood got together and went caroling, and my mother was always one of the ringleaders of this effort. But this winter she didn't have the energy to walk through the neighborhood in the cold and the snow, singing for hours.

The carolers came to our door twice that holiday season, once early in the evening and then later, so my mother could join them for a few minutes. I remember how, the second time they'd rung the bell, one of the neighborhood men laughed and said to my parents, "This time, we've weeded out the non-singers!" by way of explaining why our house got special treatment. When of course it was because everyone knew about my mother, that the second visit was because of her cancer, because maybe she wouldn't have another year of caroling in her future.

We had the Christmas tree, the presents underneath, the special breakfast on Christmas morning, followed by church and our typical elaborate Christmas dinner with way too much food. We did it all, even though my mother could barely eat, even though she wore a kerchief over her head because she was bald, signaling to everyone in the pews at mass who hadn't known she was sick that she was. We did it all because we had to, because this might be our last Christmas together. We were approaching that six-month mark, the one the doctor had given us after her surgery, the looming date of her possible death.

I didn't tell my parents a thing while I was home.

I was still hoping they wouldn't have to find out.

There was no familiar handwriting on the outside of the envelope in my hand, no return address printed in the upper left-hand corner, nothing to alert me it was from him. My address had been typed, the envelope run through a printer. It looked like one of those cards you might get from your dentist, or some other peripheral person in your life, who sent out a mass of holiday cards to clients.

The office where I was sorting through my mail was dark because it was night and most everyone was still on break. The only light in the room was the one I'd turned on over the staff mailboxes. The quiet was eerie. Usually this place was full of people bustling about, activity and noise everywhere. But the peace and the silence were nice. I'd already opened the first of the Christmas cards in the pile, then another and another, until I'd gotten to this one.

I was starting to feel happy again, and hopeful. Starting to put the pieces of my sanity back together. The ground was feeling steadier, my footsteps surer. My professor hadn't contacted me, not once. Not over the phone, not in

Rhode Island, not at Georgetown—not since our phone call. I hadn't received any letters, except for a couple of stragglers he'd sent before we had our one-sided conversation. I'd had a blissfully professor-free Christmas with my family, and I was relishing this.

I'd gotten through to him.

He'd listened to my words over the phone. *Finally.* Finally, he'd heard me, really heard me, heard my no. Each thing I said, each request I'd made of him, each action of his toward me that I forbade, one by one, as I read from those pages out loud. He'd heard my words and he'd listened.

Things were going to be okay. It seemed almost too good to be true.

I still had a lot of damage control ahead, and I knew this, too. I still hadn't told my mother that our lunch date at the Coast Guard House in Narragansett was canceled, that he wouldn't be coming to Rhode Island or be writing her any longer. I didn't know how to tell her this without upsetting her, without also telling her the truth, which I didn't want her to know. I needed my mother to keep her faith in the Catholic Church and its God and its priests, because they were part of her recovery, her lifeline of hope. I didn't want to clip it, this thing helping to keep her alive.

I still hadn't figured out what to do about grad school either, and the reality that he would be all over the building where I went for classes, that he had every right to be there since he was a professor. He had more of a right to be there than I did; it had been his place of employment for years. There was the problem of my program as well, the fact that he was the head of my concentration, the fact that he taught all of the major courses I needed to take before I could finish my MA and get through my PhD requirements and move on to my comprehensive exams.

There was also the daunting reality that I would likely need him to be on my dissertation committee, if not be my dissertation director. I wasn't sure how to finesse these complications, how to get around them or if I could get around them. Could I continue to avoid him without having to explain why to anyone else?

But I wasn't ready to scale those walls yet. I was learning to breathe again, learning to stand upright after being hunched over for so long. I decided I was allowed a few weeks of doing nothing, nothing other than taking in the experience of living my life without his constant interruptions. Without feeling like I was under siege. Without the fear that every time I turned a corner or opened a door he might be standing there. Without the dread of wondering what he would think of next to integrate himself further into my life and my family. Maybe someday soon I wouldn't worry about leaving my classes or passing through the stairwells or walking from the parking lot into my building. These simple things were what I wanted. They were *all* I wanted.

Only four people in the universe at this point knew what happened: Dan, the woman professor we told, me, and him. I wanted it to stay that way. I wanted to erase the story from my being and move on. I was repulsed by this man, but even more than this *I repulsed myself by association*. I felt I was disgusting, that other people would see that I was disgusting, too, if they knew. Christopher. Maybe even Hannah.

Before I started wearing sweatpants and stopped showering before class, before I started trying to disappear, I'd stood out at my graduate program. I'd been fashionable Donna, in a place where no one else knew or likely cared about clothes and outfits. I stood out because of the way that I dressed, and because I inherited that big personality of my mother's, embodied it wherever I went. Everyone knew me, my professors liked me, were kind to me, were excited that I was in their program, getting a PhD. I was told I was "a breath of fresh air," and I liked being that fresh air, blowing through the department, making people smile and look up as I passed.

But these things would also be the same ones that would cause people to blame me if they found out, to suspect me of being at fault. I was sure that if people knew the truth, I would never make anyone smile or laugh again. People would think I was terrible, that I'd lured an innocent, celibate professor with my charms, with those high-heeled boots and short skirts, that I'd enticed him to break his vows. I would never be able to hold my head up again or look people in the eye. I would rather quit my PhD program than allow this to get out. The shame was like a plastic bubble around me.

If he had been a different professor, maybe I would have felt differently. If he had been handsome, if he had been taller, if he had not been a priest. Men who are not priests are at least expected to look at women, to flirt, to think about women in a sexual and romantic way, even if they aren't supposed to look and think about their students that way. Maybe if other people found him handsome, if they saw him as a sexual person, too, then if they knew my secret they would look at me differently. As less disgusting, less reprehensible, less like a harlot. Perhaps they would have found his attention to me romantic. Perhaps *I* would have found it romantic.

A friend of mine said recently that it sounded like puppy love. That even though he was a much older man, accomplished in his profession, it seemed like he was a twelve-year-old boy when it came to love and sex, that I was his first crush, that he had no idea how to handle his feelings for me or even what they meant. She said this after I'd told her about the kiss in the car, how he'd blurted out "I *like* you" and then run away.

I think, on one level, she is right. He might have been older and accomplished, but because he'd chosen to become a priest when he was a young boy, he had grown into a man who was sexually stunted, a man who had never matured. He might have been an esteemed professor to all who knew him and read his work, but in fact what I had on my hands was a young teenager, barely out of middle school. I'd caught his eye and now he didn't know what to do with all these powerful feelings coursing through him while he watched me out on the playground.

But, of course, he wasn't a teenage boy. A teenage boy I could have handled. He was a man with power and resources, resources that included access to all of my personal information, sway over my coursework, my PhD concentration, the ability to make or break my graduate-school experience and my future along with it. He was a monk and a priest in the Catholic Church, an important academic who enjoyed all the privileges that went with these roles.

And this wasn't a middle-school playground, this was my life.

Whether it was puppy love, an innocent crush, or something far more sinister, he freely availed himself of his power and used it to influence me, to find me, to follow me, to harass me endlessly, even as I did my best to get away. He wielded his power like a club, and if there was any innocence to how he felt about me, that innocence was twisted and tainted, corrupted by the old man who embodied it.

Months before, I'd started likening him to E.T. when people asked about him. I wanted people to see him as harmless, as meek, as a strange little alien figure, scurrying about, ugly, yes, but who ultimately couldn't hurt a fly. But to me, by then, he was very much the grotesque, hunched-over monster, a kind of Gollum in my life, frightening and obsessed. I couldn't see him as not-a-monster anymore, the way he went about the world in his flowing robes, his neck sticking up and out from them, his back curved and bent, head jutting forward. His voice was deceptively mild, even weak, but then he would use it to lash out when he was angry. He was a eunuch of sorts, a man who had mutilated himself when he took his vow of celibacy, who had self-castrated, unsexed himself, yet was still trying to act the man to a woman, even though he was only and could only ever be a half man.

I tore open the card in my hand. It was maybe the fifth or sixth one I opened in the pile. The front of the card itself was innocuous—I don't remember what was printed on it. But the inside I remember clearly.

I recognized his handwriting immediately. It was tiny, and it filled both the left and the right sides of the card, thin line after thin line of prose that continued onto the back. It was angry, he was angry.

How could I have cut things off between us? How could I do this to him, to us? He'd done nothing wrong, he'd never done anything remotely close to wrong. I must have misunderstood everything, all of his intentions. What was my problem? He'd only wanted to help me. How could I do such a thing to a friend like him? I had to change my mind, I absolutely had to change my mind and restore things to how they were before.

Worse still, he wrote, how could I do such a thing to my mother?

How could I ask him to cut off contact with her, of

all people? Didn't I know how much she needed him right now? Didn't I realize how important priests were in her life, to her cancer survival, how important he was specifically? By cutting off their correspondence, by not allowing him to go to Rhode Island to meet her, I was going to be the cause of her suffering, her terrible, terrible suffering. I had to change my mind not only for his sake, and for *our* sake, but for my *mother's* sake. I had to, I must. He refused to accept the alternative.

I stood there in the dim light of that vacant office, holding the card, reading and shaking, legs shaking, arms and hands shaking. He'd taken that phone call like a breakup, like a relationship breakup, and now was urging me to reconsider, needed me to, was desperate for me to, and refused to accept the alternative. The emptiness around me no longer felt peaceful, but frightening. I was alone, but was I really? Was he lurking somewhere in the office right now? Was he waiting somewhere for me? Would he pop out from behind a door, a building, a tree, when I walked back across campus to my apartment in the dark, alone?

In a way he was right. I had been wrong about everything.

He hadn't heard me on the phone that day. He still couldn't hear me. He refused to hear me, wouldn't hear me no matter what I said, not until I gave him his yes. I'd fooled myself into thinking otherwise, into thinking my life was returning to normal when really it was just business as usual, business that involved his inability to hear my nos no matter how I said them, not even when they were written out in a lengthy list and spoken forcefully and clearly, one by one, in a carefully orchestrated context.

I didn't tell anyone about the card. Not at first.

Once again, I wasn't ready. I didn't want to acknowledge that the plan hadn't worked. I didn't want to acknowledge this because I couldn't bear the thought that I wasn't free. I couldn't bear the thought that there was nothing that I, alone, could do to make him go away. I went home that night, stepping carefully, looking around me constantly, jumping at the slightest noise, the slightest blur out of the corner of my eye.

Another card arrived a few days later, also unmarked. This time it came in the form of a business-sized envelope, again with no return address, and the font used to print my address was different from the one on the card. It didn't occur to me that it was from him when I was ripping it open. By the time it was mid-January and my Christmas break was ending, I'd received three of these unmarked cards. I began to fear the mail, fear opening any and every piece with my name on the outside of it.

It was then that I widened the circle a little more.

I told Christopher, even though I didn't tell him the whole story, only the vaguest contours of it. I didn't want to discuss it any more than I absolutely had to. I told Hannah, too, but again, only the most essential details. Both were horrified that I'd kept this inside, that I'd been so afraid, so unwilling to tell anyone, even them. They trod gingerly around this issue, careful not to prod too much, as if they sensed I was a deer, frightened and ready to bolt. The only person to whom I'd told every last detail was Dan. Even when I shared the barest bones of what had gone on, the hatred I felt was so potent, too potent for me to recount more than a few spoken details. The hatred I felt was not for him, though. It was for myself.

The same night I told Christopher, I also called my mother. "Have you heard from Father L. lately?" I tried to ask this as normally as possible. I didn't want to raise any alarms.

"Oh, yes," she said. "I got a letter from him the other day. He's looking forward to his visit with us."

I got off the phone, my hands, everything, shaking. I was always shaking now. I was right back in that place I'd been for so long, shattered, desperate, bent, and broken. Once more, I met with Dan. It was time I did something official.

PROFESSIONAL INTERLUDE

There's an old bank vault I pass all the time near my apartment.

It has the most magnificent door, thick and gleaming, the gears round and intricate. The bolts are fat, they look like brass, these mechanisms for keeping out would-be robbers a gorgeous feat of engineering. It reminds me of an intricate clock, like something designed for a fantasy movie full of magic. I can see the door through the dusty windows of the empty historic building that houses it. The owners are in the process of renovating its upper floors. The vault door is always open, so people can admire it while walking by, swung wide in front of its now-empty chambers.

I have a door just like this in my brain.

I have often thought this as I've studied that vault on my way home from Whole Foods, arms laden with groceries, or after leaving my friend Mary's apartment, where I am often visiting.

My brain built that door for me. My brain is the master

craftsman. But my brain is not keeping out would-be robbers, it's shutting him and everything to do with him inside that magnificent feat of human engineering, locking him away and hoping I'll forget he's still lurking in there, living in there, inside my head.

The other day I was giving a talk about Title IX and consent at a university in the Pacific Northwest. The students sitting in the rows before me were engaged, their eyes on me. I could see the wheels turning in their minds, could sense that they were listening and cared about this topic.

They seemed like nice people.

During the course of the evening, I mentioned I'd written a book about Title IX and consent on campus that would be out in a few months. I explained that the central thesis was about how universities seem to have forgotten that they are universities, forgotten how to be universities, as evidenced by decades-long failures to address systemic sexual violence within their campus gates. I told the students how it made me sad that a federal law and the threat of losing government funding were what it took for most universities to finally acknowledge the problems of sexual harassment and violence within their communities, that it took the threat of national scandal to make universities care. But I told them, too, that I had hope, that this turn in attitude was an opportunity for a new beginning, a chance to find a way to change things.

The entire evening as I spoke and then listened to students' questions and comments, I thought about the fact that I'd had to make a Title IX complaint myself during graduate school.

It was on the tip of my tongue:

"I made a Title Nine complaint once. Back in the late nineties."

This line burned in my mouth, I could taste it, feel it tingling my vocal cords. I wanted to tell the students, to just blurt it out, confess it. It almost felt like lying *not* to mention it. For a solid hour and forty-five minutes while staring out at those earnest faces, I longed to tell them my secret.

I didn't.

The event ended and I hadn't done it, hadn't found the nerve.

The words hovered on my tongue, but I still didn't know how to get them out of my mouth, I am not practiced enough with this statement to allow it to leave the shelter of my body. I *wanted* to find the strength to say it, with conviction, with *pride,* even: "I have a Title Nine complaint, people! I shall not be ashamed!"

But the fear of what people would think, that people would think it inappropriate of me to have mentioned such a thing in public, to the public, *during an academic lecture,* was still greater than the impulse to speak it. That while standing at the podium in that beautiful theater full of students, I was once again two people, two women, one a scholar and researcher of Title IX, consent, and sex on campus, the other a girl who, scared and ashamed, made a Title IX complaint herself once and then tried her best to erase this fact from her being.

A part of me wishes for a do-over, to go back and just *say it* this time.

But the other part of me simply hopes that the next time I'll find the courage to actually own it as mine.

For the last twelve years, because of my research about sex on campus, I've spoken at nearly two hundred colleges and universities, in situations just like the one where my tongue was tied. Since 2011, Title IX has been a large part of that conversation, ever since the Obama administration forced colleges and universities to reckon with the relevance of this law to sexual violence and harassment on campus.

For the longest time, I've held this law far from my own body. As if it has nothing to do with me and my personal history. As though it is and has been only a professional concern, never a personal one.

Trauma is funny like that. It helps a person bury something so deeply they literally don't remember it's there—until they do. Until they are holding a document that proves this fact in their hands, reading it after twenty years have gone by, as I did myself, just recently.

All these years, as I've traveled around the country to talk about my research, to raise the subject of Title IX in relation to it, I'd never thought about the fact that I, too, was forced to make a Title IX complaint when I was in graduate school. I've operated in the role of scholar and speaker and expert as though I didn't even know that I, myself, had used this law to help when I needed it, to hold my school accountable, just like the other young women in college are doing in droves, lately. As a researcher and scholar, I know a lot about Title IX, more than most people, as much if not more than the Title IX coordinators who currently hold the responsibility of enforcing this law on their campuses. I've written a nonfiction book that has Title IX at its center—the book I mentioned to the students in that lecture. But it was only in the process of working on that book that I began to realize, began to *remember*, that I, too, *might* have made a Title IX complaint decades ago. I only knew for sure that indeed I had after I'd dug out the file from this time in my life, a file I'd buried under other boxes in my house.

I know this must sound strange, even impossible. How could I possibly not know? How could Title IX be so

central to my research and my academic identity for a
decade, without my being aware that it's also central to
me, as a person, as a former student myself?

It's not that I didn't know about my own history—I
did know, somewhere in my brain—but it's also true that
I didn't *realize,* because the part of my brain where I've
stored this kind of knowledge functions differently than
the rest of it. It seems to have its own timelines, its own
will, and I am at its mercy. The knowledge has been
lodged in a part of my mind that I'd sealed off. By the time
I began my research about sex on campus, I was well into
my life as a scholar, and my experience with this professor
was far from my consciousness. I'd banished him and all
the memories that went with him. I'd boarded them up,
paved them over once, then again, then another time for
good measure. I shut them behind that magnificent vault
door and turned the wheel, locking them inside. Then
I lived as though they never happened—or I've tried my
best to do this.

In the first few years after everything ended, I never
spoke of this professor—and I mean *never.* I didn't tell
another soul, and only a few people close to me knew the
whole story. Dan. Christopher. Hannah. Except for these
friends and eventually the person I married, most people
in my life had no clue this had happened, and I wanted to
keep it that way.

Whenever I did speak about graduate school, I talked
of it like it was one of the best times of my life—because
it was. With the exception of everything related to this
professor, I'd flourished in graduate school. I'd gotten
nearly perfect grades, I was a beloved student of my other
professors, and I was considered promising in my field.
Because I'd split my memories of that time in two, I could
decide to recall either one set of memories or the other. In

one set, all had been well, all had been wonderful, actually. In the other, it was all darkness and shame and living under the perpetual gaze of a man who repulsed me, who tormented me, who relentlessly stalked me and, because of this, threatened to ruin my life and future. I never let the two sets mix. *Never.* It was imperative not. My career and my life, I felt, depended on this.

But eventually the memories and the accompanying behaviors I'd learned as coping mechanisms caught up with me. They would come flooding into my consciousness, taking over my brain as though this professor were waiting for me outside the classroom where I was now teaching, in my new life as Professor Freitas, far away from where he still taught himself. And eventually, because these experiences got worse and worse, I underwent years of treatment for post-traumatic stress disorder.

Because the memories, the associations with what and how I lived back then have their own timelines, their own will, because they are locked away in that vault in my brain, it has taken me years to comprehend what I went through for what it was, and the myriad ways it still affects me, sneaking up on me in places and moments and situations when I least expect it. My memories of him behave much like he did.

It was the same thing for me with the Catholic abuse scandal. When it broke, I read about it, read all the articles in the newspaper, about the ways the Catholic Church covered up crimes and abuses committed by its priests for decades, how it evaded public scandal, paid victims for their silence. I felt the same outrage and shock everyone around me felt, discussed it with friends and colleagues—all without realizing that maybe what happened to me with this priest was related to the scandal. It would be *several years* after the news broke before it even occurred to me that my professor was an abusive priest, and that part of the ensuing cover-up and silencing I endured with my university—a decidedly Catholic university, full of priests and affiliated with high-ranking bishops—involved the same method for deception and silencing victims employed by the Catholic Church for decades.

I've lived two lives, simultaneously, and have two different memories of those lives, accordingly. I generally live along only one track, but occasionally, very rarely, I'll jump over to the other for a bit, often not by choice but because something in my present evoked something in this part of my past, opening that vault door a crack. For a long time, I didn't know, not consciously, and I didn't want to know, that this professor's actions would haunt me for the rest of my life, that they would haunt my relationships, my daily activities, and my career. I didn't want to give him that kind of power. I still don't. But in so many ways, he still has it. He'll always have it, if I'm honest. And each time I feel his power getting a grip on me, I do my best to yank it away immediately.

Even though I know all of these things about myself, about how my brain is divided along the lines of the life I want to remember and the life that I do not, it is strange to try to come to terms with the fact that for a solid decade I did not notice that my work about sex on campus, and sexual assault and harassment in particular, the ways that schools have been burying incidents of it, has relevance to what I lived myself. That when I was out there talking about Title IX, I was also talking about myself. Well, I didn't realize it until, one day, I did.

Maybe the worst part of this story begins here.

It's difficult to decide which is the worst part, though. Was it all that unwanted attention from a professor I once admired who'd become a man I found repulsive? The relentless calling and showing up and letter writing and inviting me here and there and the chastising when I refused to go? Or was it the part when I began to ask for help from my university, a university I assumed I could trust because it was a university, and universities were my most sacred sanctuaries, and that university lied to me and determined that the only course of action was to ensure that I went away, that my voice was silenced for good?

I think it might be the latter.

20

It was a cold January day when Dan and I went to see our chair.

This professor, Dr. H., was the man who recruited me to this graduate program, who found more money to support me there than any of the other schools where I'd been accepted. I remember how he had called—when I was in Hawaii, working for a few weeks on an education program for high school students—to make me an offer, to *up* his last offer, to try to get me to commit to his program. I said yes on that call. I was so excited. And this man was one of the professors I was most excited about in the program because he taught hermeneutics, and I was still and always would be a philosophy geek because of Georgetown.

Dr. H. was tall and thin and always smiling and laughing. He was also a priest.

This felt like yet another test. I'd told Dan, who was thinking about becoming a priest, then we'd told our woman professor, who was the kind of person who might roll her eyes at a priest, but now we were about to tell another professor, this one a priest himself and one of the professors I most admired in the entire program. What if he didn't believe me? What if all that enthusiasm he'd shown for my presence in the program evaporated the moment he heard this story? What if he came to regret that phone call to me in Hawaii and the accompanying offer of financial support so I could attend his school?

Dan and I didn't make an appointment. We just showed up at Dr. H.'s office. It was a couple of days before the holiday break ended and our spring-semester classes would start. Dr. H. was always around, a fixture in the department, greeting students and inviting them to chat. He was friendly and approachable, one of the most social professors in the school. We told his assistant we needed to speak to him, but not why, and soon she was ushering us into his office.

The light was gray. The blinds were slightly open, the dirty snow outside visible beyond them. It was a big space, but everything about it was old, like a principal's office from the 1980s with its worn, knotted wall-to-wall carpeting and a heavy metal desk messy with stacks of paper and a fat, hulking computer.

In my hands was the grocery bag with the letters that survived my periodic tosses into the garbage can, including the unmarked ones he'd sent most recently. I'd shoved the books he'd given me in there, too, and they sagged at the bottom. There were six or seven of them.

Dan and I sat down. This professor had an area with chairs and a coffee table in his office. The three of us made a little triangle, Dan and I on one side of the table, Dr. H. facing us on the other. At first I didn't know how to begin. Then I took the grocery bag and placed it on the table.

I pointed at it and said, "These are from Father L."

Then, as I'd done with Dan, I began to recount the details.

"It started when I agreed to go to the theater with him a year ago."

I stopped. Backtracked.

"Um. Maybe not then. Maybe it's because I went to his office hours every week my first semester here." I stumbled once more. Tried to right myself. "Well, really it was probably more than once a week. Sometimes twice. Really I was doing it all the time, going to see him."

As I spoke, I could see my fault written into every word, every sentence I uttered, embedded in them. Guilty. *Guilty*. I was obviously guilty.

But I kept going. Dr. H. sat there, listening, his ankle resting near his knee, like always, hands clasped on top of it, a position of repose, of peace, of patience. He wore the exact same outfit I was used to seeing on Father L.: the black shirt and pants of a priest, white collar around his neck. Nearly all the professor-priests in my program wore this uniform.

Dr. H.'s friendliness, his smile, disappeared as I spoke.

His mouth became a tight, pressed line as I went down the list of the various things Father L. was doing. Phone calls. Invitations. Mail. Going into my file. My mother.

My mother, my mother, my *mother*.

When I finished speaking, finished an edited version of the longer story I'd told Dan, but still a more detailed version than the one I'd given Christopher and Hannah, I was exhausted, shaking, that new permanent state of mine, just slightly, just a tremor, but I felt it, could see it in my hands. I wondered if other people could see it too and wondered how they might read it—whether they'd understand it as fear, as fatigue, or as an admission of guilt.

I was scared to hear Dr. H.'s verdict.

They were professors together. They were *priests* together. They were colleagues on multiple levels.

Dr. H. leaned forward, peered into the grocery bag again. Then he looked up.

"Donna," he said quietly. He seemed to be searching for the right words.

He was about to condemn me. This was it. Probably. Right?

"This is unacceptable," he said. "Unacceptable."

Which part? What he did or what I did?

Then, "I'm sorry," he said, just like Dan had.

He sounded so certain. So confident.

Not me, then. Not me. Okay.

Dr. H. kept talking. He was appalled. The sheer quantity of the correspondence in the grocery bag appalled him, and it was only a small sampling, around forty items or so, because the other letters were long gone. Dr. H. was so definitive. Something was wrong, we were right to come to him and tell him, and he was going to do his best to help make the behavior stop.

I remember feeling stunned.

I'm not sure if it was all relief that followed. Relief was a part of it; Dr. H.'s confirmation of what I'd long suspected meant I wasn't crazy, that I hadn't been inventing dramas and overreacting to innocent behavior. But having another person—a *professor and priest himself,* one with so much authority and so much of my respect and admiration—confirm there was a problem meant that there probably really was a problem. And I still wanted to get out of this without it being a problem, without *causing* problems—for myself or anyone else.

Dr. H. immediately promised me several things. One, that I would never have to take another course with this man, that we would figure a way around the requirements he taught; Dr. H. would make sure of this. Two, that I could stop worrying about needing this man on my dissertation committee, because there was no way he was going to allow that to happen. And three, Dr. H. was going to hold a meeting with this professor to inform him that he was to have no further contact with me, to reinforce all of the things I'd originally said over the phone, the demands that he no longer approach me or call me or write to my mother.

But Dr. H. made me promise him something, too.

That I was going to march over to the office at my university that handled sexual harassment and file a complaint, that I was going to do this right now, the moment I left his office. He told me he was going to pick up the phone when I walked out the door to let the woman in charge know that I was on my way.

I agreed, but this was definitely not what *I* had wanted. None of this was what I'd wanted. I'd wanted things to go away quietly, secretly, without anyone else's knowledge. The more people who knew, the bigger a deal it would become. But Dr. H. reassured me that it was essential I do this, that it would help put in place the official measures necessary so he could do his job on my behalf.

It's funny, I know that Dan was there with me for the entire meeting. I remember him accompanying me, I remember walking into Dr. H.'s office with him, sitting down with him there, but once my story starts, *that story,* I can't see Dan anymore. It's like he disappears from the room in my memory. It's like I erase him, or maybe he quietly tiptoes out.

I remember only Dr. H. and I remember him so clearly, the tone in his voice, how strong but also caring, how concerned he was that this was happening to me, and how sad he was that I had been afraid to tell anyone before now. The entire time I was in his office and he listened as I spoke, heard what I had to say, he never flinched.

I would eventually come to understand Dr. H. as my Academic Dad.

The father who was also a father; a father squared. This man, this priest, this professor, who had recruited me to this program, who had called me with his exciting offer of financial support, would become the mentor I'd originally believed Father L. to be. But Dr. H. was my mentor for real.

From that day in his office and going forward, Dr. H. rose like a wall around me, dug and filled a moat around my intellectual endeavors, doing his best to clear a bright, comfortable space so I could once again roam safely on the academic playground that had once been my happiness. He would become the counterforce to all that would happen next, the person who defended me against the people with far more power than both of us who would not be on my side. He would become the professor for many of my remaining classes, and he would eventually become my dissertation director, the most passionate believer in the possibilities of my intellect. He would prove to me that Catholic priests could still be good. That the university was still my home. That I had still had some luck remaining when it came to professors. That I was going to be Professor Freitas myself, someday soon, regardless of this mess—he never let me forget that part either. He used to address all of his letters and eventually his emails to me with *Dear Future Professor Freitas.*

I credit Dr. H. for the fact that today I am a writer. By directing my dissertation, by the *way* he directed it, through his rules for how to get through one, he taught me how to write a book. Those rules are burned into me, they go wherever I go, they are there when I sit down at my laptop every morning, as is his faith that I would see my dream, that I would write many books, all kinds of books—he was convinced of this and told me it often.

Many years into the future, my first novel would be dedicated to his memory, and to my mother, and my grandmother, too—to his memory because he would die, unexpectedly, just a few months after he handed me my diploma. I would lose him, just as I would lose my mother and my grandmother, too, all of them a few months apart.

I think maybe before I showed up in Dr. H.'s office that day, Dr. H. and Father L. had been friends. At the very least, they had been colleagues. They were both smart men, gifted intellectuals, exceptional ones, vibrant and dynamic as they spoke of ideas. This is why I'd been attracted to both of them during graduate school, albeit with very different outcomes.

And it *was* an attraction, a kind of eros I felt, but of the intellectual kind. With Father L., that attraction became twisted and wrong, something I viewed as a punishment for marching into the traditionally male territory of the life of the mind, of philosophy and theology, unafraid of what I might find there, naïve about its buried potholes and hidden cliffs, its darkness, its punishments for the brazenness and boldness of women. But with Dr. H., I would find an altered landscape, bright and colorful and sunlit. A place where I belonged and flourished.

If Dr. H. and Father L. had been friends that day I showed up in the former's office, they certainly stopped being friends by the time I left.

Before Dr. H. would die, he'd give me a precious gift. He restored my belief that a professor could become a mentor and only a mentor, seeing me as a student and only a student. That I could go to a professor repeatedly, sit in his office, full of questions about a reading or about my dissertation, talking excitedly, hands gesturing, face smiling, without having him interpret this as something other than what it was—a student, engaged by her graduate work, eager and alive with ideas. I could do all of this while wearing high-heeled boots and cute outfits and not have this matter, that it had never mattered what I wore or what I looked like, that my intellect was why we were really there. He reassured me that a professor could go with a group of us to see the new *Star Wars* movie, hang out with Dan and Christopher and me and play football on the grass outside the theater as we waited in line, and not have this lead to something sordid later on, something dark and unwanted. That I could be a human in his presence, sad about my mother, fearful she might not get her wish of seeing me graduate with my PhD, and have him not see this as a selfish opportunity. He reminded me that a Catholic priest could act like a Catholic priest and not something entirely other.

What I didn't know then was that Dr. H. was helping me into the career that would become my trade-off when my dream fell apart. Writing, my non-dream, in exchange for being a professor, my true dream.

Dr. H. didn't know that then either, and it wasn't his intent. He thought he would be around for years to help me navigate the professional minefield created by my situation, tell me to move right instead of left, head off the questions that would inevitably be asked regarding my job applications and what was conspicuously missing from all of them—a letter from Father L. Academic specializations are small, and everyone knows one another, knows who went to what school and who must have taught them at that school. Which is also why eyebrows go up when an applicant appears without a recommendation and supporting phone call from the person in their specialization from their graduate school.

I forfeited my recommendation from this man that January day in Dr. H.'s office.

By telling on Father L., I was taking the letter I would need each time I threw my hat in the ring for an academic position and setting fire to it, watching it burn. We were all watching it burn, the three of us, Dan, Dr. H., and me, in his old office with the dirty snow visible through the blinds. It would always, always be strange when I showed up for a job interview without Father L.'s stamp of approval. I'd known this as I answered the phone a thousand times when he'd call and as I piled the letters he sent me higher and higher on the windowsill of my office, but the fact of it had gotten blurry. The only thing I could see clearly that dreary January was the need to get Father L. out of my life completely and permanently. He was a stain on my person, and I wanted him scrubbed out. I would worry about the job problem later.

But when I told on him to Dr. H. like a little girl telling on the playground bully, I was sealing my fate, ensuring that I would always have trouble down the line as I tried to get an academic position. From that day forward, my applications would always have this off quality, an unpleasant smell that, for me to explain, for me to justify, would require confessing to the fact that my missing letter involved sexual harassment—which I would not do, could never do, and which would doom my candidacy anyway if I did. I would need someone who knew the story to finesse the missing letter for me, to lobby on my behalf despite it, which Dr. H could have done, did do for me at the very beginning, when he was still alive. And then suddenly he wasn't, and I would have no one.

21

In February, a friend at graduate school, not Dan, needed to talk.

It was important, she said.

She'd come running toward me while I was outside, walking up the hill from the street parking that lined the edges of campus. I was still avoiding the lot near his office windows, trying to avoid being seen on my way into the building. My friend was smart, a minister herself, poised and graceful. She and I had immediately established an easy rapport during our first semester of classes even though our lives were so different. She was married with children, with an entire church of people who depended on her, and I was single and mostly agnostic by then, though still bordering on atheist. We were of different faiths and different beliefs. But she was intellectually quick and socially fun, and one of the few women students in my program with whom I connected easily, with whom I could go to lunch and talk for hours.

During December, when I had been debating what to do, whom to tell, I'd considered speaking to her instead of Dan. Like Dan, she was someone I admired, fair-minded, careful in her judgments, someone who was not inclined to drama or overreacting or who would jump to conclusions. And like Dan, she knew this man and knew him well, respected him greatly, had taken more than one class with him already and enjoyed them immensely. But unlike Dan, she wasn't thinking of becoming a Catholic priest, and also, this man was the head of her specialization, too. I didn't want my ruin to ruin her. I didn't want to take from her what was taken from me. In the end, I needn't have worried, because he did this to her on his own.

When she approached me that day, she had in her hand a letter. The other held an envelope, ripped open at the top. Her face was a mask of confusion, of worry, the pace of her walk a bit frenzied, which was unlike her. This friend moved through the world with the calm surety of a ship across peaceful seas, steady, unhurried, relaxed. It was one of the things I loved about her, one I wished I could embody myself. It was another way that we were different. I was always a bevy of hurried, quick, bold gestures, but my friend was the opposite, which was also why the moment I saw her speeding toward me I knew something was wrong.

We greeted each other, barely, and then she looked at me—hard. "Is there something wrong between you and Professor L.?"

My stomach did one of those looping motions, swooping up and around and then dropping straight to the sidewalk with a *thunk*.

"Why?" I asked, stupidly. I should have known even before she told me, but as with so many things he did, sometimes I failed at my duty of anticipating the lengths to which he would go to forge another road into my life and everyone in it.

"He's been writing to me and then he's called me," she went on. "And then he's been trying to talk to me about you. He came up to me a few minutes ago."

My eyes sought the ground, joining my stomach. "Oh?"

"Donna." Her voice lost its edge.

"What did he want?" I asked, studying the concrete below our feet.

"To convince you not to be angry at him. To talk to him. He's desperate to speak to you. He knows that we're friends and thought you would listen to me."

I stopped breathing, looked up into the eyes of my friend. I thought I might sit down right there, on the cold ground of the sidewalk. Everything about my body was lead. But my heart was beating so fast I thought I would faint.

"*What* is going *on?*"

"I'm afraid to tell you," I said. "I don't want it to affect you."

She jerked the letter in her hand. "It already has."

The woman in the university's office of human resources had short hair, curls all over her head, like my mother's before she lost it to cancer. She seemed nice, she was serious, she nodded a lot as I spoke. I remember thinking how she reminded me of Tootsie, Dustin Hoffman's character in the movie of the same name, like she might be from another era, the 1950s, if I had to pick. A woman in her fifties, probably.

Did she have children? A daughter like me? Would that have made a difference?

I don't remember how tall or short she was because she was always behind her desk, as though she never got up from it, as though it had her pinned to her chair permanently. She didn't smile once during the long hours I'd spent in her office back in January—the first visit of what would soon become many.

That January, on the same day I'd met with Dr. H., I fulfilled my promise to him and went straight to see the woman in charge of sexual-harassment complaints at my university. I went to see *this* woman. Tootsie.

When I was done speaking my part on that first occasion, it was her turn to speak, and as I listened, hope bloomed inside me, pushing against the bomb that had taken up so much space for so long. Tootsie promised me so many things: consequences, admonishment, official conversations and communications, correction of what had obviously gone wrong, protection most of all, protection from *him*. A stop would be put to his behavior, immediately. She seemed outraged on my behalf, so strong and sure of what had to happen next. Like she knew exactly what to do, like she knew exactly what she was doing.

I trusted her completely.

I offered her the kind of faith my mother wished I would reserve for God and the Catholic Church. She seemed like the feminist goddess I'd been waiting for, that I'd been reading about in my gender-studies classes, a divine figure masquerading as a 1950s housewife look-alike, powerful and poised to come rescue me, to fix what I'd gotten myself into. And why not? Hadn't I been taught on that very campus from my feminist professors that the divine can take many forms, *any* form, especially the form of a woman's body, even a motherly body, *especially* a motherly body? It never occurred to me, not once, that this woman might not have my best interests at heart. Or any interests whatsoever to do with me.

★ ★ ★

Tootsie *looked* like someone I could trust—and my parents had raised me to be trusting.

My mother was and my father is a good person. They worked hard, went to steady jobs that paid little but sustained our family. Before my grandmother became the first woman manager at Raytheon, she'd been the secretary. She joined the company on the ground floor, when they were still operating out of a garage in Newport, with a sum total of four people, one of them her. Eventually she was promoted from secretary to something a bit higher, then promoted again and again until she was an important woman boss, going to work at 5 a.m. every day, coming home by three to watch her favorite soap opera, *General Hospital,* with me on the couch.

There was a simplicity to our life. There were things that were good and things that were bad. Good things were the people around us, the nice neighbors, the nice parishioners, the nice teachers at my mother's elementary school and my high school. The Catholic Church was good, the government was good, people in charge were good, and you always gave people the benefit of the doubt because most people were good at heart.

My parents and grandmother believed in the Gospel of Hard Work. Do your best and you'll be rewarded. Be diligent, get everything done that people ask you to do, and you'll find that things will work out, enough to keep you going, enough to sustain you. This was America, and my parents, the son and daughter of immigrants, believed wholeheartedly in the American Dream. They raised me on it, were certain I was evidence of its truth, with my success in school that had gotten me into Georgetown, the second person in our entire extended family to go to college. I learned to work hard just like they'd shown me and was rewarded for this by being crowned valedictorian at my graduation before I left Rhode Island. God sees when people are good, my mother believed, and most people are good—it's that simple.

The bad things were cut-and-dried, too. Disobedience, lying, ignoring someone who is in need, not going to church on Sundays, not offering to help your mother, your grandmother, your father, when they needed a hand, not keeping your room clean. The really bad things happened on television, on the news, to other people. The really bad people were in the movies and at the theater, on the stage. They were characters in stories that were not our own. They were in someone else's life.

This woman, Tootsie, sitting behind her big desk, everything neat on top, unlike Dr. H.'s desk, which was full of chaos, in her long narrow office, was the woman in charge of me now. I assumed that I should listen to her. Obviously, she would see that I had done my best even in this situation and reward me accordingly. I'd been a good student and initially had tried to comply with this man's wishes. Then I'd tried to let him know, subtly and politely, so as not to hurt his feelings, that I no longer wished to comply with his wishes and requests. Only when this didn't work had I turned to more forceful yet still polite declines, then less polite ones. Then I'd tried to handle the situation on my own, so as not to upset anybody or cause any scandal, with that December phone call. *And only after all of this* did I tell Dr. H. And *he* was the person who sent me to her office.

Tootsie was my absolute last resort. I was not a tattletale. I was not a girl looking for trouble. I wanted help of the most basic sort from her and nothing more.

I wholly believed in this woman's authority, her good-will, that she would see all that I had tried to do, how I'd tried so hard not to throw my problem in her lap, how

I had not wanted things to turn out this way and how I still wanted things to be settled quietly, so no one else had to know. Of course she would help me. It seemed like a perfectly reasonable request.

What no one knew then, not my parents or any of our neighbors and fellow parishioners or the rest of the American Catholic Church and certainly not me, was that the Catholic Church was not good as an institution. That it was corrupt, that it was criminal in situations exactly like mine. At the time, no one knew the Catholic Church had a long-standing plan for responding to exactly the kind of complaint I'd brought to this woman, a standard operating procedure, and it did not involve doing the right thing.

Then, doubly problematic, not only was I talking to a woman representing the Catholic Church because I attended a Catholic university, but I was at an institution of higher education, one of many that we also now know have fostered methods of ignoring victims in order to protect the institution from harm. In this instance, *I* represented the potential harm, the person who might injure the institution by making a claim against one of its own. Because my claim could result in public scandal, *I* was the enemy, and what the woman sitting behind the desk in front of me was really in charge of doing was protecting the university and the Catholic Church from *me*.

So, this woman who looked like Tootsie, who seemed so benign, like someone who could be a fellow teacher at my mother's school, a woman with whom she might sit on the beach, a woman who Dr. H. truly believed was going to help me, took my faith and distorted it, turning it into something pathetic, something laughable. She took full advantage of my trust. She knew exactly what to do with it, how to transform it into something for the institution's benefit, for his benefit, for his own protection, not mine.

She knew just how to exact it from me, squeeze it from me, until I was wrung dry.

I stood there on the sidewalk, blinking at my minister friend, the letter from him in one of her hands, the envelope it came in gripped in the other, trying to decide what to tell her, how much to tell her, if I should tell her anything or try once again to lie for him, concoct another story that would make his behavior seem okay.

But I couldn't think of one.

So far, I knew that Dr. H. *had* talked to him, had met with him, had done his best to put protections in place on my behalf. But the reason Dr. H. wanted me to report to human resources was because he could meet with this professor all he pleased, but in the end, they were just colleagues. At the time Dr. H. was a chair, and so was this professor. They were equals, both heads of programs and specializations. Dr. H. wanted someone who had real power over this man to put restrictions in place that had traction, and that person had to be Tootsie.

Tootsie, in addition to her promises to me of consequences and other admonishments, explained that there would be a formal letter sent to this professor, informing him of all that he needed to comply with, outlining specific consequences, including a demand that he stop contacting me in every and all ways. Tootsie promised I would receive a copy of the letter as soon as it was sent.

Weeks had gone by, the semester was progressing, and still I hadn't received this letter. I assumed someone simply hadn't gotten around to getting me a copy. It never occurred to me that there were no plans to ever give me the letter, because the letter Tootsie actually wrote was nothing like the one she'd described, and she didn't want me to find this out.

Meanwhile, my professor had continued to lurk in my vicinity, outside my classes. He continued to write to my mother. The beginning of the spring semester had been different in the sense that the amount of contact from him diminished, but the contact that continued now felt amplified, a million times more sinister for its defiance, for its clear desperation.

At first I figured: he hasn't yet gotten the letter from Tootsie. She must not have met with him yet. He must not know about the consequences yet. Because of course, he wouldn't dare go against a no-contact directive from the powers of his own university or his Church. He would never jeopardize his job or religious authority by violating what they demanded of him.

At the beginning of that spring semester, back in January and the first weeks of February, I'd done my best to immerse myself in my classes, to do some thinking other than the thinking I'd grown so used to about this man and his behaviors that had dominated my brain for over a year. I convinced myself it was just a matter of time before the contact *really* stopped for good and in every way. Soon it would be over. Soon.

But now here was my friend with a letter from him, a letter he'd written to her about *me,* talking about phone calls from him to her about *me,* of finding her in the hallway and going up to her to persuade her to talk to *me* about *him.* A friend who needed this man for her own degree, and for this reason definitely did not need the way he was currently imposing on her.

I was reminded, again, of middle school, of how middle school it was of him to try to get to me through a girlfriend, to try to persuade the girlfriend to persuade me to talk to him. He was acting like a twelve-year-old boy who'd gone through a breakup in the lunchroom, who didn't know how to accept being broken up with, so he'd decided to try to talk to his former crush through her friend; as though her friend could save the day, as though she could make me see sense when I obviously couldn't see it myself. Then I reminded myself yet again that he was *not* a middle-school student, that he should know far better than to do what he'd just done with my friend, and even worse than this, he probably did know better and still could not control himself.

A chill was spreading over me.

My friend and I went for coffee. I told her the abbreviated version of what had been going on now, for over a year.

She was outraged.

She went straight to Dr. H. and told him she also wanted nothing to do with this professor ever again. Then Dr. H. sent me to Tootsie's office to make an additional report.

And once again, I told Tootsie what happened, how fearful and upset it made me.

She promised another letter would be sent immediately.

I asked her if I could have a copy of the first one, explained that I hadn't received it yet. She seemed perplexed by this, reassured me that it must have gotten lost in the mail, that I would be receiving it very soon, along with the new one, the second one. Her assistant wasn't around, otherwise she'd have the woman dig up the first one and give me a copy right then and there, before I left the office.

I thanked her. I believed she was telling me the truth.

22

One day in March, I was studying with a fellow student. He turned to me and asked, "Is your mother friends with Professor L.?"

I stared at him, unable to form words.

So he asked another question. "Do they write to each other?"

I kept staring, speechless.

"Because I think I've read her letters to him," he went on. "You know, in one of my courses."

"I don't understand," I managed, still feeling dumb about what he could possibly mean.

He went on to tell me that in their class that spring, his professor—*that* professor—was focusing on suffering, the nature of suffering, the stories people tell about suffering. That each week, he had been passing out photocopies of letters from a woman with whom he corresponded, a woman suffering from cancer, a woman possibly dying of cancer, who was also a woman of great Catholic faith, a woman with a daughter, a woman who was terribly worried she would not live to take care of her daughter much longer, that her daughter might lose her soon. The name of this woman at the end of the letters had been blacked out. The professor often brought up the concern she expressed in these letters for her daughter. This fellow student and the rest of my peers in this class, he explained, had spent well over a month now, nearly two, talking about the mother-daughter relationship she described in a new letter each week.

It had occurred to my fellow student, because of the content of the letters combined with what he knew about me, that I might be the daughter she spoke of, that she might be my mother. Everyone in my department, both the students and the professors, knew that my mother was sick and might die. There were prayers up for her on the wall of the Etc. Room, where we ate lunch and got our coffee and tea. It was not a secret that she had cancer, and it was not a secret that I was struggling because of this. So this fellow student knew enough to guess that the letters might be hers.

He'd asked me his questions as though the writer's identity were a mere curiosity, a mysterious puzzle he just happened to figure out, a small "aha" moment that cleared up a question he'd been carrying about the woman's identity, not a pressing one, but still it was there. He was a nice person, jolly, even, tall and a bit rotund, with a great red beard and a deep, raspy voice. He had no idea that informing me about what he and his peers were studying in this professor's class would be my undoing—if he'd known, I doubt he would have said a thing.

"Yes," I told him now, because I didn't know what else to do or say, "my mother and he used to write to each other."

His brow furrowed. "They still do," he said.

Some of the letters he'd read were recent, he told me. As recent as last week. There was a kind of ongoing chronicle of their correspondence at the start of each class.

It had been a long time since I'd asked my mother if my professor was still writing to her, and if she was still writing him back. In truth, I hadn't wanted to hear her answer. I was afraid to. I still had not told my parents what was going on. I still couldn't bring myself to do it.

"Oh," I said, and shrugged.

My fellow student and I went back to studying.

But my mind could no longer focus.

How many students had wondered the same thing about the mystery-woman letter writer? Had any more guessed it was my mother?

That a group of students was using the correspondence of my mother, *my* mother, who was fighting cancer and living through the pain of chemo, who was trying to be brave in the proximity of her own death, as a source for classroom debate, like any other book or academic article, *as this professor led the way,* was beyond my ability to comprehend. I sat there, taking in the fact that my peers had spent the semester discussing *me* as the daughter in the equation. They were likely picking apart my mother's prose, how it conveyed our relationship, trying to glean the deeper meaning in her words as though her letters were mere texts, like any other readings in a class.

Was he trying to punish me? Was that what this was? Or did it not even occur to him I might find out? Was it some bizarre new way of drawing me close without my knowledge, of keeping me in his life through my mother, by bringing us into his classroom, the one place where he would always have power, where he would always rule, the place where he was king?

I had to get the letters back. I could not allow him to keep them.

I excused myself from the study session. I went straight to Dr. H.'s office and gave him this new information. He was astonished. His colleague's newest behavior was reprehensible, inappropriate to a degree that surpassed anything else the man had done before this moment. Unforgivable. Dr. H. promised he would talk to him once more and demand he give my mother's letters back. He sent me once again to Tootsie's office to report this latest violation.

I went.

I am not a violent person.

I hide under the covers during violent scenes on television shows, or sometimes I leave the room and come back when all the noise seems to have died down. I can't watch anything gruesome. I'm not one for getting angry either, or one for conflict. It takes a lot to provoke me, as my close friends know.

But I began to have violent fantasies about this man.

I began to think about scratching his face with my pink painted nails, leaving bloody trails down his cheeks and across his eyes. I began to think about pounding my fists against his head, taking his skull and smashing it against a wall, crushing his rib cage, beating him until he could no longer stand.

The person having these thoughts seemed so far away from the person I was, or believed myself to be. I didn't know that I could become violent if pushed far enough, hard enough, brutally enough.

But using my mother's letters in his class with my peers was so far beyond what I ever could have imagined him doing, or thinking to do, that I found myself in this place where thoughts of violence, scenes I could not bear to witness at home on the television, became appealing, so appealing that they were a comfort. I couldn't stop myself from having them, and at some point I stopped caring that I was.

I'm going to give Tootsie the benefit of the doubt for a moment. Put myself in her shoes.

Or I'm going to try to, because it's also true that I came to hate her, and I've hated her ever since, with an outsized rage, decades now of hate, as though she were somehow worse than him. And maybe she was, in a sense, because I thought she would help me, and instead she lied.

But maybe Tootsie did what she did, gave me the run-around, made it so that my life fell into an even greater hell than when I first came to see her, because she, too, was trapped. Maybe she really did care about me, really did worry for me, really did feel horrified on my behalf, but she was stuck in a system that would never allow her to do anything to help me, not really, or to stop him, not really. Maybe she wanted to, badly, but this would require her to stand down the Catholic Church in addition to her university bosses—bosses who paid her salary, who put food on the table for her and the daughters I imagined she might have at home, bosses who were also bishops and other high-ranking members of the Catholic hierarchy.

In the news recently, because of the tidal wave of sexual harassment and assault accusations moving through our world thanks to #MeToo, I have read articles warning women that HR representatives are not—that they never have been—our friends in situations like harassment and assault. Though they may be the people we are supposed to report to when incidents occur, their real job has nothing to do with protecting us, and everything to do with protecting the bosses and the reputation of the company itself. They represent the institution, not you, the articles have warned. They are not your advocates, they are the bosses' advocates, the company's advocates.

But those articles have also spoken of the terrible dilemmas of these HR reps, most of them women themselves, how they, too, are caught in a corrupt and dishonest system, just like the women who go to them in order to report horrors in the workplace. How these HR reps often *wish* to help these women, believing it is the right thing to do, yet by doing so may lose their own jobs in the process.

Isn't this a disgusting thing for all of us to realize?

The reporting system in place supposedly to protect us—that was supposed to protect *me*—is not there to protect us at all. The reporting system is there to do the dirty work for the company, the institution, the men in charge, there to collect information that the bosses need to know about, so as to better and more quickly squelch it, silence it, before it can ever come to light. A system designed to let the bosses know whom, exactly, to fire, the very moment a potentially fireable offense is committed, however outlandish and far-fetched the so-called offense might seem. Whom, exactly, whether student or worker, to brush under the rug.

So maybe this system was behind what Tootsie did and didn't do. Maybe she was a victim of sorts in her own right, walking a tightrope, trying to keep a job that was tied to a corrupt—no, a criminal—system put in place decades before at my university. Maybe she lost sleep at night over the impossible situation she was in, with regard to me and others who had made similar complaints in the past. Maybe she wasn't as callous as I began to believe, callous and cruel and uncaring about what I was going through. Maybe when she made all those promises to me, she really believed she could come through on them, maybe she wanted to, maybe she even tried to deliver on them and then was told no, absolutely not, by her bosses.

Or, maybe she knew exactly what she was doing, maybe she had her job because she was good at this, at lying to victims, at pretending she cared. Maybe she believed in the cause. Maybe she believed that what she was doing was the right thing and that I was in the wrong, that in the end I was just a crazy girl who'd misunderstood a friend-ship with a professor—which was how she described my claims in the letters she'd written to this man, the ones she was refusing to let me see, the ones she would eventually be required to show me because I'd gotten a lawyer to force her to show them to me.

Tootsie, as always, was a flurry of concern when I went to report my professor's latest transgression, his discussion of my mother and me in his classes. And, as always, Tootsie was awash in confusion as to why I still hadn't gotten copies of the letters she'd sent to him after the other occasions we'd met.

Did she have the wrong address, perhaps? she asked me. Had I changed apartments since we'd spoken?

As usual, no one was around to help her dig them up, but as soon as the person returned, she'd have them do so. She apologized for the third time for not following up with a phone call after her meetings with my professor to report that they had happened—yet another thing she'd promised each time I met with her, then never did. But this time, she quieted my growing dismay at her lack of follow-up and the failure to produce the promised letters with a proposal far more attractive than anything she'd suggested in the past.

Would it help if he was placed on sabbatical? she asked me.

Would that make me feel at all better? Safer?

I nodded vigorously. "Yes. Yes, it would," I told her, nearly shocked at the suggestion, that it was even an option. I was stupid to believe her again, I know, I know. But at the time, I was so tired, and she'd dangled something so appealing. He would be placed on sabbatical the next year, as a way of forcing him to stay away from me.

Would the school really do that? I wondered.

Of course, she told me.

It seemed like such a big consequence. Tootsie was acknowledging that what was happening was serious—very serious. The spring semester was nearly over by then. There were about six weeks left.

Could I keep my head down and make it to summer? she wanted to know.

Yes, I could, I told her. I would force myself.

I *believed* she would make a sabbatical happen. I walked away from her office *believing* that when I returned for classes in the fall, I would no longer have to worry about running into him, about him lurking near the rooms I was in, about meeting him in the stairwell, or about him peering through the blinds of his office window as I walked by.

23

My mother passed the six-month mark and kept on going.

Summer arrived and she was still alive, she'd survived chemo, survived cancer, for now.

Little by little, she recovered. Her doctors were stunned the cancer had disappeared, for now. My father and I took her to the beach when she was strong enough. She was anxious to return to teaching in September, to go back to her classroom once or twice a week, whenever she was up to it. She missed her tiny nursery-school students, their parents, her colleagues.

My father and I were elated.

We'd braced ourselves for the worst, and instead we enjoyed the ocean and sand with my mother in July and August, my mother the quintessential beach bum who'd drag us there at 7 a.m. if we were willing, toting a cooler stocked with sandwiches and cut-up watermelon. That February, March, and even in April, she'd been sure, we were *all* sure, she'd never set foot on the beach again, never march up to the place by the lifeguard chair where she sat like she owned it, like she'd purchased it in a sale, setting up the familiar orange-and-white-striped umbrella we'd had since I was small, the one that marked her spot and told everyone that she had arrived.

The students in my residence hall were gone for a blissful three months of peace, so I could travel without having to ask anyone to cover for me. I went back and forth to Rhode Island as often as I could to enjoy this reprieve from my mother's cancer. I went back and forth to Tennessee, too, as much as my boyfriend, Christopher, wanted to go.

Despite everything that happened, my grades were good from the previous spring semester, nearly perfect.

I'd somehow done the impossible!

I commuted to help with my family, kept up with my schoolwork, held down a job at Georgetown that could be all-consuming, maintained a relationship with a boyfriend and also my friendships, all while being traumatized by one of my professors, and all while preventing my other professors (save the two I told) from finding out what was going on—and keeping my parents from finding out, too. They had enough to worry about. I had contained the damage, mostly.

I even looked forward to starting classes again, to returning to the version of life where I worried about nothing other than pursuing my intellectual curiosity, to stoking the excitement that never left me about ideas, philosophy, feminist theory.

Tootsie had promised a sabbatical.

I relished what that sabbatical was going to be like, fantasized about it all summer.

I would be able to walk across campus, walk from my car into the building that housed my department, without worrying that someone was watching, that someone was waiting for me beyond the doorway. It was going to seem like last year never happened.

Best of all, I hadn't heard from him. Not a letter, a postcard, a phone call, not a glimpse of his mousy self, peering at me through a window or popping up when I rounded a corner. I stayed away from school during those hot and humid months, and he stayed away from me.

When my mother reached the one-year anniversary of her diagnosis, in August, and passed it, I did my best not to remember what else had happened that day the year before. Instead I reveled in her continued presence with us.

I had a lot of reasons to hope by the close of that summer.

I dwelled there, treading water, legs working to sustain that suspended state. Above the surface I was calm and collected and smiling.

School started again, and he was around like always.

There was no sabbatical, no consequences. Just him teaching his classes, as though it were perfectly fine that he'd been using my mother's letters as a tool for analysis and discussion with my peers. As though it were absolutely aboveboard that he'd brought a friend of mine into this mess, pressing her to make it all better, trying to get her to convince me that I should forgive him. As though it were no big deal that a professor had been following around a student for over a year, refusing to take her nos for an answer.

When I stepped onto campus and realized he was still there, teaching and lurking in the halls like always, I was livid. I was also confused.

Why? How could the school have let this go? Hadn't Tootsie promised me he'd be gone? Hadn't she sworn to provide me with peace and security for the first time in ages?

Maybe this was my fault.

I should have insisted the last time I left her office that she find those letters, demand that she make copies and hand them over or I'd refuse to leave. Just as before, she hadn't followed up with me over the summer.

Stupid, stupid me.

I was so desperate to move on, to move forward, to forget about everything, that I didn't call her office over the summer, not once, demanding information, asking to know his status, if the sabbatical had indeed worked out.

I went to Tootsie's office now.

The way there was familiar.

But this time, *I* was different.

I wasn't the nice, demure student asking for help. I was the angry student, unstable, really, the ground seeming to crumble under my steps as I walked. Nothing was as it appeared, or as anyone told me it would be.

I wanted him to be on a *fucking* sabbatical, and he *fucking* wasn't. I wanted him to suffer some *fucking* consequences for what he'd done. Hadn't I suffered plenty of *fucking* consequences because of him? What the *fuck?*

While I'd been willing to have faith the previous spring in all that Tootsie promised, the curtain had been pulled back, and finally I was able to see that there was nothing behind it. That there had been nothing all along. How could she have done this to me? How could she have lied to my face when I was so scared and desperate?

"Where are the letters?" I demanded, standing before her, refusing to sit when she asked me to. "You told me you wrote letters, that you'd give me copies. Where are they? I want them *now.*"

I seethed. Today, I wouldn't leave without them.

In truth, she couldn't give them to me, she explained. They were private.

Then why didn't she tell me this before? Why had she said otherwise? *Why was he not on sabbatical?* Why, why, why?

I was leaning over her desk. I wonder if she was afraid. I was afraid of myself in that moment. Tootsie was speechless, made no more promises. She must have known I would no longer believe them, that it was useless for her to say anything. I left her office, zigzagging across campus. I was like a drunk person.

I ended up at the provost's office. I demanded to see him immediately. Said I wasn't leaving until I spoke to him. The secretary kept her eye on me as she picked up the phone. She watched me carefully, as if she could see a bomb strapped to my chest, underneath my clothing.

The provost at this university was a VIP. It was a big university, so going to see him was akin to showing up to see the president. He had power, real power. And like so many other powerful people at my university, he was also a priest.

It wasn't long before the secretary ushered me into his office.

The provost was skinny, gray-haired, unsmiling.

Not at all like Dr. H., even though they were both thin. Dr. H. was a runner, so he was thin and strong. But this man was thin and frail, skin pale, like maybe he didn't see much sunlight. I don't even remember whether he said hello to me or if we exchanged small talk before I launched into my reasons for being there.

I told him everything.

Every little thing this professor had done, every clever, creative means he'd found to worm his way into my life and that of my family. It took a long time. At least an hour, maybe more. I don't remember. When I started speaking I'd tried to be calm, but by the time I was ten minutes in I was enraged, my voice going up and down, growing louder and quieter, louder and quieter, as I forced this man to hear every last thing I had been through at his university, because of one of *his* professors, one of *his* priest-professors, one of *his* colleagues, and because of *that woman* who did nothing to help me even though she told me she'd take care of things.

Fucking Tootsie.

Did he not already know what had happened? I asked, once I finished. Had no one informed him? Or had he been informed and he simply didn't care?

He didn't answer. He just stared at me with the same blank expression he'd worn the entire time I'd been telling him the story of my time as a graduate student, all the way back from my first semester. I waited and waited for him to say something, anything, but all he did was look at me like he wished he were a magician and could make me vanish from his office. Then I realized that what I'd originally thought was confusion, even emptiness in his eyes, was really contempt. He watched me with contempt.

I started to cry.

"Don't you care? Don't you care what's happening to me? Don't you want to help me?" I was saying, over and over, my voice rising to a yell because I couldn't believe that he might not care. And because I couldn't believe he was regarding me like a piece of garbage, the stench offending him. Then, "You don't care, do you? You don't care, you don't, you don't, you don't care at all." My voice grew quieter and quieter, until it disappeared.

Still he said nothing, looked down his nose at me, stared like he wanted to be anywhere else than with me. He showed no compassion, no sign that my grief, my fear, my despair, moved him, not even a tiny bit.

Abruptly, I got up, turned around, and left his office without saying goodbye, sobbing. His secretary looked at me like I was crazy, some deranged girl student she was glad was leaving. And I was crazy, wasn't I? I was acting crazy because I felt crazy. Crazy was where I'd landed.

It had become my home, suddenly. It happened so fast. One minute I was hopeful, serene, excited, the next I was deranged. I went to Dr. H.'s office.

He was there, like always, he listened to me sobbing and, like always, he was kind, he was worried. But this time his response shook me.

"I have done all I can on my end. I have tried to get your mother's letters back and L. has refused, saying she freely wrote to him so her letters are his to keep and to do with what he wants. I have met with him multiple times and with others at the university about what's been going on." He looked at me in a way that I knew was meant to say something without words, but I couldn't decipher what. Then he said out loud, clearly and definitively, "Donna, it's time."

"Time for what?"

I really didn't know.

"You need a lawyer. You need a lawyer now. You must get one."

I dumped the grocery bag full of unopened letters on my coffee table.

Even after everything, I'd still been too allergic to touch the correspondence that remained from this professor that hadn't gone into the trash. Too repulsed and sickened. Too full of dread to make myself do it.

But now, I had to force myself to look.

One by one, on the very same couch where I'd read his article the previous August about the goodness of priests falling in love with young women and having affairs, I opened the last letters he'd sent me before I'd made the phone call in December, telling him to go away forever. Among other banal things, like accounts of what he was up to and chronicles of trips he had taken, there were love poems.

There was no accompanying explanation, no *Dear Donnas* at the top of the page or any *Sincerely, L.*s at the end. Just love poems, typed out or written in his hand, nothing else.

Over the next few days, I went to see a number of people.

Because I worked in Residence Life at Georgetown, I knew what to do if a student came to you with a complaint of sexual assault or harassment—I'd just never thought to apply the process to myself. Georgetown was ahead of its time back then; they'd hired a sexual assault services coordinator and someone else for sex education. They were wonderful women, and they happened to work in the offices on the first floor of my residence hall. They were always just steps from my apartment door, but it had never occurred to me to ask their advice or for help before now. Finally, now I did, and once I was there, talking to them, real women who treated me like a human being, who looked at me with honest concern and sympathy, women who would keep their promises to me, I wondered why it had taken me so long to go to them. I regretted not seeing them earlier. Soon I would regret this even more.

From there I went to visit one of my women professors from undergrad, and then a second one. I told them briefly what was going on and asked them what they thought I should do. Soon I had four women, four adult women, mothers themselves, who would walk with me the rest of the way I had to go, far beyond the terrain that the lawyer I was about to get would cross with me.

I called my father.

"Dad," I said. "Um, do you know any lawyers?"

There was a long pause. "Why?" Then another long pause. "Are you in trouble?"

"No, no, no," I told him. "I'm fine. Everything is fine.

I just...am in a situation. And I was advised I need a lawyer. So, um, do you know any?"

Yes, he told me, and gave me the man's name and number.

"Are you okay?" my dad kept asking.

"Yes, I am. I swear. Don't worry, don't worry, don't worry."

"Did someone...did someone *hurt* you?" he asked in a gruff, fractured voice.

"No," I told him, firmly and decidedly. *"No."*

I think my father wanted to know if I'd been raped, was scared maybe I had. Once I confirmed this wasn't the case, he was able to let go of anything else that might have gone wrong, since I suppose nothing could seem as bad as that in his mind.

"Don't tell Mom about any of this," I begged him before we hung up. "Please."

"I would never," he said. "Your mother has enough going on."

When I called my father I knew I could probably get away with asking him my question without him forcing me to say what was really happening. With my mother I never could get away with this. When I called him, I also knew that one of his best friends was a lawyer, a small-town lawyer, but a man who was nice, who had always been kind and friendly. Even though he didn't have any experience with situations like mine—then again, who did at the time, this was the nineties—I called him and he said he would help. I made him promise not to talk to my dad about anything. He told me he didn't need to promise, that as my lawyer he was legally obligated to keep what was between us only between us.

Things happened fast from there.

Formal letters with demands were dispatched to Tootsie, as well as a Title IX complaint to the Department of Education with claims of sexual harassment and a failure on the part of my university to respond. Letters from Tootsie finally arrived at my lawyer's, letters that did not say what she'd told me they said, but something else entirely, something to the effect of how everyone at the university knew that *I* was at fault, that I'd misunderstood a friendship with my professor. The letters repeatedly spelled my name wrong, *Frietas* instead of *Freitas,* a detail that bothered me deeply, that still bothers me deeply, errors that pierced my already raw skin. Tootsie couldn't even bother to spell my name right. Long days of formal interviews were scheduled, interviews where I would have to spend hours explaining everything I'd gone through again and again. And eventually, after many, many letters back and forth between my lawyer and the school, my professor was finally placed on sabbatical.

But there would never be any consequences.

Not real ones. Not while I was a student, not afterward either, not ever.

In fact, soon this man would be promoted within the university's administration. He would be a celebrated professor for many years to come, for more than a decade.

Tootsie, my university, had known exactly how to handle me the moment I showed up in her office, exactly what to do to make it more likely that consequences, real ones, would never be suffered by this man no matter what he did to me, and that there would never be any consequences for the university or the Church either. Tootsie was as clever in ensuring this as he was at stalking me. She knew she'd win before she actually did.

My lawyer confirmed this pretty much the moment I first called, that I didn't have a leg to stand on with the school and my claims, that likely nothing would or could happen despite all this had done.

Had the human resources woman explained to me the

first time I went to her office, my lawyer asked over the phone, that the moment I made my complaint, a clock started ticking?

No, I told him. She hadn't. What clock?

The clock for the statute of limitations, he said. The clock that gave me six months total to come forward with a formal complaint of sexual harassment to the Department of Education. Once the six months passed, there would never be the possibility of court, or the threat of consequences for a university from a judge. Any complaint from me would be dismissed immediately for this reason.

By the time I called a lawyer, a little over eight months had passed.

The statute of limitations had run out over the summer.

24

My mother died shortly after I received my PhD, at the end of my first year as a professor. Dr. H. had died about eight months before she did, not long after he first called me Dr. Freitas and my dissertation committee popped a bottle of champagne to celebrate my transformation from just Donna to Dr. Freitas.

I'd finally begun to live my dream of being a professor after the lengthy process of becoming one, and it turned out to be one of the saddest years of my life.

To add to my misfortune, soon I discovered that I had "landed badly," as it is sometimes put by my fellow academics, at the college where I'd gotten a tenure-track position.

With professor jobs, you either land well or land badly, and this depends on the makeup of your department. Women professors especially are at risk of landing badly, and women professors in my field are especially, especially at risk since our field is mostly male and run by men, though this is changing, slowly. I found out, through the grape-vine of other professors at my school, that my department of only tenured men had never wanted a woman teaching alongside them. Worse still, I was their *third* attempt at hiring one. They hadn't wanted to hire me either, not really—they'd been forced to hire a woman by the school. The two women who held my position before me had undergone six years of torment by my new colleagues, and then were each in turn denied tenure and sent packing. This, apparently, was to become my fate as well.

My new colleagues were terrible to me, and now there was no Dr. H. to call.

And when my mother went into a coma in early May of my first year as a professor, the tenured men in my department saw this as an opportunity. They used my ab-sence at graduation, among other events, as marks against me in my evaluations, as evidence that I was not commit-ted enough to the school. They would use my ensuing sadness about losing her to cite me for other failings, too. So I knew, early on, that I had to leave that place, but I also knew that I would be short two important letters if and when I tried—the most important ones, Dr. H.'s and Father L.'s.

The year after my mother's death my colleagues were cruel, crueler than I ever could imagine anyone being when a person is grieving, though at the time I was in a fog and would take in the scope and depth of their cruelty only later. I asked these men, then pleaded, then begged them for some understanding, and the answer was, sorry but *no*. They did not consent to my grief. They used the power of non-consent forcefully and enthusiastically, with all the intelligence and power of their positions, knowing full well that when it came to power in my department, I had none. And once again, in the context of a university, I had no agency. I went on the job market again and again, desperate to leave.

I would never get another position as a professor. Not a real one.

One day, about nine months after my mother died and well into the terrible treatment by my colleagues, a friend and I went to a small diner near her house. She and her husband lived in a beautiful, tiny Vermont town about a forty-minute drive from my Burlington apartment. I loved going to visit them, and I loved the little shops and restaurants that dotted their picturesque Main Street. She was a psychology professor from school, and we'd become friends the first week we'd started teaching. Over coffee and breakfast, I made a confession.

"I think I might be going crazy," I told her.

I was dismayed, I was ashamed, I was at my wit's end. She asked me why, and I began to explain, listing my symptoms, one by one.

Lately, I'd become afraid—of everything. I was afraid of the mail, for example. Like weirdly afraid of it. Like when I walked through the lobby of my apartment building on my way home from teaching, I would avert my eyes from the long line of silver mailboxes on the left-hand wall. I didn't want to touch or go near them. What's more, after I managed to force myself to pick it up, the mail would sit in a pile, unopened, for days. Weeks. Months. I resisted even looking at the stack on the counter. Going near it, picking up a single envelope, tearing it open, required such effort, such tremendous effort.

So yeah, there was the mail.

But there were other issues. I was having trouble getting out of my car when I went to school to teach. I would drive into the parking lot and pull into a space near my building, turn the ignition off, and sit there. Hands on the wheel, staring out the windshield, the clock ticking toward the start of a meeting or one of my classes. *Come on, Donna. What are you waiting for? Get out of the car. Get. Out. You're going to be late.* Eventually I would grab the handle and open the door. Then I'd look at the blacktop. I'd stare at the white painted line that marked my parking spot, door open, even when it was freezing. Then, eventually, I'd take deep breaths, deep, deep breaths, and set one foot outside the car, then the other, and shut the door behind me. Still breathing deeply, I'd walk the few steps to the building and up the stairs to the second floor, where my office was, sick, utterly sick to my stomach the entire time.

Once I got to my office, I then faced the inability to *leave* it. My classroom was a problem as well; not entering the classroom but leaving it after class was over. Thresholds had become an overall challenge, though only at school, for some reason. I would sit in my office chair, trying to persuade myself to stand up and walk out the door so I wouldn't be late for my students, or I would stand inside my empty classroom once my students had gone, unable to move. My heart would pound, my lungs would heave. I couldn't breathe. I would talk to myself, cheer myself on, scold myself. *Come on, Donna. Just go. Just go. You can do it! What is your fucking problem? Stop being crazy. Go, go, go!*

The more I explained to my friend what I was feeling, doing, going through, the crazier I felt. Crazier and more ashamed.

This friend also happened to be the only person in this new chapter of my life as a professor that I'd told about what I went through in graduate school. I'm not sure why I told her, what had possessed me to. There were still very few people in my life who knew anything about him; people who'd known me for years still had no idea. But this friend has a calm about her, a kind of peace and openness that invites intimacy, so I'd confided in her one day. And she also happens to be a psychologist.

She listened carefully as I finished going down the list of behaviors I'd been exhibiting while I picked at the food I would never actually eat. When I stopped, she told me that in graduate school for her internship, she'd worked at Veterans Affairs and had counseled a lot of veterans with post-traumatic stress disorder. She explained what PTSD was, because I didn't know, explained about the brain and how it can react to trauma, how as a survival mechanism it can bury certain experiences and all the emotions that go with them. Then, unfortunately, new experiences in life—experiences that have nothing to do with the trauma—can trigger the brain into thinking the trauma is still happening. The brain reacts by flooding a person with all the same feelings and emotions they felt when the trauma was taking place.

It occurred to her that the seemingly innocuous things, like getting the mail or leaving my car or crossing the threshold of my classroom, sounded an awful lot like the behaviors I'd developed because of that professor from graduate school I told her about. She wondered if I was experiencing PTSD, which would make sense, she thought, given that I'd lived under siege for quite a long time.

And maybe, she theorized, my mother's death, maybe everything surrounding it, including the awful treatment from my new colleagues, had triggered me. Maybe school and all that went with it—each time I arrived and had to go up the stairs to my office, willingly surrounding myself with these cruel colleagues each day, going in and out of classrooms when I'd once been afraid to do just this in graduate school—were triggering me, flooding my brain and my body with the same emotions I felt when the professor was stalking me. Maybe PTSD could explain my sudden fear, my repulsion, my sickness, regarding the mail, *especially* that sickness regarding the mail.

It would make sense, wouldn't it? He'd sent me so much mail, and eventually letters that were unmarked, mail I couldn't anticipate or prevent myself from opening because I didn't know they were from him. It was my comment about the mail, really, that helped her make the connection, she explained.

I should see someone who specialized in this, she urged. I wasn't crazy, I just needed to learn how to reconnect the part of my brain that had buried these experiences and memories to the rest of it. There were people who could help me learn how to talk myself through the dread and the flood of emotion, to tell myself I was safe, that my professor wasn't right around the corner, lurking, that I was okay. Eventually, she told me, I would stop feeling so out of control, so crazy, and I really would be fine again.

I did see someone, and it turned out my friend was right, I had PTSD.

And eventually I would be fine. I was fine and I am.

I never did tell my parents what happened, though. Not really.

Each one of them knew *something,* but neither one of them knew everything.

I remember a day when my father came to visit me in Vermont. My mother had already died; there was snow on the ground. We were walking back to his car after having lunch.

"Do you want to know more about what happened in graduate school?" I asked him.

He was aware of what "more" I meant. He knew I'd hired his friend, the lawyer, for something having to do with a professor.

"Do you want to tell me?" he asked back.

"No. I don't know. No," I said. "I guess not."

This was the truth. I didn't *really* want to tell him. But I worried I *should* tell him.

Shouldn't I?

We got in his car, drove off, and never spoke of it again.

The only thing I ever told my mother about was the letters. I'd called her up during that spring semester when they were still writing to each other. I'd decided to talk to her over the phone rather than on a visit to Rhode Island so she couldn't see my face. If I did this in person, she would have been able to read in my eyes that I was lying. Or, at least, that I wasn't telling her the whole truth. Only a slight sliver of it.

"Mom," I began, "I need to talk to you about Father L."

"What about him?"

"I need you to stop. Writing to him, I mean."

There was a long pause on the other end.

"Sweetheart," she said, "is something wrong?"

"No, no," I said. "Everything is fine! But can you do that for me? And can you tell me if he writes you again?"

"Ohh-kaaay?" She sounded hesitant. Doubtful.

I changed the subject. She didn't ask anything more. The conversation moved on, my breathing steadied again. I was through the worst of it, my mother mostly unscathed.

I don't know if my parents ever discussed that phone call about the letters, or if they talked about my getting a lawyer. I don't know if they spent time wondering what was happening to me, if they considered trying to sit down, the three of us, and make me tell them what was going on. Maybe they knew more than I realize. Maybe they guessed some of it. But aside from the occasional "Donna, are you *okay?*" asked with a certain tone, one that I knew was referring to this thing I was dealing with that we were not discussing out loud, they let the subject go.

We tiptoed around it from then on, so quietly the topic went completely unexamined. I think my parents could sense I was going through something serious during graduate school, but they never asked for specifics. I don't think it's that they didn't want to know, though maybe in a way they didn't. But they are very private people, of a different generation, far older than most of my friends' parents— my mother had me when she was thirty-three, which was considered ancient for someone of her generation to be having a child. But even more significant than my parents' age was the fact that they'd been raised by my immigrant grandparents during the Great Depression. They were of the mind-set that hardship was part of life, and your duty was to survive it, without much complaint. You didn't talk about it, you just plowed through everything until you got to the other side. There was no sense dwelling on it, since dwelling wouldn't get you past it.

I am certain they wanted to respect my privacy, that they assumed if things got too dire I would turn to them, as when I'd asked my father for the name of a lawyer.

As hardworking, good people who didn't talk about their problems, not even to each other, my parents raised me well, had faith in my judgment, and believed that they had a daughter who could hold her own and make good decisions. In a way, I think, it was their faith in me that allowed them to close their mouths and not press me for more. They felt they had a daughter with a good head on her shoulders, a capable person, and that I could handle whatever came at me, even if it was difficult.

I don't judge them for not asking. There was so much going on during that time, so much chaos in the house because of my mother's cancer, my grandmother's Alzheimer's, so much sadness and fear, that what I was going through seemed to pale in comparison. I didn't have cancer, I wasn't dying. I would get through this, like I'd gotten through everything before it.

But sometimes now, looking back, I see the gulf this created between me and my family, one that I couldn't figure out how to bridge, one that I eventually didn't want to bridge because I was desperate to forget, to move on, to pretend that what happened never happened. I got used to standing there on the other side, alone, while we all agreed not to notice the chasm that was spreading out between us.

PART FOUR

25

The aftermath of sexual harassment is quiet.

You learn quickly not to speak about it, not to say anything, because it makes other people uncomfortable. No one knows what to say to you, how to fix things, what might help. It makes people uneasy to know that this thing happened to you, this strange, ugly thing they don't know how to remedy. So, to not make anyone else feel awkward, you don't tell people, you don't tell anyone at all.

Soon, you are alone in it, you are alone with it, for years.

So, the aftermath of what I went through is also lonely.

Even now, decades later, I still don't have a handle on how to tell the story of *my harasser, my stalker,* as I have learned to refer to him, to call him and call it (my story), as though he's something I acquired or earned, like my PhD or my job. I like to forget that he exists, that he is a part of my history that I can't shake off no matter what I do. On the rare occasion when I do tell someone, a friend, a confidant, I realize I still haven't figured out how to tell it, that I haven't mastered this story yet. The means to tell it with grace and confidence still eludes me, despite the fact that it happened so many years ago and despite the fact that *I am a storyteller by profession.* It has become my professional responsibility and duty to tell stories and tell them well.

When I do try to give voice to this part of my past, I realize I am not only terrible at telling it, but I get lost in the telling. It's like a labyrinth that pulls me in and confuses my brain. There is so much of it, *so much story,* and so many things that he did because he was so creative at stalking me, that I have yet to master the part of being the stalkee. There are so many twists and turns and gotchas in the story that they are a maze I can't find my way through, a maze that takes me in and messes me up all over again, never letting me out. There are so many details—and it never suffices to share just one, like the biggest among them: *I was sexually harassed once, stalked, really, by my mentor, for a couple of years.* If only I could stop with this central detail, the fact of the stalking, the harassment, but I cannot. One detail begets another and another, and as soon as one detail is out, the rest want to follow. I don't know how to end the story, because it is seemingly endless. I don't know how to get out of the labyrinth of details once the first one has fallen from my lips. I can't stop them, just like I could not stop him.

The sheer piling up of details has a purpose: my need to prove to the listener that I wasn't imagining things, that I didn't, couldn't have misinterpreted my professor's behavior, that I didn't make any of this up, that anyone would have eventually realized that something was wrong with behavior like his. *Right?* One terrible detail isn't enough to prove I was a victim. I need hundreds or no one will believe me, will think I made a big deal out of nothing. My self-doubt still, after so many years, pulls me under and overwhelms me. My self-doubt and my shame are still that profound, my worry, my fear that what happened was because of something I did. I am my own best and loudest victim-blamer. I am the first person to blame myself and I invite anyone I tell to blame me, too.

But is there such a thing as trauma without shame? Isn't shame an integral part of what causes an event or series of events to become a trauma?

Back then, during graduate school, I believed I must be the only person to whom something like this could happen. I don't mean that I thought myself special or unique in a positive way, like I had been lifted up and singled out for this attention. I mean it in that terrible, shameful way, where I felt that somehow I was being punished, that there was something about me that had attracted this unwanted attention, that I had lured him. I was unique only in that I'd done something particular, expressly to attract him. I'd given him a signal by accident that brought this experience to my doorstep. I was, am, unique only in that the stalking was somehow, at its foundation, my fault.

And yet, I am not some shrinking violet either.

I am fierce, I am outspoken, I am intelligent, I fight back, I am a flirt, I am sexually confident, I go after things, I am strong, I am my mother's daughter.

I am all of these things, even though I am also someone who suffered this other thing, and everything that went with it. I don't quite know how to reconcile all that I am in relation to this one ugly part. But both things are true. I am a force to reckon with, ask any of my friends, and I was broken by this, and my friends could tell you that, too.

My friend the psychologist talks about *but* versus *and* with respect to the specific language women use to describe their struggles with motherhood. Women will say things like "I love my baby, *but* my baby drives me crazy" and "I love being a mother, *but* I am also terribly depressed because I am a mother." She talks to clients about replacing the word *but* with *and,* about how two seemingly opposing things can be held in tension, that they need to be held in tension. A woman can love her baby *and* be driven crazy by that baby. A woman can love being a mother *and* be terribly depressed about being a mother.

In that same vein, I am fierce, *and* I am polite. I am strong, *and* I am vulnerable. I want things, *and* sometimes I don't want things. I am a good judge of people, *and* sometimes I am too trusting. I am an ardent, insightful, committed feminist, *and* I let the patriarchy walk all over me.

And I still blame myself when I look for the reason for what happened to me. I still search for that reason by looking within myself.

What is wrong with me, what failure was there in my upbringing, what shortcoming in my character, what crack in my self-understanding, my sanity, what thing or things did I do to cause this man to prey on me, specifically? What about *me* turned him in my direction? What about *me* made me tolerate something so palpably repulsive for so long? What amount of stupidity in a person is necessary for them to not see that *they themselves* are the offense, in the eyes of officials? How dumb does a girl have to be to fail to see the truth before her own eyes?

I know, intellectually, rationally, that I should be shifting the blame somewhere other than me. I know, with everything I am, that if someone stood in front of me and tried to blame my mother for what happened, blame the way she raised me, the way she taught me right and wrong, I would scream at them in a rage for blaspheming against her. But I know, too, that if this same person insinuated, even suggested outright, that I was to blame, at least partly or even completely, I would likely be willing to concede their points, to accept their arguments. To nod my head and agree that yes, yes, everything that happened, all that I've recounted here, is completely and totally my fault. That's probably right, yes.

Because I am both a survivor *and* still a victim, and somehow I will always and forever be both.

26

I never heard from him again.

Not directly.

I hear from him all the time from the place he came to occupy inside my body, inside my brain. My brain chemistry changed to accommodate his actions and my reactions to them. The change seems permanent. I've worked hard to switch my brain back to the way it once was, undivided, but so far my success has been limited.

His behavior stopped a full year and three months *after* I made that December phone call, pleading with him to go away. The letters, the lurking, the contact with my mother, the peering, the popping up and out in hallways and stairwells, the constant phone calls, all of it finally came to a halt. I'd grown to believe I'd never be free, and then I was.

I celebrated with Dan. We went to dinner because I wanted to mark the precise moment when I got to move on and forget all of this ugly business. It was a fancy dinner.

I remember I ordered duck—it was expensive, and it was the first time I'd ever eaten it. I believed I would now live as though none of it ever happened. I drew a clear line around it, around myself, and then I stepped over it, out of the circle, believing it contained, imprisoned, never to emerge again. I put up fences and walls and barbed wire, hired a guard to defend the rest should it try to escape. I acted and lived as though this part of my life never existed, immersed myself in my studies and went to conferences. It was blissful, truly blissful, for a while.

I had help.

Dr. H. worked on my behalf while he was still alive, forcing Father L. away from me during the last year of my studies, after he returned from his sabbatical. Father L. was forbidden to attend my graduation. My family would be there, and Dr. H. ensured I would be able to enjoy the ceremony in peace, assured I wouldn't even catch a glimpse of him, because he was banished from campus that day.

But still, he existed, unfortunately, and there were moments when I did catch sight of him, when I glimpsed him scurrying down a hallway or walking out of the building. There was also the problem of conferences— conferences I would attend because it was important for me to attend them, to present papers to establish myself in my field, which was *his* field. Dan acted as a one-man advance team, checking out rooms before I entered them, doing a sweep of a reception or panel, making sure I could safely walk inside the door.

It's not as though I asked Dan to do this, and we didn't plan that he'd do this—it's just what he did, instinctively, because he is a good person, a true friend. Most of the time, we didn't acknowledge this man's existence or his presence at the conference. Dan did his work silently and invisibly. And when it was discussed, it was done so only cryptically.

"Let's not go to that reception now," he'd say. "Let's wait thirty minutes and then go."

Or, "Why don't you come with me to this other talk instead?"

Or, "Maybe we should leave the book fair and get lunch?" he'd ask. "I'm hungry."

"Oh, sure," I would answer. "Okay, great."

And that was that.

The moments when I did catch sight of him, or ran into him at a conference because Dan wasn't there to steer me away from the confrontation, were the same moments I realized I had not moved on. My whole body would flush, my skin hot and crawling, my vision blurred, heart pounding, the blood rushing in my ears, head dizzy. The reaction was physical, and it was total.

The worst was in Miami.

It was June, the conference was small, maybe a few hundred people, with keynote lectures peppered throughout the schedule. For those, everyone would gather in the same hall to listen. Some colleagues and I headed off to lunch after the morning session ended. There was a group of maybe ten of us. We stepped out into the heat and the sun, startling after the cold, stale air of the conference hotel. I was in a good mood, it was hot and the warmth felt wonderful. I was walking along, chatting, letting the swirling sea of conference-goers set the pace, people out in search of a place to eat in the welcoming weather. Our group came to a stop at a red light, and we waited for the signal to cross. I was engrossed in a conversation and wasn't paying attention to the other people around us.

Then I glanced at the walk sign to see if it had turned, and I saw him.

He was standing right in front of me, close enough to touch, not even a foot away, the closest I'd been to him since the very last time I saw him, at my graduate school. He was facing front, but he knew I was there, knew I was right behind him. He was watching me, head angled just enough so he could see me.

The world tilted, I saw stars, I began to hyperventilate.

The light went from red to green, people began to cross, he didn't move.

At first, neither did I.

Then, without thinking, I walked away from the crowd, away from my group, away from him, onto the grass of a small park next to the sidewalk. I didn't even know what I was doing, didn't think of how I'd appear to the colleagues I was with, I just knew I wanted to get away, away, *away*, and immediately. No one else there had any idea about him and me, our history. To those colleagues, this man was an esteemed scholar, someone they admired, someone to revere, someone with whom they might try to strike up a conversation. Even invite him to come to lunch with us.

I sat down in the grass.

Strange looks were sent my way. There was some uncertainty about what to do among my colleagues, about why in the world I was sitting on the lawn in my conference attire, in my high-heeled sandals and my long, flowing summer dress, probably getting grass stains; about why I was flushed and panting. The friend I'd been talking to, a woman colleague from Minnesota, told everyone to go on without us, and she came over.

She got down on the grass with me. "What's wrong, what can I do, can I get you some water?"

I shook my head. He was still standing on the corner, not looking at me, but not going anywhere. I couldn't swallow, I couldn't speak. Worst of all, I was humiliated. I was so, so mortified. How could I possibly explain what

I was doing, and eventually what I had done, when I saw those colleagues again? I was acting like a maniac in the middle of a professional meeting. More and more people were streaming out of the hotel doors and onto the street on their way to lunch, passing by us, glancing at the two dressed-up women sitting in the grass, complete with conference badges dangling from our necks. Some of these people knew who I was, knew who she was. I don't know what they were thinking, but it couldn't have been good.

Meanwhile, he finally moved on. He made his way down the street and around the corner until he disappeared from view.

"Oh my God," I was saying to the woman with me in the grass, "oh my God, I'm so embarrassed, I'm so embarrassed." I was still panting, I thought I might pass out. "I don't think I can move."

My friend was kind, she didn't ask too many questions, didn't pry, other than about my well-being, about helping me find my way back to a sense of calm and safety. We ended up going to lunch, just the two of us, and she talked and talked about all sorts of things, anything other than what had happened. The conference presentations, the feminist theory we were both teaching in our work, some projects she was planning on doing, on writing. She got me water and made me drink it, then got me a glass of wine from the waitress without asking me if I wanted or needed one. She got herself one, too, and the two of us drank them down before we returned to the hotel for the afternoon sessions.

"I'm not sure I can go back there," I told her.

I was so angry at myself. I hadn't known he was attending the conference. I hadn't looked, hadn't checked the roster of participants before I got on the plane, which wasn't like me. This was what I got, wasn't it? I let my guard down, didn't do my homework, and this was my punishment.

"I'll be right with you," my friend said. "You just tell me if you need to go and we'll go somewhere together."

People can be so kind.

People like my all-male colleagues at my first teaching job could be so cruel, that is also true. But plenty of people are generous and understanding. That much I've learned from dealing with this strange affliction I've never quite known how to tell anyone about. I was grateful for this woman's unquestioning willingness to be by my side and help if necessary, without requiring an explanation.

The rest of the conference was a miserable trial. I couldn't get ahold of myself. I couldn't banish him from the forefront of my mind and go back to enjoying being there. The conference was too small for that. In the lobby of the hotel, where everyone was milling about between panel sessions and keynotes, I was now on high alert, glancing around frantically, scared he'd pop up again when I least expected him, certain he'd be watching me from across the room or from behind a plant. I couldn't come down from my panic. It was a ledge, and I was chained to it for the duration.

I was so defeated. I was so angry at myself, I was a failure all over again. I'd wanted to forget, to stop caring, to overcome the jumble of emotions that would assault me whenever I allowed myself to think of him, when I tried to reckon with his presence in my brain and body, and still I couldn't. And maybe I never would. I was angry at him, too, I was enraged by his existence, my hatred for him bubbling to the surface of my being. But I was forced to reckon with the reality that he still made me fearful and repulsed, that I was still a scared little girl in the face of the situation I'd gotten myself into, that he'd *put* me into.

At that Miami conference I was right back where I was in graduate school, as though everything were happening all over again.

Why, why, why was I still so afraid of him? Why couldn't I see him for what he was—a pathetic, physically harmless mouse of a man? Why did he cause me to react this way after so many years had passed? Why couldn't I be stronger, more courageous, the brave young woman I often understood myself to be, that others did, too? Why did I let him get to me so totally? Why? Why me? Why did he pick *me?*

And that is the question that I couldn't seem to shake, that I would always come back to—that I still come back to—why *me?* What did I do to make him pick *me?*

I'd gone to the conference as myself, as the feminist professor who wore heels and lovely long dresses, who was put together and accomplished, and in the span of a single moment she vanished and I became a nervous, confused, insecure girl, who saw the foolhardiness in her attire, in her self-presentation to the world, in her attention-grabbing outfits that were capable of grabbing the wrong attention, that were practically screaming for the wrong attention.

That was about ten years ago.

I haven't seen him since.

After that Miami conference I stopped going to meetings in my field. I dropped out of my field altogether and moved on to other things, other subjects of inquiry. A different profession entirely. I let go of being the professor I'd always wanted to be. My dream as I'd envisioned it was dead.

27

There is a way in which this man broke my heart.
Maybe he would be happy to know that. Maybe
it would make him feel good to realize that he did, indeed, work his way into my heart in such a manner that
he could shatter it. But he didn't break my heart in a romantic sense. He broke the heart in me that had turned
itself completely toward the end of becoming a professor,
my truest desire. I trusted him to respect this desire,
trusted him automatically because of his role as professor,
as my mentor. Because of that trust, my consent to just
about everything he asked, at first, was total and unwa-
vering. He represented my heart's desire, and I wanted
what he had.

Consent and trust go hand in hand. To say yes to someone is also to communicate "I trust you." I trust *you*, this
person to whom I am saying yes, to consider my well-
being, my happiness, my pleasure, my vulnerabilities, my
value and my worth, my desires, my interest, my likes and

dislikes, my boundaries, my limits, the heart in my body that hopes and yearns and dreams.

We are consenting to people constantly, to our friends and to our loved ones, to acquaintances and to co-workers and even to people minding the cash register at a store. To reduce consent to something relevant only to sexual situations is misguided and wrong. It's to misunderstand the complexity of consent, its role and constancy in the everyday of our lives.

Consent is our default mode of operations.

Our lives are generally tuned to consent, and it hums as we move about the world like soft radio static, a buzz underneath everything we do and all the people with whom we spend our time. This default mode of consent changes only when we get into situations of sexual intimacy (and sometimes not even then), situations of sexual and romantic relevance. Only then do we start constructing walls to block a person from reaching us, often from literally reaching us, physically, bodily. Only then does consent become an act of which we become self-aware because the rest of the time our consent is unconscious. It is "ready-to-hand," as Heidegger might say.

I loved Heidegger as an undergraduate. I loved most of all his concepts of "ready-to-hand" and "present-at-hand," concepts I've gone back to repeatedly over the course of my intellectual life, because they seem to apply to just about everything.

For Heidegger, things are generally ready-to-hand and become present-at-hand only when we are forced to notice them. Ready-to-hand things are ones we don't have to worry about because they are performing their everyday functions without fail. For example, a door is typically ready-to-hand. We walk up to a door, we go through it without noticing what we are doing, without thinking much about the door, as though we don't even see the door. The door becomes present-at-hand only if, when we are trying to get through it, we grasp the handle and it falls off, and we can't use the door as expected. We are forced to reckon with the door, to notice its existence, to figure out why it stopped functioning, so we can fix it and return to not worrying about it anymore.

For Heidegger, our "being" is typically ready-to-hand, too; we don't think much about the fact of it, about how our being functions and goes about the world. But when our being becomes present-at-hand, suddenly everything we are, that we know, that we believe, our understanding of how to exist, is called into question; suddenly we need to think about the fact of our existence, deal with it, and this can be paralyzing. Much like the door that is broken and stands in our way of moving through space, our being becomes broken, and we must attend to it or else remain stuck, treading water, unable to go anywhere, do anything, or find meaning in our own existence.

Consent, the concept of it, has become present-at-hand for all of us, recently.

We're not sure, anymore, as a society, a culture, what consent is and isn't, where it belongs and where it doesn't. Who controls it and who has the most power over it and whether we can get that power back, distribute it more equitably. We need to figure out its function, what's gone wrong with it, so wrong we can't stop talking about it, debating what it is and isn't.

For me, consent with my professor broke down, like the door handle that stops working. Consent became present-at-hand, it became the only thing I thought about, the substance and heartbeat of my every move and action during those years when he refused to stop seeking me out. Consent no longer was effortless but was my every effort and momentary concern. Consent and its opposite were all I knew. And in the confusion and the loss of it, my being broke down, too.

We cannot sanitize every comment, every come-on, every gesture in our efforts to stamp out harassment and assault. We cannot sanitize all of our spaces, we cannot make them irrefutably safe from words and acts and behaviors. We are humans, and our emotions and desires make us into complicated creatures. Sometimes we are nervous and awkward. We misjudge and we make mistakes and we dream of things that will not happen, of people we want to be with who will not want to be with us. We muster our courage and go for someone who seems unattainable to see if, by some miracle, it turns out they like us back, and this is not a crime.

But we can certainly do a better job of teaching people how to understand romantic feelings, how to read signals, how to back off when someone says no, how not to keep pursuing someone when they have rejected us, about what is appropriate and what is inappropriate in certain contexts, in professional and educational circumstances. We must become better thinkers—*critical* thinkers—about this aspect of our lives, better communicators on every level with respect to consent and non-consent. We may not want consent to be present-at-hand forever, but we should not want consent to go back to being invisible, so invisible that we don't notice its function, that we don't care or refuse to care or even see when it has been ignored, disregarded, when this disregard has caused someone else to suffer, to become traumatized, when it has changed her life forever.

And yet I also know, *deep down to my core,* that when I began to say to my professor, clearly and loudly and forcefully, no, he blocked out my no. He became an Olympic champion at refusing to hear my no. I said no at every turn, I said it in so many different ways, I tried every no I could think of—nos using words, nos using actions, nos of silence, of avoidance, of not showing up when I said I would. Kindly nos, mean-spirited nos, angry and frustrated and exasperated nos, careful, sweet, and understanding nos, nos with a great deal of explanation and justification, nos that I would use for a man who was hitting on me at a bar. But it didn't matter how or under what circumstances I said these nos. He was unable, or refused, to hear and accept them.

I do not believe that a Title IX training at his university, or the kind of trainings people are devising at colleges all over and at businesses and stores and every possible place of employment to combat harassment and assault, would have changed him or stopped him from what he did to me. I just don't believe it. I don't think that a national conversation about consent would have made this man realize what he was doing to me. I don't believe that any effort would have prevented him from being unable to hear or respect the word *no*, unable to read any signals from the person who'd become the object of his desire. I think people like him will always work to justify and rationalize what they're doing, no matter what it is or how awful the effect. I think some people are beyond our reach to educate, that *he* was beyond reach. I believe that some people are beyond hearing, beyond listening, beyond teaching. To teach him, to make him understand, would require far greater change than we can possibly expect from all of our trainings and our national conversations. That kind of conversation doesn't exist, not yet, and maybe not ever. It might require a miracle, or magic. There always will be people like him, and that is one of the unfortunate facts of reality. And an enduring, unfortunate fact of my reality is that I happened to run into someone like him, and he happened to turn his gaze on me and refused to look elsewhere once he had.

What we *can* change, what we *must*, are the people around him, people like Tootsie, people like that awful provost, the attitude of a university, a workplace, a corporation, that works to protect the bosses, the company, the college's reputation, the football team's reputation, over and above and beyond any concern whatsoever for the person whose consent was disregarded so completely and totally that she will suffer for the rest of her life.

Looking back, I would have been so grateful for anyone and anything that could have protected me from what I endured. I wish someone could have prevented what happened to me.

Maybe I'd be different, happier, less anxious, less existentially dark, had I not spent years dodging a professor's convoluted overtures. Maybe I'd have a better professional life, maybe things would have been less rocky and today I would be a traditional, tenured professor instead of a nontenured, nontraditional one. But then, maybe I never would have lived that glorious intellectual awakening at Georgetown if I had been prevented from being the way that I was with my other professors, if I had been warned against becoming close to them, or if *they* had been trained not to take an interest in my life, dissuaded from communicating to me that I mattered, that I was more than just another student to them, convinced by their institutions that letting me know such things could put all of us in jeopardy. Maybe I never would have discovered the academic joy that has defined and inspired me to do things I never dreamed of doing as a kid, read Hegel and Heidegger and Nietzsche and Kant and Gadamer and believed myself completely capable of such achievements, become a writer of books, of novels, a person who stands up in front of a room of thousands of people and talks about her research.

I am certain, so certain, that the behavior of most of us, the bits of effort on our parts to reach out, to get to know each other, our students, the children in our lives, the co-workers who are new and inspiring, the ways we try to help and connect, professionally or personally—efforts I have made myself with my own students over the years— are vastly different from a series of *three thousand efforts and comments and invitations* from one professor to one single student, a student who is pleading, "No more, please, no more." Enough comments and compliments and efforts to pry and possess that they piled all the way to the ceiling of my Georgetown apartment, surpassing the roof and climbing toward the sky like droplets of water, rising to the heavens to form heavy clouds overhead.

28

I have always loved going home.

Rhode Island, it's in my bones, it calls to me, wraps its sandy, briny arms around me and holds me close, whispers to me in its vulgar accent, and I relax. I love it with all my heart, I love its twice-convicted felon, the former mayor of Providence, that it's always up-and-coming yet never quite seems to arrive. Rhode Island flows through me like the ocean that borders every nook and cranny, every edge of it. Its people are my people, or at least the people I grew up with are, a mix of working-class kids with a few summer residents thrown in, most of whom were working class, too, because it used to be that way in Rhode Island—you could "summer" down in Narragansett if you lived in the city by renting, or buying if you were lucky, a falling-down beach shack.

Rhode Island, its beaches, those kids, my parents raising me there, gave me the kind of childhood that people get nostalgic about in movies and television series, full of roaming the woods, building forts, combing construction sites for discoveries, and most of all, endless days on the sand building dribble castles, collecting sea glass, searching tide pools for hermit crabs and other treasures we would carefully place in our pails so we could pretend they were our pets for a while, until our mothers made us return them to the sea. My summer nights were filled with flashlight tag, kick the can, capture the flag, and ghost in the graveyard.

Leaving home for college, leaving Rhode Island, this place where I was happy, was difficult, but I also couldn't wait. My brain, my mind, yanked me away, my questions pulling me elsewhere. But my heart and my body also wished to root themselves forever where I'd grown up.

The only other person I was close to who also left Rhode Island for college was my childhood best friend. We'd met in second grade, and by high school we were inseparable. We were valedictorian and salutatorian of our class, and we gave our speech together onstage at graduation. The *Providence Journal* came to interview us, the best friends who were number one and number two. It is one of my favorite memories.

But I think she, like me, could feel how this marked us among our friends. We were still *theirs*, we were a part of things, the hanging out, the parties in the sand dunes, the going off to hockey games and dances, but we were also *not theirs*, too. We were smart in a way that would take us places, that would take us *elsewhere*, whereas most of our friends weren't going anywhere—and they didn't, certainly not out of state. The price of our intellects and the pursuit of an education was *them*, or at least the ways we were with them before she and I left.

It was the same thing with my parents. They wanted for me what they never got—opportunity, the kind of education that would take me places, that would change my life and financial circumstances. They worked their entire lives to give this to me and then suddenly I had it, just as they wanted, but there was a price. Richard Rodriguez, one of my favorite essayists, talks of how an education can separate a family when parents work to give a child what they never had. He writes of how much his parents wanted him to learn perfect English, which he did but in the process lost his ability to speak to them, since they spoke Spanish. There was an uncrossable distance that grew between them.

My parents opened the doors that eventually made me valedictorian and that eventually got me into Georgetown, and Georgetown opened the door to things they couldn't have dreamed of for me because they didn't have the language, the academic vocabulary, the experience, to comprehend them. Georgetown opened the door to my PhD, and it was a long time—too long, I think—before I was self-aware enough to comprehend the relational cost of this pursuit, of the ways my education turned me into a person my parents no longer could understand very well, or knew how to talk to anymore, whose new dreams were foreign and strange, almost incomprehensible. Pursuing my educational dreams made me into a person who turned her back on where she was from, its people, her family, arrogantly so, condescendingly so. It shames me to think about it. For a long time, it didn't occur to me that I might want to go back someday, that I might need to, that my circumstances might change and I would require the shelter of both the place and family where I grew up, the safety of an earlier time, the familiarity and security of it.

So, there is a way in which my PhD cost me a sense of place, and the place itself, Rhode Island, a home where I could settle, the family I once had before I left them to go away, planning to never return.

And then *his* part in all of it cost me the other place I'd hoped to someday call home, that I believed was my rightful home, the academy, the university that would welcome me with open arms and take me into its intellectual embrace, that I assumed would do this because I was worthy, and then it didn't.

But lucky for me, Rhode Island, and my family—unlike the university that never fully opened its arms for me, not truly—always welcome me back.

Today, I am half professor, half not. I live in the place between, hovering in that liminal space of being a part of yet not being a part of something, of my profession. He put me there, in this no-woman's-land, the same territory where so many women in my situation have come to dwell.

We are unable to be a part of our chosen profession because of abusive men, because we were paid to go quietly, because once we are paid to go, we no longer hold the resources to go elsewhere. We lose our recommendation letters, our letters of reference, the support of our colleagues. We either risk becoming the sources of rumor or our secret makes it impossible to justify our search for another job. We are left with the choice of outing our history and scaring our interviewers, resulting in not getting hired anyway, breaking our silence and legal commitments, or we stay quiet, allowing our interviewers to suspect the worst possible reasons for our lack of the right references. For why we are in the job market at all.

I had idyllic notions about the university, all universities, about being a part of academia, about one day living the storied life of the college professor. The university is the magical castle of the bookworm, the enchanted fairyland of bespectacled youth. Georgetown, my undergrad, preserved those notions, then grad school destroyed them.

One man held the wrecking ball at just the right angle, then a group of administrators swung that wrecking ball with all the force it had straight into me.

As a sometime professor now, I still hold these fantasies, these ideals, about the university. I hang on to them tightly, refusing to let go. For one, I still want them to be mine someday. But for another, I still believe in the university as an institution, as a beacon of hope and a force for good in the world. Maybe that makes me stupid, but I am unwilling to give this up. Universities were, are, my home. Though if this is really true, then today, I suppose, I am homeless.

I am still Catholic. But it, too, is a sometimes painful, restless part of my identity.

I never learned to love the mass, not even after I studied the liturgy and its history in graduate school. I learned to appreciate the ritual of it, the notion that it was like a portal, a door we could enter when we wanted to move from the profane into the sacred, to hover near God, that the mass itself was a liminal space, liminal like me, a place where you could move between worlds. I learned to love the idea of the Eucharist, its social-justice underpinnings, that Catholics took the body of Christ each week as a reminder that we are all one body and that as one body, if a part of the body is sick and in need, then we, as a people, are called to heal the wounded part of us. There are so many things I learned to appreciate, but in the end, they were all intellectual, and when I tried to go back to mass and soak it up like my mother did, to love it like she did, I couldn't. I always found it as boring as ever, as boring as when I was in the first grade and would fidget endlessly in the pew alongside my family, desperate for the homily to be over, anxiously awaiting communion, which for me signaled that mass was almost done, we would be leaving soon, and nothing deeper.

Then my grandmother died, and my mother shortly afterward.

One day, in Brooklyn, where I live now, I went to Sunday mass because I'd recently met the priest who oversaw the parish across the street from my apartment. I told him I'd go, so I went, and I was surprised. I loved the mass that day in a way that I never had before, in a way I'd always wanted to love it but never could. It wasn't because of anything the priest said, and in truth I have no idea what he spoke about for the homily or even the readings for that moment in the liturgical calendar. What I loved was that my mother and my grandmother were suddenly there with me.

The mass had given them back to me for the precious hour I sat in that little church, listening, reciting the prayers. The ritual had finally performed its magic, become a portal for me to enter a space where I could dwell for a few moments in the company of my mother and grandmother as though we were all still together. My mother always told me she thought the mass was beautiful because of the unseen things it could evoke, because it allowed us to be in the presence of the communion of saints, how she could feel them there whenever she went. I never understood what she meant until that moment, until the words and the ritual of the mass, a ritual I knew by heart, had transported me to that place she'd told me about, and I found her there when I arrived. The Catholic mass had given me my mother back, my grandmother back, too, and from that day onward it always has.

Every time I go to mass now, I can hear them with me, saying those words, because I heard them next to me doing just this for so many years as a child and then as a young adult.

Nothing, no one, can ever take that from me. Not a cardinal or a bishop. Not even Father L. Especially not him.

It was a gift from the women of my family, and as long as the mass exists, I will always have it, cherish it. I am grateful for it. To me, it is grace.

There is a defiance rooted in my choice to remain Catholic, too.

I have joked with my students about how if the Catholic Church is a big house with a yard, I am usually somewhere on the porch, swinging in a hammock, or standing on the lawn—not fitting snugly inside, but definitely still on the premises. I also tell them that sometimes I am just across the street, picketing, or heckling the men of the hierarchy on their way in and out of the front door.

A big part of my Catholic identity resides in refusal—my refusal to go away, my refusal to stop being Catholic despite the inexcusable ways I've been treated by bishops and cardinals and the other men who rule this tradition. It isn't only Father L. who put me in their crosshairs. My work about sex and consent on campus has made some men within the hierarchy angry at and fearful of me.

But I remain Catholic also because I am Italian and I am Portuguese, because my mother and grandmother and father passed on this tradition to me as a tradition of my family, all the saints and the Sunday meals and the masses, and I am unwilling to let this go. I am unwilling to let someone take this from me, steal it from me, wrest it from my arms. Doing so is akin to letting someone rob me of my mother and grandmother, the memories I have of my family as a child. Letting go of Catholicism would require me to let go of them, and I simply will not.

And then, Catholicism to me does not equal the silly, pathetic, corrupt, and shortsighted men who rule it. At the heart of this tradition are people like Dr. H. and the many nuns I've known and loved throughout my life, that professor-priest who was slow like a turtle but quick to smile and laugh. It's my mother, who was a devoted Catholic until the day she died, and her Catholic colleagues who donated their vacation days to ensure she could take the year off, and it's the Jesuits I grew to admire at Georgetown. They are Catholic, too. And I am Catholic like them.

29

Around once a year I google him.

It's a strange thing—to realize I can search for him. Despite a world where everyone, all the time, is googling everyone else—where it is so easy to type a person's name in the search bar and find out everything they've ever done, find information you've never dreamed of finding—it almost never occurs to me to google him. Well, it occurs to me only that I could, if I wanted to. Some of this has to do with my detachment from social media and all things online, my inherent resistance to them, which is also due to him. And then, I still mostly go through the world as though he doesn't exist, because I don't want to give him that much power over me. When I open the vault door in my brain and allow myself to peer inside that space, sometimes it is difficult for me to figure out: What is mine, and what is his? What in my life is exclusively of my own making, and which things has he influenced, permeated? This is a difficult question with which to live, so I do my best not to dwell on it. I also avoid thinking about the possibility that this man might google *me,* that I am quite googleable, unfortunately, despite my attempts to not be. I try to imagine that he has never googled me, not once. That it would never occur to him to type my first and last name into the search bar. And maybe he never has.

Decades later, he does feel far from my life for the most part—until the moments when it suddenly feels like what happened was yesterday. Or when the mail piles up in my mailbox if my husband is away, or when the stack of letters with my name on it is teetering dangerously on the kitchen table. I have mostly worked through my aversion to the mailbox. I can go to the mailbox without wanting to vomit, but I still avoid what is a simple, daily act for most people.

The last time I did google him, I felt incredible dread— dread that he might be dead.

You would think I would feel the opposite, that I would want him to be dead, that I would rejoice at this information if I should happen upon it. I thought it strange myself that, when I typed him into Google and waited to see what came up, it occurred to me that his obituary might appear—and how much the possibility upset me. He is old by now, after all. It took me a few days of struggling to understand why I didn't want him dead to realize the reason behind this worry—especially since I used to wish him dead all the time, wished he would die a painful death back when he was writing my mother and he was teaching her letters to my peers in his classes.

The reason I dread his death is because I have things I want to say to him, things I'd like to tell him before he dies. Things I'd like him to know. And if he dies before I do this, I will have lost my opportunity forever.

★ ★ ★

No one ever said they were sorry.

Not my university, not the Catholic Church, and certainly not him.

I wanted him to say it, most of all.

"Don-*na*, I'm sorry for what I did to you."

I wouldn't care if he did it in that singsong, scolding tone of his. I would care only that he would have finally acknowledged what he did do, that he did *something*.

The fact that there was never any *sorry*, any apology, any acknowledgment that something had indeed happened to me, something out of my control, something that someone should have tried to stop, him ideally, the school eventually, once I told them—this kills me to think about now that I am older. That the only response I got was a demand that I pretend none of this ever happened, that I never speak of it again, had the effect of making me doubt that anything of substance did actually occur.

I understand that universities, the Catholic Church, wanted to—still want to—avoid any and all acknowledgment of wrongdoing; that they believe if they say they are sorry, if they offer an apology to a victim, this is an admission of guilt, an affirmation that something wrong happened, something that may even be considered criminal. I get that institutions want to protect themselves, that this is always their interest in situations like mine—to silence the victim, to force the victim to sign away her life in exchange for something like help, at the very moment when she is at her most vulnerable and desperate and will do anything for that help, even the tiniest bit. But it is an act of cruelty visited upon this person, a young woman who has just started on her way, who is at the very beginning of her professional life; an act that will hobble her for decades to come, this compelling her to pretend that all that she lived never occurred.

I wanted an apology from Tootsie, too. I wanted her to look me in the face and admit what she did, lying to me all those months, letting the statute of limitations run out, never telling me that our first conversation started a clock, hoping I wouldn't know that it had, realizing that every day that passed from then on I was wasting time, I was giving away all my rights.

Maybe Tootsie wanted to say she was sorry but couldn't. Maybe they wouldn't let Father L. apologize to me either. Maybe my school told him he wasn't allowed. That the agreement we all struck together—me, Tootsie, the university, him, the Catholic Church—was so strict and binding that even private apologies were forbidden, any and all acts of contrition. That even though he was a man who could oversee the sacraments, including confession, he was not allowed to confess himself. Maybe they said it would be unbecoming for a man with his professional stature, a man who was a priest, to admit he had forsaken one of his vows, that he had hurt another person, a young girl. Maybe he thought about contacting me to say words of apology. Maybe he wished he could. Maybe he's gone to sleep nightly during the last two decades wanting to get this off his chest, wanting to ask my forgiveness.

But I also wonder what he would say, today, if I asked him what happened all those years ago. Would he know that what he did was wrong? Would he realize how totally and completely he traumatized me? How much his behavior terrorized me, hurt me, ruined me for a while? Does he feel any remorse? Or does he think it was all a misunderstanding on my part? A friendship gone awry?

He must have known the Church would cover for him. I mean, did all priests know this at the time? Did he think he was unlike his abuser colleagues because he didn't rape me? Because I wasn't a twelve-year-old boy?

He was powerful enough to know that the Church was moving people around. Maybe he thought he was being clever by not touching me. Maybe he knew that he was the untouchable one.

If you asked him today what happened between us, I wouldn't be surprised if he said it was all my fault, that he was just trying to be a good friend to me, that he was just trying to help me with my career. Maybe over the last two decades he has convinced himself that this is the real truth. Or maybe he didn't have to work that hard to convince himself. Maybe he believed this was the truth all along.

"Don-*na*," he might say, "*you* were the one who was terrible to me."

It's also true that lately I've been *hoping* that he might realize what labels apply to his person because sexual harassment and assault have been in the news so constantly, so everywhere we turn. I've been wondering if now, today, he might be able to name himself as the perpetrator in the situation that was ours.

And then, in this particular moment in our nation, I've also wondered whether, if this professor's behavior had been happening right now, in this Title IX, consent-education-centric era of the university, would *I* have known to tell someone sooner? In this post-Catholic-abuse-scandal era, would *I* have been able to name his actions as inappropriate much sooner than I did?

One would hope. But I don't know.

It's not like I can go back and do everything over, do everything differently. I'm sure so many women wish they could go back and change what they did. Tell someone sooner—far sooner. For their own sake and that of others who would come afterward.

Were there others after me?

Were there others before me, too?

★ ★ ★

To this day I don't know if he was a kindly man, benign even in his stalking of me, a victim of circumstances that stunted his knowledge of love and sex, so much that he was powerless to understand his feelings for me and the way he expressed them. Or if he was a calculating monster who knew exactly what he was doing the entire time. Sometimes when I think of him, he is an evil little thing, hunched over, eyes gleaming red, demonlike, his mouth twisted into a sneer. But sometimes when I think of him, he is a sad little old man, lonely, frail, a being who has always been unloved, unloved in a real way, at least, who has never felt the connection he obviously so desired with me. In that version of him, I see another human being, a broken, suffering human being, and I feel sorry for him.

I swing wildly between these two interpretations, depending on the day, the hour, what novel I'm reading, or the particular news update I've seen. I think, probably, the truth is somewhere in the middle.

This is a man who entered the priesthood at a very young age, far too young, who committed to celibacy likely before he could fully comprehend what celibacy meant, what it required, how it would shape his future life and relationships, how it would forbid him certain types of relationships. He joined the priesthood during an era when the Catholic Church was in denial about the sexual desires of its priests, when the Church was still burying the issues that accompanied a life of celibacy. The Catholic Church refused to deal with the complications of this vow, the wicked crimes now attached to it. Instead it became masterful at denial, at burial, at looking the other way when its priests raped children. It sacrificed the lives of so many children to save the lives and reputations of its priests and the institution. So, in many ways, this professor was, is, simply another problematic priest from that pre-sex-scandal era of the Catholic Church, among so many others just like him, among the *thousands* of others just like him. He's just the one who happens to be mine.

Then again, maybe he always knew more than I've assumed about what priests were doing and getting away with. Maybe his friends in the priesthood were all in on it together, completely self-aware about the wrongness of their behavior, laughing when they got home over their cocktails and dinner served by kindly, unsuspecting Catholic ladies doing their duty and taking care of these heroic, celibate Catholic men. Or maybe he had no idea at all, and he was bumbling about like a drunk, vision blurry, a slave to his desires, desires he was hiding from his fellow priests, hiding from himself even, desires that he simply did not know how to control or stop, desires he knew were highly problematic given his vows. (And he *did* know, I will remind myself here, at least eventually, because he wrote about their forbidden nature in that article he sent me.) Maybe at night he suffered a terrible turmoil about having feelings he could not restrain, feelings he'd never known before, feelings he couldn't stop no matter how hard he tried.

Or maybe I'm giving him too much credit again. Maybe I'm giving myself too much credit, too, and I was not his first love. Maybe I was his second, his third, his tenth. Maybe he did to twenty other young women, girls, the very same thing he did to me, and the Catholic Church buried his actions with them as it did his actions with me. I don't think I will ever know the answer to any of these questions, and as with so many other things, I simply have to accept this.

★ ★ ★

One evening, at happy hour, one of my closest friends asked me his name.

I turned to her, mouth half-open, ready to utter the answer.

But then, I didn't.

"Almost no one knows it," I said. "Not even my husband."

It's not that I don't trust you, or that I wouldn't tell you, I stammered. But I...I...I just...can't.

I said this, then sat there, at the bar, sipping my drink and trying to understand *why* I couldn't tell her. Why, really, couldn't I? Why not? What was the big deal? It's been forever since all of that happened.

And this friend is a person I trust completely, have always trusted, with whom I have shared some of the most intimate moments a life can force on us. Not long ago, I stood by her while her husband took his last breaths in a hospital room, watched with her as the monitors ticked each of the final beats of his heart, as they got slower and slower until they stopped and he was gone. So, intimacy is not a problem between us. We have plenty of it.

"I wouldn't google him if you didn't want me to," she offered.

"I know you wouldn't," I said, and meant this, because I knew *she* meant it.

Her question forced me to try to understand why I couldn't speak his name, why I never do, not to anyone, ever. I am afraid that somehow—even with promises not to look him up—knowing his name will allow friends and loved ones to find out who he is, that it is inevitable they will find out, and then, from that day forward, *his* face, his image, will be an overlay across *my* face, my body, like film or plastic wrap, I will be trapped beneath him, he will be suffocating me for the rest of my relationships with these other people. The possibility tortures me.

"I couldn't bear it if, when we got together, you associated me with what you saw of him," I told her finally, the best explanation I could manage. "I don't want you ever to associate me with him."

This is another of the ways I have banished him from my life, or tried to, another method of splitting myself, of maintaining the person I am now, who has done her best to wash herself of this man's filth, even though I know this is not technically possible. Even though I know that, in a single moment, the world will tilt, and I will be the girl I was back then, as raw and bruised as when he was still in my life, still refusing to go away.

A few months ago, I was walking with this same friend through Brooklyn, and I told her that I was considering writing this man a letter. I told her about the dread I felt when I'd googled him, the strange fear that he would die before I could say what I wanted to say. It's not that I've never thought about what I might say to him, I told her, I just never thought I would actually ever say it, and lately I kind of wanted to.

Before, it had always seemed too dangerous, too much like a bad idea to contact him. It was never a real consideration, the thought of writing him, because I was so afraid he would write me back, that he would find me again, that he would take any contact as an invitation to be in my life once more. That like an addict of alcohol or drugs, he would again become addicted to me, because he really was like an addict of me, as disgusting as that is to admit.

But as the source of my dread about his possible death came to light, I realized something else, I told my friend as we passed through Fort Greene, which is this:

I am no longer afraid.

I am no longer afraid of him contacting me, or writing to me, or emailing me, or even showing up at my door like he used to, unannounced. If he showed up at my door today, I think I would laugh in his face. I think I would laugh because it would be a pathetic act on his part. Until recently, seeing him again would have undone me, but I don't think it would now. His power is gone in that respect. It's true that he will always have power over me because what happened still lives in my brain, and because of the way he affected my professional life and current reality. But I now know that the power of his physical presence lies in the past and not in my present. Anything he did today would roll off me, I think.

"You know what you could do," my friend said. "You know what you *should* do . . ."

"What?" I asked. I could tell she liked the idea of whatever it was.

"You could find every email address he has and ever has had," she went on, "you could find his home address, his work address, every place that has his name associated with it, even the church where he preaches if he still preaches, his social media accounts, every location where he can possibly be contacted. And you could send him unmarked letters at every single one of them. Use different fonts, don't put a return address. Give him a taste of his own medicine. Do to him what he did to you. Just once. So he knows what it feels like."

I laughed. It never occurred to me, likely never would have occurred to me, to do something like what my friend suggested. I liked contemplating the thought of doing it, even though I also knew it would be cruel. He is an old man and likely won't be around much longer. I should have more sympathy for him, shouldn't I?

Let him go to his grave without a last communication from me?

I don't think I ever will write him, though I do think about it, though I still have things to say, though I would still like an apology, and likewise would like him to ask me if I would forgive him, because I would like him to acknowledge that he needs my forgiveness.

I do not forgive him and I wouldn't and I won't.

30

There is a way in which this story has never been mine. For one, I didn't want it.

Who would? What person, what young woman, what young feminist, would want these ugly, unflattering experiences to be part of her past?

I've spent decades burying this story, hiding it, covering it up as best as I can manage, much like the cover story I invented to keep my reality a secret from the people around me. I've put as much life, as much living and experience, as possible between me and that time. I've spent my energy putting distance between me and him.

So, this story wasn't mine because I didn't want it to be.

Because I refused it.

But for another, this story was taken from me.

It was taken away by my graduate school, by the administration there. It was officially stricken from the record, from any records. It was expunged. I was paid a small fee for my silence and my denial. I remember my lawyer explaining to me what it was.

"They're giving you a nuisance fee," he said.

Nuisance.

That word has run through me for decades. I am, I was, a nuisance. Like a gnat that flies around someone's face on a hot summer day. I was, I am, the equivalent of a gnat to my graduate institution, to the Catholic Church, a harmless bug to swat at, to squash. All that I lived because of that man, and *I* was the one deemed a nuisance.

But the thing is, the story still exists.

He, and they, gave me this story.

The story is *mine*.

I am the protagonist now, not them, not him.

I am the story.

Because I am still me, I am still here, and it happened to me, no matter how much I would love to deny it, and no matter how much my graduate school would love to deny it. All of these things happened to me, and I have them in me. I carry them in my heart.

I am fusing them with the person I am now, a person who can study this story like a scientist, under a microscope of words and memories, turn it around, look underneath it, hypothesize about it, analyze it, offer it to others to study and think about and debate and judge.

I am claiming it. I am naming it.

One of the first things I learned in my feminist education was that for millennia, men have controlled women's stories, they have written us into their stories by writing over us, writing over our voices until our voices could not be heard, until our voices did not matter. That men have believed, have known, that by controlling the story they could control us *through the story;* that they would always have us because of this, they would always have power over us, because the story would always be theirs.

But feminism also taught me that even though men

might have told the stories of women for millennia, even though men have assumed this right as though it was theirs all along, their right to be and become our voices for us, women can speak up and claim our stories for ourselves. We can take our stories back from them and rewrite them according to our actual experiences, what we actually think, what we've actually lived, from our perspective. We can stop being characters in the stories of men and become the protagonists in our own stories.

The stories of women.

This man forced this story on me decades ago. He wrote this story and I starred in it. He wrote this story for me, about me, without my permission. Then my graduate school wrote over it, rewrote it, chose to erase it, because they knew I was young and I was afraid and I was desperate and, because of this, I would let them erase me along with the story. They took the soft side of a pencil and rubbed it over my features, my outline, my being, until I ceased to exist. They wrote me out of my very own story.

Or, at least, they tried.

ACKNOWLEDGMENTS

This is not a book I ever imagined writing. Its existence depends upon the people in my life who were willing to listen when I was ready to speak, and to forgive my struggles to speak this part of my story. I will always be grateful for your patience, support, and belief in me—you know who you are. I live in gratitude to you every day. You are my friends, family, and loved ones.

I want to say a special thanks to my editor, Judy Clain, and to everyone at Little, Brown for having so much faith in this book, and of course to Miriam Altshuler, my agent, who has been a mentor, a cheerleader, and a friend for so many years now, and to all my writer friends who read drafts. You have helped me make this book the best it can be.

Lastly: there is one person in particular, who wondered if, after I wrote this memoir and had the people closest to me read it for various reasons, I still felt alone in it. And I realized as I pondered her question that for the first time in my life, the answer was *no*. I don't think I feel alone anymore. I think I feel known. And that feels like a miracle. So, to the people I love and the people who love me who've spent their time reading this book to try to know me in this way—thank you, truly.

ABOUT THE AUTHOR

Donna Freitas writes both fiction and nonfiction. She is the author of *Sex and the Soul: Juggling Sexuality, Spirituality, Romance, and Religion on America's College Campuses,* among other titles. She has written for several national newspapers and magazines about life on a college campus today, including the *Wall Street Journal,* the *New York Times,* the *Boston Globe,* and the *Washington Post.* She has appeared on National Public Radio, the *Today* show, CNN, and many other news media outlets and has lectured about her research at more than two hundred colleges and universities. She lives in Brooklyn, New York.